State Department, Press, and Pressure Groups

State Department, Press, and Pressure Groups: *A Role Analysis*

BY William O. Chittick

WILEY-INTERSCIENCE,
A Division of John Wiley & Sons
New York • *London* • *Sydney* • *Toronto*

For My Mother and Father

Library of Congress Catalogue Card Number: 72–101971

SBN 471 15590 X

Printed in the United States of America

10 9 8 7 6 5 4 3 2 1

Series Preface

In a democratic society there is no more important principle than the people's right to know about their government and its obligation to keep the people informed. The role of the press and communication in the governing process has been important since the earliest days of the nation.

In the modern mass society of an international power, communication between government and people through a complex and often instantaneous means of transmission has vital implications and consequences. The explosive impact of the mass media on the political and governmental process has brought about changes in politics, public administration, and international relations.

The interrelationship between government and communication has many new dimensions that must be explored and understood. The "Wiley Series on Government and Communication" was conceived to probe and provide greater understanding of those new dimensions.

Some of the books in the series deal with the way in which governments (local, national, and international) communicate with the people, either directly or through the press and mass media.

Other books in the series discuss the way in which the people, usually through the press and mass media, obtain information from government.

Finally, some of the series books deal with the problems that arise at that intersection of society at which government and people meet through the media. These are problems of the social, economic, legal, and political implications of the communication process when dealing with government, the problems of restriction and censorship, of distortion and propaganda, of freedom and national security, and of organization and technology.

Certainly the future of democracy may depend to a large extent on the success with which we understand and deal with the problems created by the relationship between government and communication in a new age.

RAY ELDON HIEBERT
Series Editor

Preface

This study deals with four groups caught in the apparent contradictions of democracy and foreign policy. The four groups are State Department policy officers, State Department information officers, foreign affairs reporters, and leaders of nongovernmental organizations. These groups form a distinct social system, and the purpose of this book is to analyze the role each group plays in this system. The book contains my answers to three questions. First, how do these groups affect the content of public opinion and foreign policy? Second, to what extent do these groups perceive antagonism in their professional relations with each other? Third, does perceived antagonism among them demonstrate the incompatibility of democracy and foreign policy?

The idea of using role analysis to study problems of democracy and foreign policy first occurred to me after Frances E. Rourke recommended that I read a selection by John S. Dickey[1] in my graduate student days at The Johns Hopkins University. I was fascinated by the role which the information officers in the State Department could play in the formation of public opinion and foreign policy. Accordingly, I wrote my Ph.D. dissertation on *The Domestic Information Activities of the Department of State.* After two years of military service, I began a more comprehensive and scientific study of my subject. This book is the result.

[1] John S. Dickey, "The Secretary and the American Public" in *The Secretary of State,* ed. Don K. Price (Englewod Cliffs, New Jersey: Prentice-Hall, Inc., 1960).

The book is based largely on the official record, including some unpublished material, and two sets of interview data. I am grateful to those individuals who gave me access to their old files, especially the late E. Taylor Parks who guided my search for documents in the State Department. My thanks also go to those institutions that supported my field research. An initial set of exploratory interviews in 1962 was made possible by funds provided by The Johns Hopkins University and the Ford Foundation under the program of Small Grants for Research in Public Affairs. A second set of structured interviews in the summer of 1966 was facilitated by my appointment as a Guest Scholar at the Brookings Institution in Washington, D.C. I am especially grateful to the individuals who participated in the two sets of interviews. The willingness of these individuals to share their knowledge and opinions with me make it possible to write this book.

The analysis and writing phases in the preparation of this book were supported by the Office of General Research at the University of Georgia. A number of individuals also assisted me. Delmer Dunn read and thoroughly criticized the first draft of the entire manuscript; Geoffrey Y. Cornog offered extensive comments on an early draft of the seventh chapter; and Brett H. Hawkins and Ira Sharkansky provided helpful suggestions at various stages in the preparation of the book. I am deeply indebted to each of them, both for their criticisms and for their encouragement. R. Robert Rentz advised me on the use of statistical techniques, especially in Chapter 5. I am very grateful for his willingness to explain these procedures to me. I also benefited from the services of a number of capable student assistants, including Vicki Lowe, Jane Gibson, and Boonlert Pairindra. Mrs. Elizabeth Landrum did most of the final typing. She is particularly accurate and prompt in her work. My wife, Marilyn, read and edited the entire manuscript. She has provided me with substantive criticisms and moral support throughout the preparation of the book. I also owe a word of thanks to Ray E. Hiebert, the series editor, for his patience with me during this phase of the project.

WILLIAM O. CHITTICK

October 1969
Athens, Georgia

Contents

Chapter 1

Introduction

THE GROWTH OF THE domestic-foreign interface in this country raises anew the question of whether foreign affairs can be managed on a democratic basis. To what extent can a democracy demonstrate the patience required to sustain a difficult foreign undertaking? To what extent can a democracy take advantage of momentary breaks in international developments? To what extent can the public debate foreign issues without giving aid and comfort to the enemy? To what extent can a democratic government conceal its thoughts and actions without losing public confidence?

DEMOCRACY AND FOREIGN POLICY

These questions have been raised repeatedly by those who have reflected upon the apparently conflicting requirements of democracy and foreign policy. Most critics and even some friends of democracy regard foreign affairs as an exception to the notion that the public can handle its own affairs. Commentators on the relations of democracy and foreign policy from Thucydides to Lippman have been intrigued by the apparent difficulties that democracies face in the conduct of diplomacy. Even the father of liberal democracy and constitutionalism, John Locke, created a separate power—the federative power—to deal with foreign affairs so that it would not be subject to direct popular control.[1]

Contemporary democratic theorists acknowledge the low level of direct popular participation in representative democracies. Nevertheless, they stress the importance which such participation plays in the maintenance of democratic political systems.[2] It is the requirements of popular participation in democratic decision-making that supposedly conflict with the requirements of effective decision-making in foreign affairs.

First, genuine participation by the people in decision-making requires that the public be adequately informed. Since it is usually not possible for a government to communicate with its domestic public without also providing information to foreign countries, including enemy states, information on foreign affairs must sometimes be withheld from the people. To the extent that secrecy, rather than publicity, is characteristic of the foreign policy-making process, some argue that democracies are unable to conduct foreign relations effectively.

Second, popular participation in government requires ample time for deliberation. Since foreign policy must be responsive to a host of constantly changing external forces, there is often little or no time for effective consultations with the public. To the extent that speed, rather than deliberation, characterizes foreign policy decision-making, some believe that democracies are incapable of making the quick decisions necessary to deal with these fluid external circumstances.

Third, public participation in policy decisions is most meaningful if people can express opposition to the government on a continuing basis. Since foreign relations often require the communication of firmness, decision-makers discourage public dissent with foreign policy. To the extent that unity, rather than dissent, characterizes effective decision-making in foreign affairs, some believe that democracies are incapable of pursuing difficult and unpopular policies to a successful conclusion.

[1] John Locke, *Two Treatises of Government,* ed. by Thomas I. Cook (New York: Hafner Publishing Company, 1947), p. 196.
[2] Peter Y. Medding, " 'Elitist' Democracy: An Unsuccessful Critique of a Misunderstood Theory," *Journal of Politics,* August 1969, p. 652.

On the basis of these arguments it seems plausible enough that democracies encounter special difficulties in the conduct of their foreign relations, but this proposition is by no means universally accepted. There are innumerable factors which could contribute to the conflict between the public and the official leadership over the conduct of foreign affairs. The fact is that most studies linking the friction between the public and foreign policy officials with conflicting requirements of democracy and foreign policy are highly impressionistic. There is great uncertainty about sources of conflict between the government and the public over foreign affairs. The question remains how compatible are democracy and foreign policy?

NEW APPROACHES

The inability of students of foreign affairs to resolve this question results in part from the character of their studies. The traditional literature on the problem of democracy and foreign policy seldom tested the assumptions upon which its conclusions are based. New approaches to the problem by political scientists and others may make a greater contribution than these earlier studies to the recurring debate over the existence and sources of conflict between the public opinion-forming and foreign policy-making processes in a democracy. What is new and appealing about these approaches?

Most early studies of democracy and foreign policy fail to accept the stratification of the public and consequently pose the problem of democracy and foreign policy solely in terms of the relations between government officials and an undifferentiated public.[3] The need to distinguish between various segments of the public was recognized by Gabriel Almond as early as 1950. In his book on *The American People and Foreign Policy* Almond identifies four key participants in the opinion and policy process: the general public; the attentive public; policy and opinion elites; and the official policy leadership. Each of these

3 Gabriel A. Almond, *The American People and Foreign Policy,* rev. ed. (New York: Frederick A. Praeger, 1960), pp. 137-139.

participants performs a distinct function: the official policy leadership makes foreign policy and seeks public support for it; other policy and opinion elites compete for public support and policy influence; the attentive public is the informed and interested stratum before whom this discussion and controversy takes place; and the general public participates in indirect and primarily passive ways. The value of Almond's structural-functional analysis is that it focuses attention upon those participants who are most directly and actively engaged in the opinion-policy relationship: political elites; bureaucratic elites; interest group elites; and communication elites.

Despite this breakthrough, it was almost a decade before political scientists began detailed and systematic studies of the relations between these elites. James Rosenau contends that the reason that earlier writers failed to describe the direct communications between elite groups is that they were preoccupied with the futile effort of trying to demonstrate a causal nexus between public opinion and foreign policy.[4] Rosenau helped to overcome this roadblock by emphasizing the opinion-submitting process as a missing link in the opinion-policy process and by identifying the discrete individuals who play roles at critical junctures in the opinion-policy process.

In the last few years political scientists have conducted a number of empirical studies in which they have drawn inferences about the existence and sources of conflict in the relations between selected groups in the opinion-policy process. Two of these studies have received wide recognition: Bernard Cohen's analysis of the relations between government officials and foreign affairs reporters in *The Press and Foreign Policy*[5] and Dan Nimmo's exploration of the relations between government information officers and reporters in *Newsgathering in Washington*.[6]

---

4 James N. Rosenau, *Public Opinion and Foreign Policy* (New York: Random House, 1961), Chapter 2.

5 Bernard C. Cohen, *The Press and Foreign Policy* (Princeton, N.J.: Princeton University Press, 1963).

6 Dan D. Nimmo, *Newsgathering in Washington* (New York: Atherton Press, 1964).

These studies have contributed to the literature on public opinion and foreign policy in a number of ways. First, by focusing attention on interactions of elites, these authors have described aspects of the relationship which have not been described previously. For example, there have been a great many studies of the value of the press in disseminating information to the public, but Cohen is the first to describe what policy-makers extract from the press. Second, by studying interactions among discrete individuals these authors have generated new hypotheses about the relations between them. Nimmo, for instance, has drawn some inferences about the competition among information officers and reporters on the basis of his description of varying role expectations between and within these two groups.

Despite these hopeful developments, there are several short-comings in this emerging literature. In the first place, these authors do not present a very comprehensive picture of the relations among policy and opinion elites. Nimmo limits the value of his study of government information officers and reporters by not taking into account sufficiently the impact of government policy officers on their relations.[7] Cohen commits a less serious error when he fails to distinguish sufficiently between information and policy officials in their relations with foreign affairs reporters. Moreover, there are no comparable studies of the relations between information and policy officers, between these officials and nongovernmental organization (NGO) leaders, or between NGO leaders and foreign affairs reporters.

In the second place, these authors do not present the findings upon which their carefully worded and supposedly cautiously accepted statements about the relations among these groups are based. The only empirical findings explicitly recorded in either study describe one or more of the interview samples.[8] Neither author attempts to establish statistically the existence of the relationships he discusses. Since these studies are strictly

7 Bernard C. Cohen, *The American Political Science Review*, Vol. LVIII, December 1964, pp. 1005-1006.
8 See Nimmo, *op. cit.*, pp. 246-248.

exploratory and descriptive, there is an obvious need to test the validity of the findings.

A ROLE ANALYSIS

The purpose of the following explanatory study is to establish empirically the existence and sources of perceived antagonism among all four of the relevant elites: government policy officers, government information officers, foreign affairs reporters, and leaders of NGOs. Do these groups perceive antagonism in their professional relations? Is perceived antagonism for one group equally shared by members of other groups? If not, what are some of the correlates of perceived antagonism among members of one group for another? Finally, what are the implications of these findings for theories of conflict between democracy and foreign policy?

The focus for this research is the relations between the State Department, the press, and pressure groups. The State Department is the agency under the President which has the primary responsibility for conducting American foreign relations. Although the State Department is accountable to the democratically elected leadership of both the Executive and the Congress, the press and pressure groups serve as its principal intermediaries in direct relations with the public. A systematic and detailed study of the interpersonal behavior and attitudes of those most directly and actively engaged in this relationship should reflect some of the problems of democracy and foreign policy in the government as a whole.

The relations between the State Department, the press, and pressure groups are highly structured, and the individuals who are most directly and actively engaged in these relations can be readily identified by the positions they occupy in their respective organizations. The first set of position holders is State Department policy officers. They hold positions of responsibility for the conduct of some aspect of foreign relations. Although in Department parlance the term "policy officer" is usually reserved for generalists at the level of Assistant Secretary or above, generalists or specialists who hold positions as country officers, division chiefs, office directors, and country directors, as well as higher-level position holders, are considered policy officers in this study.

The second set of position holders is State Department information officers. The job of an information offcer is to conduct the public relations of the State Department. Many of these positions are located in the Bureau of Public Affairs, but others are scattered throughout the Department as each principal officer has his own public affairs advisor.

The third set of position holders is foreign affairs reporters. They are the members of news organizations who have the job of personally gathering information and opinions from the State Department. They serve a wide variety of news organizations: newspapers; newspaper chains; wire services; news services; radio and television networks; news magazines; trade and ethnic press; and so on.

The fourth set of position holders is NGO leaders. They are the ones who conduct the international programs of nongovernmental organizations and maintain group liaison with the State Department. These positions have been created by a wide spectrum of pressure groups, including business, labor, farm, professional, religious, veterans, and women's groups.

These four sets of position holders are mutually dependent. Department information and policy officers share decisions on information policy. Department officials depend upon reporters and NGO leaders for information and for help in building public support for Department policies. Reporters depend upon Department officials for foreign policy information, and pressure group leaders rely upon the Department both for information and for access to decisions affecting their special interests and attitudes. Reporters rely upon NGO leaders for information; NGO leaders depend upon reporters both as a source and as a channel for information.

The interactions among these four position holders in the opinion-policy process constitute a distinct political system. This system can best be studied by means of role analysis. The term "role" refers here to the socially prescribed behavior of a position holder. The standards which position holders use to judge behavior are called role expectations. Role theory posits that position holders will behave in accordance with both their own role expectations and those of counter position holders. In short, role theory claims that the behavior of position holders is a function of their role expectations.

There are at least two reasons why this research takes the form of a role analysis. First, it is necessary to rely at least in part upon data based on role expectations because these position holders are sensitive enough about their relations with each other that it is not always possible to get hard data on role behavior. Second, role expectations (whatever their relation to role behavior) are the normative criteria by which position holders judge behavior, and these standards may be correlated with perceived antagonism among position holders.

The research design for this study is described in Appendix A. The interview schedules used for each of the four groups are found in Appendices B-E. The statistical basis for selected findings in the book are shown in Appendix F.

PATTERN OF ORGANIZATION

This book is organized in three parts. The first part deals with the setting in which the opinion-policy relationship will be analyzed. It contains a brief description of the evolution of the relationship between the State Department and the domestic press and pressure groups (Chapter 2). It also includes a discussion of the way that Congress, which sees itself as the link between the State Department and the public, has sought to limit the public relations of the State Department (Chapter 3).

The second part of the book concerns the policy and opinion elites in this study: State Department policy officers, State Department information officers, foreign affairs reporters, and leaders of nongovernmental organizations. First, the discussion centers around the positions which each of these four groups occupy and the characteristics of the individuals who occupy them (Chapter 4). Then attention is focused on the role expectations and attitudes of these position holders (Chapter 5). In the process of describing these participants in the opinion-policy process, the variables or factors which distinguish one set of position holders from another as well as those which distinguish the occupants of any one position from each other are described in detail. The identification and discussion of these variables provides the basis for the systematic analysis of the relations among these position holders which follows.

The interactions of participants in the opinion-policy process is the subject of the third part of the book. The analysis begins with the interaction between information and policy officers in the making of State Department information policy (Chapter 6). It is followed by an analysis of the relations between these Department officers and foreign affairs reporters (Chapter 7). This in turn is followed by an analysis of the relations between Department officers and the leaders of nongovernmental organizations (Chapter 8). The final section deals with the relations between foreign affairs reporters and the leaders of nongovernmental organizations (Chapter 9). Each of these chapters contains a discussion of the community of interests shared by counter position holders as well as the conflict of interests between them. In each case correlates of perceived antagonism among them are identified, and the implications of these findings for the opinion-policy process are discussed.

The overall pattern of perceived antagonism among participants in the opinion-policy relationship is described in the concluding chapter (Chapter 10). Correlates of perceived antagonism among these four groups are summarized in this chapter along with a discussion of these findings for the problem of democracy and foreign policy.

PART I

Setting

Chapter 2

The Public Dimension of American Foreign Policy

THERE HAS BEEN a veritable revolution in the relationship between the American people and the Department of State in the last fifty years. Less than a half-century ago a small coterie of professional diplomats in the State Department handled the foreign relations of the United States with little direct communications with the American public and its constituent interest groups. Except for the publication of selected documents and a few press releases, the Department of State made no effort to enlist public understanding and support for American foreign policies prior to World War I.

In contrast, there are information officers scattered throughout the State Department today, and their primary function is to promote public understanding and support for United States foreign policy. This remarkable transformation in the public relations of the State Department reflects an entirely new dimension in the conduct of American foreign policy.

This public dimension of American diplomacy consists of a two-way flow of information between the State Department and the American people; the Department of State finds it important not only to keep the public informed on foreign affairs but also to keep itself informed regarding the state of public opinion. This dramatic change in the public relations of the

State Department may be attributed largely to four interrelated factors:

1. The changing content of American foreign policy.
2. The extension of the democratic idea in the United States.
3. The rise of mass communication.
4. The growing public character of international relations.[1]

The impact of each of these factors on the public relations of the State Department will be discussed separately.

THE CHANGING CONTENT OF AMERICAN FOREIGN POLICY

The public dimension of American diplomacy first reflects the efforts of the United States to cope with an essentially new international situation: the challenge of bipolarity, the revolution in military technology, and the emergence of many newly independent states. Between the two world wars the United States could afford to pursue an isolationist foreign policy based in part on unilateral and often negative declarations of purpose. This approach was symbolized by our failure to join the League of Nations in 1919 and the International Court of Justice in 1935, as well as by our naive faith in the Kellogg-Briand Peace Pact of 1928 and the Neutrality Legislation of the 1930s. In order to cope with the international situation during and after World War II, however, the United States adopted a cooperative foreign policy based on positive international commitments throughout the world.

This transformation in American foreign relations began even before this country entered World War II. As early as 1939, an Advisory Committee on Postwar Foreign Policy was established under the auspices of the Department of State to plan an international organization which would correct the

[1] These four factors were first discussed by John S. Dickey. See Dickey, "The Secretary of State and The American Public," *The Secretary of State*, ed. by Don K. Price (Englewood Cliffs, N.J.: Prentice-Hall, 1960), pp. 140-142.

perceived weaknesses of the defunct League of Nations.[2] The official leadership elements in this country apparently considered America's failure to participate in the League as one of the important reasons for that organization's demise, and they wanted to assume an active role in forming and ensuring American participation in the new international organization.

After the war, the United States participated in the United Nations organization, and played an active role in virtually all of the international institutions which have grown up under the aegis of that body. When the cold war prevented the United Nations from serving its peace-keeping functions effectively, the United States took the lead in building regional economic, political, and military organizations for mutual defense and development purposes. By the mid-1950s the United States had formally allied itself with some forty-four governments, and had informally reached understandings with a host of unaligned governments. The resulting complex of bilateral and multilateral ties demonstrated America's new willingness to collaborate with other nations.

This policy of collaboration took numerous forms: the Truman Doctrine, the Marshall Plan, the North Atlantic Treaty Organization, the Mutual Security Program, the Trade Expansion Act, and the Nuclear Test Ban Treaty. Any one of these measures would have been considered beyond the scope of American foreign policy just a few short years before it was adopted, and yet each of them was apparently accepted by a majority of the American people as a necessary feature of this country's foreign policy.[3] Moreover, this policy of collaboration encompassed a fantastic variety of concerns and interests: trade, science, space, education, information, housing, cultural exchange, and so on.

Another dimension of this change in diplomacy is the enor-

2 Harley Notter, *Postwar Foreign Policy Preparation 1939-1945,* Department of State Publication 3580, February 1950, pp. 63-65.

3 This conclusion is supported by the surveys of the National Opinion Research Center of Chicago, the Roper Poll, and the Gallup Poll. See the files of the Public Opinion Studies Staff, Department of State.

mity of this country's commitment abroad. As the leader of the Free World, the United States has accepted a tremendous burden for the military defense and economic development of vast areas with huge populations. Besides maintaining a large nuclear deterrent to hostile acts in vital areas around the world, the United States has stationed well over a million troops overseas and spent over a hundred billion dollars for economic rehabilitation and development and defense support abroad. In fiscal year 1969 the United States stationed over 500,000 troops and spent in excess of $25 billion in South Vietnam alone.

The sheer size and scope of this policy has had a profound impact on the relations of the Department of State with other departments and agencies of the Executive, with Congress, and with the American people. Beginning with World War II, the State Department required the active participation and support of most other departments and agencies of the government, both houses of Congress, and the general public because it could not conduct the foreign policy of the United States without their assistance.

Other Departments and Agencies

The dependence of the State Department on other departments and agencies increased tremendously during and after World War II. The armed services in particular assumed a very substantial role in the conduct of foreign relations during the war. New agencies were also established to handle economic, information, and other programs abroad. These agencies included the Office of War Information, the Office of Strategic Services, the Office of the Coordinator of Inter-American Affairs, the Foreign Economic Administration, and the War Shipping Administration. In addition, many domestic agencies undertook programs connected with the war effort. The influence of all these departments and agencies in the field of foreign affairs was considerable.

The armed services emerged from the Second World War with the largest presence abroad despite the rapid demobilization of troops. Moreover, the prominence which those in the national security field had had in the formation and execution of American foreign policy during the war was fully maintained in the postwar years because of the cold war. New structures were created to increase the effectiveness of the agencies concerned with national security: the armed services were brought together under a single Department of Defense; a Central Intelligence Agency, National Aeronautics and Space Administration, and Atomic Energy Commission were established; and the National Security Council was formed to ensure that these agencies would have a continuing voice in foreign affairs.

The postwar growth of civilian departments and agencies with a primary responsibility for foreign affairs was equally spectacular. The foreign affairs agencies which were established on an emergency basis during the war were incorporated into the State Department in the immediate postwar years. While each of these agencies now functions independently, they remain closely linked to the State Department. Some, like the Agency for International Development and the Peace Corps, are formally part of the State Department. Others, like the Arms Control and Disarmament Agency, are separate agencies with directors who report directly to the President but have formal ties and responsibilties toward the State Department.

In addition, there are perhaps twenty domestic departments and agencies with overseas programs and personnel systems, including the Departments of Treasury, Justice, Agriculture, Commerce, and Labor. These agencies often have a substantive overseas commitment in their area of specialty. In some cases their representatives overseas are integrated into the United States Foreign Service. In other cases these agencies have established separate personnel services.[4] There is scarcely an important domestic department or agency in the United States government which does not administer some overseas program or activity.

The tremendous increase in the number of other departments and agencies involved in the conduct of foreign affairs created essentially new tasks for the State Department within the Exec-

---

[4] See Robert E. Elder, *Overseas Representation and Service for Federal Domestic Agencies,* Carnegie Endowment for International Peace, 1965.

utive branch. As the principal organ of the government in foreign affairs, the Department had the responsibility to help form and coordinate the actions of these other departments and agencies. Department officers were frequently asked to chair interdepartmental committees, and various agencies were formally required to clear their actions with the Department. The task of coordinating American policy abroad was infinitely complex. A single policy, such as foreign economic aid, might involve at least four government agencies and six international financial institutions.[5]

But the State Department's task was not simply one of coordinating the actions of all the departments engaged in overseas programs; the Department also had to gain the support of other departments and agencies of the government for the overall policy which the President and the Secretary of State wished to pursue. In order to gain the competence necessary to deal with the almost infinite variety of programs conducted by these other agencies abroad, the Department had to recruit specialists in all these fields. Then these officials had to develop cordial relations with their counterparts in other departments and agencies.

The Congress

Moreover, the State Department became increasingly dependent upon Congress for support. The provisions of the United States Constitution have always assured Congress a role in foreign affairs. The advice and consent of the Senate in particular was required both for the confirmation of ambassadors and other personnel for diplomacy and the ratification of treaties. Few treaties were proposed by the President to the Senate, however, and only a small number of those were amended or rejected by the Senate. For the most part, the State Department could operate with no new authorizations and with routine appropriations.

However, the growth of the foreign policy sector of American policy during and after World War II has given the Congress more opportunities to influence the conduct of American

5 Herbert A. Simon, Donald W. Smithburg, and Victor A. Thompson, *Public Administration* (New York: Alfred A. Knopf, 1950), p. 443.

diplomacy. Whereas foreign affairs had been the special concern of only a handful of committees prior to the war, half of the thirty-six standing committees of the two houses of Congress now deal regularly with issues of international significance. The form and content of postwar foreign policy gave these Congressional committees and even individual senators and congressmen the opportunity to use their investigative and critical powers to the fullest.

The increasing dependence of the Department and the government on Congress became especially pronounced in the area of appropriations, where the House of Representatives held special prerogatives. In 1937 the United States spent $18 million on foreign affairs—all on the traditional diplomatic functions of the State Department. In 1967 the United States spent about $5.6 billion on foreign affairs, excluding expenditures on U.S. military forces and intelligence. Of this $5.6 billion, less than 4 percent went for the general overhead of foreign affairs; the bulk of it went for overseas activities and programs.[6] This provides Congress, and especially the House of Representatives, an excellent opportunity to influence the content of American policy abroad.

The efforts of the State Department to develop a regular working relationship with Congress began with the Congressional liaison activities developed by President Roosevelt and Secretary of State Hull to insure Senate support for the new United Nations. These activities were extended to other foreign policy areas in the immediate postwar years. The fact that a Republican-dominated Eightieth Congress was in power when the Democratic administration was striving to deal with cold war problems made it especially important that the State Department establish bipartisan approaches to Congress. As a result of mutual consultations between Executive and Congressional leaders, the "do-nothing" Eightieth Congress became one of the most productive ever in the foreign policy field.

The State Department continues to work closely with key

---

[6] Charles L. Schultze, *Hearings* before the Subcommittee on National Security and International Operations of the Senate Committee on Government Operations, "Planning-Programming-Budgeting," Part 1, 90th Congress, 1st Session, p. 28.

members and committees of Congress in order to insure Congressional understanding of current foreign policies and actions and to enlist Congressional support for new programs and activities. The Assistant Secretary of State for Congressional Relations and his staff maintain a number of services for senators and congressmen with an interest in foreign affairs.

The General Public

Although both the Congress and the President, regardless of party, have generally approved the basic outlines of American foreign policy since World War II, the State Department needs general public support, especially when its policies adversely affect important domestic interests. In order to obtain the annual appropriations and authority necessary to implement its policies, the State Department has constantly been compelled to augment the power bestowed upon it by Congress and the executive hierarchy with whatever power it could muster for itself. In short, the State Department has been compelled to develop its own constituency.

This quest for constituency has taken two basic forms. First, the State Department, like other departments and agencies of the government, has attempted to create general public approval and acceptance of its policies and actions so that both the Administration and Congress have cause to sustain its program. To the extent that the President and his Secretary of State can mobilize strong support for their policies among the general public, special interests will make little headway either in Congress or elsewhere in the Administration. Second, the State Department has attempted to create and maintain the active support of private and civic interest groups who for one reason or another are prepared to stand up for the Department in Congress and in the Administration. These groups help to neutralize the opposition of other special interests to the Department's program.

The State Department, however, faces a number of special problems in building its constituency. For example, unlike so many other departments and agencies of the government, the State Department does not formally represent specific groups in American society; consequently, it does not maintain programs which bring it into daily contact with people at the state and local levels. It is thus particularly difficult for the State Department to create and sustain public interest in its diverse activities at the grass roots level.

Prior to World War II, there was no systematic attempt on the part of the State Department either to obtain general public understanding and support for American foreign policy or to enlist the support of various nongovernmental organizations with an interest in foreign affairs. The change in the relationship between the Department, the public, and these interest groups can be traced as far back as the passage of the Reciprocal Trade Act in 1934. Although the impact of this measure was not fully appreciated at the time, it was destined to alter the traditional relations between the State Department, Congress, and the American people.

In the spring of 1934 the Administration sought permanent authority to reduce certain categories of tariffs by 50 percent. In the course of preliminary deliberations on the Hill, however, Administration leaders agreed to accept the three-year limitation proposed by Congressman John W. McCormack of Massachusetts on the grounds that the Reciprocal Trade Bill was an emergency measure.[7] Because of the three-year limitation, it was necessary for the State Department to continue building support for a program of tariff negotiations which progressively antagonized some important domestic producers. This was the first time in history that the Department of State had assumed the responsibility for a foreign policy that had a continuing effect on domestic interests, and it taught the State Department a great deal about keeping the public informed.[8]

When Secretary Hull witnessed the last of his four successful fights for the renewal of the Reciprocal Trade Act, he was apparently so impressed with the support which various private organizations had given the State Department in Congress on

[7] See Daniel L. Cheever and H. Field Haviland, *American Foreign Policy and the Separation of Powers* (Cambridge: Harvard University Press, 1952), pp. 94-95.

[8] Dickey, *op. cit.*, p. 196.

each of these occasions that he asked John S. Dickey, who had handled this aspect of the information program intermittently since 1934, "to bring to the aid of postwar policies the type of public liaison activity that had proven itself in the Trade Agreements program."[9] On June 29, 1943, Secretary Hull formally appointed Dickey as a Special Consultant to the Department of State.[10] The efforts of Dickey to get the Department to accept public liaison activities were partially realized in the general departmental reorganization of January 15, 1944, when he was named the Director of the new Office of Public Information.[11] This Office (now Bureau of Public Affairs) is one of the primary links between the State Department and the American people.

THE EXTENSION OF THE DEMOCRATIC IDEA IN THE UNITED STATES

The public dimension of American foreign policy is also the result of the dramatic extension of the democratic idea in the American system of politics in the twentieth century. The progressive movement to increase popular control over the affairs of government was remarkably successful in the early portion of this century. By the second decade, the United States Constitution had been amended to provide for the popular election of senators, and various state constitutions had been amended to provide for direct primary elections, the initiative and referendum, and recall. By 1919 suffrage had been extended to women, and by 1965 extensive provisions had been made to guarantee voting rights to Negroes and other minority groups. The prominence of the concept of equality in American life became apparent with the acceptance of the one-man, one-vote rule as the basis for apportioning seats in city councils, state legislatures, and Congressional districts throughout the country. The progressive notion that the people could decide what

9 Dickey, *MS*, pp. 21-22.
10 Departmental Order 1167, June 29, 1943.
11 Departmental Order 1218, January 15, 1944.

was in their interests was as fully accepted in foreign as in domestic affairs. The spread of the democratic idea together with the defeat of the League of Nations proposal in the United States spurred the development of a number of pressure groups with a major concern for American foreign policy: The Foreign Policy Association (1918), the League of Nations Association (1920), the National League of Women Voters (1920), and the Council on Foreign Relations (1921). These pressure groups sought both to educate the general public on foreign affairs and to bring their influence to bear on the State Department and the government.

The activities of these organizations were gradually supplemented by the work of other pressure groups who had a strong secondary interest in foreign affairs. An increasing number of these nongovernmental organizations (NGOs) had affiliates or representatives abroad, and they took an active interest in current Department policies and actions. Some of these groups placed great emphasis upon the passing of periodic resolutions on American foreign policy. These organizations were important because they comprised most of the people who were seriously interested with foreign affairs.

Congress and Other Departments of the Government

Congress, traditionally considered the popular branch of the American government, was affected by these developments. The number and length of public hearings provide ample testimony to the efforts of various committees to be responsive to public pressure. The gradual liberalization of the rules of procedure in both houses illustrates the drive to allow the popular majority to work its will once the minority's right to have its views heard and considered has been satisfied. Indeed, Congress hesitates to take any action until the question has been openly discussed in public and its members receive some clues as to how the people back home feel about proposed legislation.

The changes in the policy-making process introduced by the spread of the democratic idea were probably even more dramatic in the executive branch of the government. As executive departments and agencies undertook more and more responsibility for the decisions which affected individuals in society, they endeavored to make themselves more responsive to popular will. As the government grew under the civil service system, it became broadly representative of the public. In many cases, individuals with good contacts with clientele groups were given key administrative positions. The government established an increasing number of advisory groups who could reflect the views of affected groups as well as the general public.

To the extent that Congress and other departments and agencies of the government with which the Department dealt came under the influence or control of important domestic interests which might be adversely affected by State Department policies, it became important for the Department to know what these groups were thinking. Moreover, these domestic interests were also exerting pressure directly upon the State Department. How was the State Department to respond to these domestic pressures?

The State Department

Efforts by the State Department to assess public views on foreign affairs may be traced back at least as early as 1942. In the summer of that year the Division of Special Research under the supervision of Joseph M. Jones began to study public attitudes on international affairs in anticipation of the nationwide campaign on behalf of a postwar international organization. Between January 12 and March 2, 1943, a series of analytical studies was prepared in the Department on "party platforms, various phases of isolationism, the activities and effects of pressure groups, and public opinion in relation to the policies of the interwar period."[12]

Thus, beginning in 1942 the Department prepared comprehensive studies of public attitudes on American foreign policy by analyzing Congressional statements, newspaper editorials and columns, organization statements, radio programs, and public opinion polls. As early as 1943, the Department contracted with the Office of Public Opinion Research of Princeton, New

12 Notter, *op. cit.*, p. 196.

Jersey to make special public attitude studies on foreign affairs.[13] In subsequent years this public opinion staff prepared daily, weekly, and monthly opinion summaries as well as special reports on specific problem areas such as Europe, the United Nations, and foreign aid.

In relation to postwar planning the Department also undertook an extensive program of consultations with private groups across the country. Department officers not only visited these organizations but even invited their leaders to the Department where they could discuss the Dumbarton Oaks Proposals for the United Nations Organization with some of the higher-ranking officials of the Department. At first these off-the-record meetings were largely exploratory in nature, for both sides had much to learn about the other's mode of operation. The organizations feared that Department cooperation would be contingent upon their agreeing to all of the proposals, and many officers of the Department were still skeptical of open diplomacy.[14] Meetings began on October 14, and by December 20 the Department had participated in some 115 such discussions.[15] By the spring of 1945 the cooperation between the State Department and these powerful national organizations had reached the point that the U.S. Delegation to the San Francisco Conference was willing to accept the representatives of a select number of such organizations as consultants to the American delegation at the Conference itself.

The idea of having 42 nongovernmental consultants at the Conference was a highly imaginative but risky operation. John S. Dickey went to the Conference as Public Liaison Officer of the United State Delegation and the consultants at the Conference. The situation was fraught with difficulties. Many organizations not given consultant status felt bypassed, and they sent

13 In 1945 the contract was shifted to the National Opinion Research Center of the University of Denver (later University of Chicago).
14 Dorothy B. Robbins, *U.S. Non-Governmental Organizations and the Educational Campaign from Dumbarton Oaks, 1944 Through the San Francisco Conference, 1945* (unpublished Ph.D. dissertation, New York University, February 6, 1959).
15 Notter, *op. cit.*, p. 378.

they own observers to the Conference. In his first session with the consultants Dickey stated that they were invited to the Conference on behalf of the United States Delegation as representatives of the American people, not of their respective organizations. Consequently, he asked them to confer with the American delegation as individuals or in small groups rather than as a bloc, and he requested them to avoid antagonizing the observers sent by other organizations by aiding and informing these observers whenever possible.[16]

The consultants to the United States Delegation at San Francisco had seats on the Conference floor and access to the Delegate Lounge when they could discuss the United Nations Charter with foreign as well as American delegates. This afforded them an unusual opportunity to participate in the formulation of the Charter. Consultants met three times a week with members of the Delegation for reports on the progress of the Conference and, on other days, among themselves to formulate views and decide on suggestions to be put to the Delegation. Daily meetings were arranged by information officers so that members of the consultant groups and others could brief the observers sent to San Francisco by nonconsultant organizations. Moreover, a number of the consultant groups and observers set up a separate organization to keep their affiliate groups informed of developments at the Conference and to urge local action on behalf of their proposals. The consultants are credited with making a genuine contribution to the United Nations Charter; their suggestions regarding the scope and authority of the General Assembly and the Social and Economic Council and human rights were particularly effective.[17]

In the postwar period the State Department has cultivated a number of formal as well as informal channels for public opinion. The Bureau of Public Affairs has maintained liaison with nongovernmental organizations, read public correspondence, made studies of press comment, and in other ways attempted to keep abreast of public views. Other bureaus and

16 Robins, op. cit.
17 Chief, Division of Public Liaison, Staff Meeting, June 25, 1945, The Cochran, Friedman and Seamans files, Department of State.

offices in the Department have also listened to public groups. Outside experts are brought into the Department for consultations when necessary, and there are a number of public advisory committees to help the Department keep informed of public attitudes.

THE RISE OF MASS COMMUNICATIONS

A third factor which helps to explain the public dimension of American foreign policy is the growth of mass communications in this century. Information on foreign affairs became much more accessible to the American public in the first decade of the twentieth century than ever before because of the invention of cheap newsprint and high-speed presses on the one hand and telecommunications on the other hand.[18] The resulting growth in the newspaper industry created a need for additional newsgathering services, and this, in turn, brought an end to the cartelization of international news sources. American newspapers began to station their own foreign correspondents abroad, and for the first time the American public had access to an independent source of information about foreign events. Public access to information on foreign affairs was further extended by the development of radio broadcasting and the weekly news magazine in the 1920s and by the development of the television industry in the 1940s and 1950s.

The impact of these new media upon the State Department and its policies cannot be overemphasized, for the advent of each successive mass communications medium greatly facilitated the flow of information between government and the public both at home and abroad. For example, it is conceivable that if Woodrow Wilson had been able to speak directly to the American people on the radio as Franklin Roosevelt was later able to do, the whole course of American foreign policy during the interwar period would have been different. But there was no radio in 1919, and President Wilson had to reach the people

18 Wilber Schramm, *Mass Communications* (Urbana, Ill.: University of Illinois Press, 1960), p. 78.

by train during his nationwide campaign on behalf of the League of Nations. Even then, he could only reach a small proportion of the population directly—relying upon the newspapers to carry his message elsewhere. Radio and television greatly enhanced the relationship between public opinion and foreign policy by providing a truly mass media of communication.

Since most of the news channels are under private control, government agencies, including the State Department, gradually attempted to influence the content of news stories by furnishing information and interpretive material. An entirely new breed of officers was introduced into the State Department. These information (public relations) specialists were charged with the responsibility for placing the Department and its policies in the best possible light. By working closely with representatives of the private media of communication, these government information specialists have attempted to create a favorable public image of the Department, its leaders, and its policies.

State Department Press Relations after World War I. The Department of State did not develop any systematic relations with the press until World War I. Prior to this century, most current information on foreign affairs reached the American public via the President and Congress or, to a lesser extent, by way of a few favored newspapermen who had access to the Secretary of State. The task of informing the press was not even formally recognized by the State Department until 1909 when Secretary of State Philander C. Knox created a Division of Information which, among other things, was to collect "information on matters of public interest as might be given to the press."[19]

The reporters assigned to the State Department were entirely on their own except for the informal meetings which the Secretaries of State, beginning with John Hay, arranged for a few of the "most experienced and trusted correspondents."[20] These

19 See Natalio Summers, *Outline of the Functions of the Office of the Department of State 1789-1943* (Washington, 1943), p. 96.
20 Bertram D. Hulen, *Inside the Department of State* (New York: McGraw Hill Book Company, 1939), pp. 141-144.

informal press conferences began to have their first real importance under Secretary of State Robert Lansing. Although Secretary Lansing met with newspapermen twice daily, he did not pretend to be able to answer the maze of questions which every hour of the day was raised by newspaper cables, and these meetings became more and more perfunctory as the United States was drawn into World War I.[21] In May 1917, Secretary Lansing instructed all officials of the Department "to refrain from discussing matters of public business with press representatives," and he ordered that "all requests for information . . . even to insignificant matters of fact or detail," were to be referred to the new Division of Foreign Intelligence.[22]

Mr. Philip H. Patching, the first Chief of the Division of Information, was brought back into the Department in April 1917, and he, along with Hugh S. Gibson, a career diplomat, became the first press officers of the State Department. The Division of Foreign Intelligence was charged not only with meeting the press but also with supplying news to all American missions abroad; because of this and the Division's relative lack of authority, it confined itself mostly to formal statements on news facts and did not attempt to provide any background or explanation of international events as they occurred.[23] In order to supplement this limited source of news, however, the Division did make it a practice to give "its confidence to one man among the correspondents and to make him responsible for the selection of those of his colleagues whom he considers worthy of being treated on this basis."[24]

It was not until after World War I that the State Department really began to place its press operation on a sound footing. In May 1921, Secretary of State Charles E. Hughes abolished the Division of Foreign Intelligence and placed the press operations of the Department under a new Division of Current Information.[25] The effort of Henry Suydam, the first Chief of this Di-

---

21 *The New York Times,* May 8, 1917, p. 1.
22 Departmental Order 82, May 7, 1917.
23 *The New York Times, loc. cit.*
24 Hugh R. Wilson, Chief of the Division of Current Information 1924-1927, "Memorandum concerning the Division of Current Information," 1924, pp. 2-3.
25 Departmental Order 201, May 5, 1921, and 206, May 24, 1921.

vision, to bring about "a general liberalization of the news sources within the Department, with a view to building up an enlightened public opinion . . . in support of American foreign policy" was largely unsuccessful, for it represented a concept of press relations which was far ahead of its time.[26] It was only after persistent demands by the press and patient but deliberate leadership on the part of Hugh R. Wilson (1924-1927) and Michael J. McDermott (1924-1944) that the Division of Current Information was able to achieve some status in the State Department.

State Department Press Relations after World War II. The new era of press relations began with the Dumbarton Oaks Conference in August 1944. At that time the representatives of the governments of England, Russia, China, and the United States met in Washington, D.C. for preliminary conversations on their respective proposals for international organization. After considerable debate it was decided to allow the press and movie photographers to attend the opening session, but the delegates were agreed that no press statements would be made without the approval of the three chairmen.[27] However, on the third day of the conversations, Scotty Reston of *The New York Times* published an article "which seemed to indicate pretty conclusively that he had had copies of all three plans in his possession."[28] While the publication of the Reston article further convinced the American group of the need for secrecy in meetings of this type, it also meant that "all of the other correspondents were catching hell from their editors and were absolutely on the warpath."[29] This incident set the stage for the first of a number of skirmishes which took place between the Department and the press during the ensuing negotiations.

[26] Henry Suydam, "Report on the Work of the Division of Current Information," the files of the Office of News, Department of State, August 9, 1921, p. 9.
[27] Under Secretary of State Stettinius, Chairman of the United States Delegation, *The Personal Diary of Edward R. Stettinius, Jr. Covering the Dumbarton Oaks Conversations,* Part 1, August 21, 1944, p. 7. The Chinese delegation did not arrive until later in the conversations.
[28] *Ibid.,* "American Group Meeting," August 23, 1944, pp. 1-2.
[29] *Ibid.,* "Telephone Conversation with Mr. McDermott on Press Relations," August 23, 1944, pp. 10-11.

On the very next day a Correspondents Press Committee handed the delegates a statement charging them with secrecy and "pointing out that this policy would result in a vacuum of ignorance which would lead to bad guesses and half-truths of rumor."[30] The press recommended "the day to day release of substantive information."[31] The delegates in turn stressed the informal and explanatory nature of the conversations, but they finally "promised to give serious consideration to the points made by the correspondents."[32] Under Secretary Stettinius, who was selected chairman at the Dumbarton Oaks conversations, concluded that "the meeting did little to correct the fundamental problem, as nothing but a complete reversal of the press policy would have satisfied the correspondents."[33] That evening Mr. Stettinius confided to President Roosevelt "that the thing I was most worried about at Dumbarton was press relations."[34]

On the 14th day of the conversations at Dumbarton Oaks, Under Secretary Stettinius held a press conference which proved to be something of a revelation to him. As he later wrote in his diary, "I met with the press at 2:30 and stayed with them for an hour and ten minutes. They asked me exhaustive and searching questions and it was a grueling experience."[35] The Under Secretary then added that "on several questions they pinned me down and made me say more than I had wanted to tell them."[36] After this encounter with the press Mr. Stettinius went directly to the Secretary's office and told him about the conference. The Under Secretary later noted in his diary that "he did not seem concerned with the fact that I had to give out some substance, saying 'the

---

30 *Ibid.*, "Correspondents Press Committee," August 24, 1944, pp. 3-4.

31 *Ibid.*

32 *Ibid.*

33 *Ibid.* An earlier example of the kind of pressure which the press can exert on delegates to an international conference occurred at the Paris Peace Conference in 1919. On that occasion the American press contingent summarily rejected the first two press officers appointed by President Wilson.

34 *Ibid.*, "Reception and Dinner at the White House for the President of Iceland," August 24, 1944, pp. 21-22.

35 *Ibid.*, September 5, 1944, p. 9.

36 *Ibid.*

world is not going to come to an end if you give the press a little information to keep them happy.' "[37]

After the Dumbarton Oaks Conference, the number of reporters seeking hard news in the Department increased so rapidly that the Secretary of State could no longer meet with them regularly or individually. As the Secretary's conferences with reporters became more and more infrequent, the Special Assistant for Press Relations began to hold fill-in or briefing sessions for the press. These daily briefings soon became a regular source of spot news for reporters, and an information officer gradually emerged as the official spokesman for the State Department.[38]

This daily briefing is held at noon since that hour probably represents the best compromise between the competing demands of reporters for morning and afternoon newspapers. As a dependable source for authoritative statements on developments in the news of the day, the noon briefing has become the event around which diplomatic reporters in Washington organize their daily schedules. Radio and television correspondents usually cover this event in the same manner as newspaper reporters, although the noon briefing does provide an occasion for sound and video coverage if the major networks feel that the situation warrants it.

The emergence of the electronic media has had a profound effect on press coverage of the State Department. Radio and television, along with the wire services, now captured most of the spot news markets. In order to compete, the daily newspapers and the weekly news magazines have emphasized the analysis and interpretation of information in the news. A number of news services, some of which are affiliated with national newspapers, sprang up to furnish the printed media with feature articles and historical material. Although the capability of each channel of communications for hard news and interpretation is somewhat different, there is enough overlap so that the

[37] *Ibid.*, p. 10.
[38] Michael J. McDermott, Hearings before the House Appropriations Subcommittee, 80th Congress, 2nd Session, January 27, 1948, p. 32.

competition which is set in motion among them has strengthened the government's hand.

Reporters use the regular noon briefings and occasional press conferences to get current information, but they normally hold their best questions for the many private interviews they have with individual officers throughout the Department. In addition to these personal interviews, groups of reporters usually arrange to have periodic private conferences with key officials. These private interviews and conferences provide reporters with an opportunity to develop their own interpretations of Department policies and foreign events. Of course, it also gives the Department an opportunity to color the news.

Indeed, the Department's willingness to meet the demands of the press for more liberal information policies often reflects its own interest in getting its view to the public directly. The press, for example, was traditionally prohibited from quoting the Secretary directly at his press conference. Beginning with John Foster Dulles, however, the Secretary of State first encouraged reporters to quote him directly from an official transcript of the press conference and then permitted the entire conference to be carried live by the electronic media. This liberalization of the press conference under Dulles was not a coincidence; Dulles was especially adept at catching the headlines with his explanations and interpretations of American foreign policy.

Of course, mass communications create new dangers as well as new possibilities for the Department. The persistent demand for news fostered by the press and related media makes it increasingly difficult for the State Department either to maintain the myth of majority support for its policies in the face of dramatic protests, or to remain silent when prudence requires it. On the other hand, the insatiable appetite for news makes the communications media especially vulnerable to Department propaganda. The information activities of government agencies almost inevitably go beyond what is necessary to create mere public understanding. Agencies usually paint their activities in glowing terms in order to sell them to the public. Mass communications thus make it at once more difficult and more important to choose between secrecy and publicity and to distinguish between information and propaganda.

THE GROWING PUBLIC CHARACTER OF INTERNATIONAL RELATIONS

A final reason for the growth of the public dimension of American foreign policy is the ease with which both information and persons can be transported today. Frequent summit conferences and other highly publicized international meetings have focused public attention on foreign affairs. Indeed, it is often alleged that the real purpose of these encounters is to set the climate of world opinion. Global and regional organizations provide permanent international forums for public as well as private discussions of world problems among governments, and these discussions receive widespread publicity during periods of crisis such as the Arab-Israeli War in June 1967.

Moreover, each of the major powers has established an elaborate overseas information service to influence foreign opinion. Although the deep ideological struggle between Communist and Western countries has intensified this development, these information programs are not directed solely at hostile states. Indeed, overseas information activities are probably more effective when aimed at neutral or friendly states because a larger portion of the population in these countries will find the information credible. These propaganda efforts tend to make diplomacy more public because those in charge of these activities have a stake in releasing as much information as possible, particularly if it is information which the incumbent government has withheld from the public.

The widespread use of mass communications as an instrument of foreign policy and the susceptibility of international news to manipulation by foreign news sources have compelled governments to perfect their own domestic information programs. No nation can afford to have its domestic public receive its first and most complete information from abroad. If the State Department is not prepared to provide sufficient background information to the press, the "representatives of other countries are generally willing, and often eager to give out their interpretation."[39] As early as 1921, the chief of the Department's press office recommended that "Information about American foreign policy should reach our own public through an American source no less effective and far more straightforward than the necessarily biased and interested interpretations and reactions put upon it in Europe."[40]

Yet the need for a strong domestic information program is not solely the result of the public information activities of foreign governments; there are all sorts of private groups and institutions within the United States and other countries which are involved in matters transcending national boundaries. Indeed, there is scarcely an important business, labor, agricultural, veteran, or service group in America which does not have branches, affiliates, representatives, or programs abroad. In negotiating and dealing with similar groups abroad or even with the governments of other states, these groups do affect American policy abroad. For example, in October 1961 the Veterans of Foreign Wars helped to reassure the Republic of France that neither the people nor the government of the United States "was associated with the reported assistance extended to injured Algerian rebels by another veterans group in the United States."[41]

Private groups and individuals can affect American foreign policy through their actions at home as well as abroad. For example, in February 1964, Secretary of State Dean Rusk stated that "foreign concerns that trade with Cuba may be jeopardizing their sales on the American market because of 'consumer reaction' against them."[42] Although Secretary Rusk denied that he was calling for a consumer boycott, the incident does indicate the kind of impact which private groups can have on American foreign relations. Moreover, some groups influence American

---

[39] "The Foreign Service and the Correspondents," *The American Foreign Service Journal*, Vol. XXV, No. 8, August 1948, p. 9.

[40] Henry Suydam, "Memorandum on the Organization of a Press Division in the Department of State," April 14, 1921, pp. 6-7.

[41] News Release, Veterans of Foreign Wars of the U.S., October 24, 1961.

[42] *The New York Times*, February 16, 1964, p. 1.

diplomacy simply by acting as domestic pressure groups. For example, in February 1964 the International Longshoremen's Association effectively blocked grain shipments to Russia by refusing to load wheat for Russia and other Soviet bloc countries until the Government agreed that 50 percent of the grain sold under future export licenses would be carried in United States flagships.[43] Since the actions of these private groups and institutions often do affect United States policies abroad, the State Department must have the means of explaining its policies to these groups and their members.

[43] *The New York Times,* February 26, 1964, p. 1.

Chapter 3

Congressional Restraints on the State Department

THE ATTITUDES OF Congress as an institution toward the public relations of the State Department are quite ambiguous. On the one hand, Congress is largely dependent on the State Department and the administration for information on foreign policy. Indeed, Congress is one of the largest consumers of Department publicity. On the other hand, Congress regards itself as the primary link between the people and their government, and it is quite critical of State Department efforts to bypass Congress and inform the public directly. Congress is also suspicious of Department efforts to obtain an independent assessment of public opinion on foreign affairs.

CONGRESS AND THE DISSEMINATION OF POLICY INFORMATION

Congress is quite wary of Department efforts to speak directly with the public. The standard congressional criticism of the Department's information activities is that they are designed to sell foreign policies and programs to the American public be-

37

fore they have been approved by Congress. Congressmen apparently fear that information activities are employed largely to strengthen the Department's position *vis-à-vis* the Congress.

Occasionally, Department spokesmen under the persistent questioning of members of Congress acknowledge that one of the inevitable results of their information activities is to influence current legislation. When Mr. Carl T. Rowen was Acting Assistant Secretary of State for Public Affairs, for example, he admitted to the House Appropriations Subcommittee that this was the effect of the Department's activities in support of the Reciprocal Trade Agreements program in 1962.

> *Mr. Bow.* The purpose of this drive you are making is to get your story across to the American people. You are hoping by reason of the American people reading this particular side of the story and reading your pamphlet that they in turn will bring pressure upon Congress to pass this legislation; is that not the very purpose of it?
>
> *Mr. Rowen.* Well, we hope that the American people will come to the conclusion that this is in the national interest, and in the process of democracy I guess they would make their views known to Congressmen.
>
> *Mr. Bow.* That is one of the purposes of it, isn't it?
>
> *Mr. Rowen.* Well, it is not directly an effort to pressure Congressmen, but that is a purpose in effect.
>
> *Mr. Bow.* It is one of the purposes, and it is what you are driving at?
>
> *Mr. Rowen.* Yes, that is correct.
>
> *Mr. Bow.* That is true of the briefing conferences, the speaking engagements and the current documentation. The whole purpose of the $64,000 you are asking for all falls into this category, doesn't it?
>
> *Mr. Rowen.* Yes it all does.[1]

Moreover, many Congressmen argue that Department publications and speeches are not information at all but rather propa-

[1] *Hearings* before the House Subcommittee on Deficiencies of the Committee on Appropriations, 87th Congress, 2nd Session, Second Supplemental Appropriation Bill, 1962, p. 291.

ganda since they contain only the views of the State Department and the Administration. Indeed, some Congressmen have argued that the Government has no right to use the taxpayers' money to state a position with which some taxpayers disagree.[2] Of course, "This principle, logically carried out, would make government impossible."[3] It is simply not practicable for the State Department or any other government agency to handle complex international issues in a way which will satisfy everyone. By presenting as complete and objective a picture of its own position as possible, however, information officers believe that they can serve the opponents as well as the proponents of any given measure, for such information provides a solid foundation for constructive criticism as well as enlightened support.

Nevertheless, Congress has tried a variety of techniques to regulate these government information activities over the last fifty years. For example, it attempts to distinguish between the public affairs activities of career information officers and the partisan activities of political appointees in the State Department. Political appointees are expected to seek public support for current administration policies and programs in their personal statements and appearances; the career information officers of the Department are not. Indeed, those who conduct the Department's information program are expected studiously to avoid activities which might give substance to the charge that they are lobbying on behalf of legislation currently before Congress.

Since World War II the Appropriations Bill for the Department of State and Justice and the Judiciary and Related Agencies has also prohibited the use of funds for "publicity and propaganda purposes."[4] Running through all of these Congres-

---

[2] See Richard Nixon, *Congressional Record*, August 24, 1951, p. 10611. Also, former Senator William Knowland, *Congressional Record*, January 31, 1951.

[3] See Elmer Davis, "Report to the President on the Office of War Information," *Hearings* before the House Subcommittee on Governmental Information, "Government Information Plans and Policies," Part II, 88th Congress, 1st Session, p. 240.

[4] See U.S. Statutes at Large, 1945-1967.

sional restrictions on government publicity is the notion that it is possible for those administering a given policy or program to maintain a sharp distinction between proper and improper publicity—between information and propaganda. Yet, the need to enact new regulations seems to deny the fact that there is any simple test by which either the Administration or the Congress can readily distinguish information from propaganda.

Congress has repeatedly modified its general strictures against government publicity in order to insure that the public and the Congress are informed on foreign policy. Even the Congressional prohibition against "the use of appropriated funds for the dissemination within the United States of general propaganda in support of the mutual security program,"[5] the so-called Dowarshak amendment, was interpreted by the conference committee so as to deny any "interference with the supplying of full information to the Congress and to the public concerning the operations of the mutual security program."[6] While no one has ever been prosecuted for violating this or any other such statute, a number of Department information officers indicate that these restrictions have had a psychological effect on the Department's information activities.

But Congress has not relied solely, or even primarily, upon these statutory provisions to limit Departmental publicity, as the paucity of funds annually appropriated for domestic information activities amply demonstrates. There have been repeated efforts in Congress to reduce, if not to eliminate entirely, various information activities and programs. For example, when the State, Justice, and Commerce Appropriation Bill for 1952 (H.R. 4740) reached the Senate floor, the then Senator Richard Nixon rose to amend the bill so that "no part of this appropriation shall be available to pay the compensation of any person employed in the Division of Public Liaison or to pay any expenses incurred by such Division."[7] Nixon's amendment failed adoption, but an amendment (Sec. 605) sponsored by Senator

5 "Mutual Security Act of 1952," Public Law 400.
6 *Hearings* before the House Appropriations Subcommittee, 86th Congress, 1st Session, p. 678.
7 *Congressional Record*, August 24, 1951, p. 10611.

Byrd of Virginia applying "a 25 percent cut against the budget estimate for publicity and propaganda activities in the various departments covered by the bill" was passed without a division of the Senate.[8]

When the conference committee later dropped Sec. 605 of the bill, Senator Ferguson of Michigan, one of the conferees, asked that the conference report be rejected unless the Byrd amendment was restored. He opposed the bill in spite of the fact that every item of the appropriation carried a personnel reduction of 10 percent, regardless of whether the budget estimate was allowed or not.[9] After a lengthy floor debate, the Senate adopted the conference report without alteration by a vote of 31 to 27. However, Senator Ferguson, joined by Senators Bridges and Knowland, reopened the matter seven days later by incorporating the Byrd publicity amendment in the Second Supplemental Appropriations Bill of 1952 (H.G. 5650). While this scheme also failed in the end, the strong opposition of key Congressional figures to the Department's domestic information activities was not readily forgotten by some of the "old-timers" interviewed in the Bureau of Public Affairs.

For the most part, however, Congressional surveillance of the Department's information activities has been less dramatic but more effective than the above incident suggests. Congress has effectively controlled certain types of Department publicity without having to place the mechanics of this control on the public record. For example, one information officer recalled that the late Congressman Taber, who was Chairman of the House Appropriations Committee, used to sit in on the executive hearings on State Department appropriations and take an active part in the proceedings although his presence and comments were systematically stricken from the record. According to this officer, Congressman Taber made his biggest impact upon the appropriations for State Department information activities after the hearings—during the mark up period for the bill.

The inability of Congress to find an effective means of distinguishing between proper and improper government publicity

8 *Ibid.*, October 12, 1951, p. 13075.
9 *Ibid.*, p. 10542.

has increasingly compelled it to rely upon its power over the purse to control Department information activities, and this in turn has had a profound effect upon the nature and scope of the Department's information program. By restricting funds for salaries and other expenses either selectively or across the board, Congress has made it difficult for the Department to develop and sustain an effective information-education program of its own. As a result, Congress has forced the Department to rely mainly upon the headline approach to international news.

Moreover, the fact that the State Department has trouble reaching the public with its own publication, speaker, and conference programs has forced the Department to rely more and more upon the manipulation of the private media of communication in order to get its story across to the American people. Thus, the success which Congress has enjoyed in restricting those information activities by which the Department reaches the public directly only serves to increase the Department's efforts to reach the public indirectly through the privately owned, mass media of communication.

In view of the partisan basis for much of the Congressional criticism of Department information activities, it is tempting to argue that the State Department should limit its information activities to those foreign policies and programs which already have bipartisan support in Congress. However, this argument really begs the question. If there is already strong Congressional support for a policy, there is often less need for the government to explain it to the public. On the other hand, it can be argued that government publicity on matters having strong bipartisan support are more likely to take on the character of propaganda since the members of both parties in Congress have a stake in promoting these policies.

The fact is that the State Department must have the means to explain its policy to the public whether it happens to be controversial policy or not. As long as the State Department is primarily responsible for initiating foreign policy, there will be tremendous pressure upon the Department to give these policies the chance they need for success by promoting them. Even Congress is often unwilling to support new measures until public opinion has crystallized on them. Of course, there is always the danger that the Department will oversell policies in an effort to develop public support for them, but that is another problem altogether. The point is that Congress cannot hope to limit the Department's domestic information activities to areas of consent. It can only hope to eliminate some of the more dangerous manifestations of government publicity.

CONGRESS AND THE COLLECTION OF OPINION INFORMATION

Congress has also been openly suspicious of the Department's efforts to study public opinion. Congressmen apparently perceive public opinion studies as a technique which the Administration uses to improve its propaganda efforts, to perpetuate itself in power, and to usurp the role of Congress as the reflection of public opinion. The last attitude was clearly portrayed in the clash between Congressman Knox of Michigan and H. Schuyler Foster of the Public Opinion Studies Staff during the hearings on "State Department Public Opinion Polls" in July 1957.

> *Mr. Knox* . . . . Mr. Foster, as a political scientist, you are doubtless familiar with the role assigned to each of our major [branches] of government—[Executive], Congress, and Judiciary, under the Constitution, are you not?
>
> *Mr. Foster.* Yes sir.
>
> *Mr. Knox.* Would it be proper to say that one of the principal responsibilities of the Congress is to represent the American people, to express American public opinion, on such matters as foreign policy?
>
> *Mr. Foster.* Yes; I would.
>
> *Mr. Knox.* It is true, however, is it not, that one of the reasons for electing a new Congress every 2 years is in response to public opinion?
>
> *Mr. Foster.* That is often stated. I think that is one of the reasons for it.
>
> *Mr. Knox.* You would say that is the reason?
>
> *Mr. Foster.* Yes.
>
> *Mr. Knox.* The election of a President every 4 years has not

served its purpose quite as well as having Congress elected every 2 years; isn't that correct?

Mr. Foster. Yes; if it were governed only by the interval between elections, that would certainly be true. Of course, that is not the only factor.

Mr. Knox. What are the other factors?

Mr. Foster. The extent to which the legislators and the Chief Executive gain accurate information, as to what the state of thinking of the people is.

Mr. Knox. Is that all the justifications you have?

Mr. Foster. Well, I don't know that that is all.

Mr. Knox. Well, then, if we are agreed that the chief and most responsive mechanism of our Government for expressing changes in public opinion of foreign policy is the Congress, what function does public-opinion polling by the President or the State Department serve?

Mr. Foster. It serves several functions. . . .

Mr. Knox. Well then, the Secretary is limited by making use of the agency of Government to which public opinion is intended to be formally expressed, namely, the Congress.

Mr. Foster. But, Mr. Knox, the primary purpose of Congress . . . is to enact laws, and not to convey from week to week, and day to day, the opinions of the American people on all topics, foreign and domestic.

Mr. Knox. Well, now, Mr. Foster, you are aware of the fact that the Secretary of State often appears before committees of Congress and testifies, which, from the questions that are propounded to the Secretary and his answers to them, certainly gives him some indication as to what public opinion is, as far as Congress is concerned, does it not?

Mr. Foster. Yes. I would think it would be more accurate, Mr. Knox, to call that congressional opinion, or perhaps, committee opinion.

Mr. Knox. Are you inclined to believe that the Members of Congress are not representing the people who elected them to Congress in the manner which was in their best judgment, and in conformity with the opinions of the people who elected them?

Mr. Foster. I, of course, did not say that, Mr. Knox, but you know many Members of Congress seem to find it helpful themselves to conduct polls, in order to improve their understanding of the thinking of their constituents on these questions.

Mr. Knox. If that is true . . . , it certainly should reflect in their statements to the Department or other agencies of the Government, should it not?

Mr. Foster. I think it does. We, ourselves, make a careful study of all those that are listed in the Congressional Record.

Mr. Knox. Well, Congress is not enough. You feel you should go beyond that. You don't think the opinion of Congress represents the American people.

Mr. Foster. I would not think, Mr. Knox, that that would be the most reliable place in which to get information on what all of the people across the country are thinking about all of the various topics of foreign affairs concerning which the State Department needs to know what they are thinking.

Mr. Knox. Did you ever have an occasion to analyze a Congressman's mail?

Mr. Foster. No; I have not.

Mr. Knox. I think if you had, you would not take the position which you do. I think the American people of today are very astute, and they let their opinion be known to the Member of Congress so that the Member of Congress has some idea as to what the people in the district are thinking.

Mr. Foster. There are many cases in which public opinion polls suggest that the mail received on particular questions comes, as of course it must, from a relatively tiny portion of the total electing population, and quite different in character, from the results obtained in the polls.[10]

The idea that State Department public opinion studies are really unnecessary is reinforced in the minds of many congressmen by the fear that the Department uses such studies to influence Congress on matters coming before that body. Some congressmen suspect that opinion information is periodically leaked to the public by the Department in order to embarrass congressmen who are opposed to the Administration's foreign policy. Still others suspect that information obtained from polls

10 *Hearings* before the International Operations Subcommittee of the House Committee on Government Operations, 85th Congress, 1st Session, pp. 206-208.

is used as the basis for propaganda campaigns designed to engineer public support for Department programs before Congress.

Indeed, Congress first became interested in State Department polls when an official of the International Cooperation Administration (ICA) leaked the findings of five nationwide polls which showed significant public support for the foreign aid policy at the same time that congressmen claimed that their mail was strongly in favor of a budget cut. These polls, which were clearly identified with the executive branch, raised serious doubts in the press about some of the assumptions that prevailed in Congress about the unpopularity of the aid program, particularly economic assistance to neutral nations.[11] In view of the influence which public opinion polls themselves may have on public attitudes, Congressman Hardy and others suspected that the results of these and other polls were being used by the Administration as a self-serving device.[12]

Although the subsequent investigation was primarily directed at the alleged misuse of funds for polling purposes, there was some concern that the results of these polls might also be used for a publicity campaign on matters currently before Congress. It was apparent that ICA officials were disturbed by the fact that the public's support of the mutual security program had little, if any, relation to the explanation which the Administration had given for it; ICA officials apparently concluded that they would have to make even more strenuous efforts to get their message across to the public. Congressmen Reuss and Hardy were both alarmed by the allusions which ICA officials made to an educational campaign. They felt that these officials were "trying to create an attitude of acceptance on the part of the public generally for the future, rather than merely trying to point out all of the factual developments of the program from the past. And when you get into that, if that isn't pure propaganda, I do not know what it is."[13]

11 E. W. Kenworthy, The *New York Times*, March 17, 1957.
12 *Hearings* before the House International Operations Subcommittee, *op. cit.*, pp. 109-110.
13 *Ibid.*, p. 285.

Another criticism leveled at the polls by legislators is that they are inaccurate. For example, the Subcommittee investigating "State Department Public Opinion Polls" was very disturbed with the interpretation which the ICA gave one of the questions asked by the State Department on foreign aid. The question was "Do you think we should or should not continue to send economic aid like machinery and supplies to countries that have agreed to stand with us against Communism?"[14] Ninety percent of the respondents said that we should continue economic aid, 7 percent stated that we should not continue it, and only 3 percent did not express an opinion. In an ICA memorandum dated February 12, 1956, however, the same figures were used to represent approval of the entire foreign aid program. Noting that on these questions the Department did not distinguish between informed and uninformed respondents, Congressman Hardy questioned a number of administrative officials on the value of the polls.

> *Mr. Hardy.* Well, I could understand how a question like that might have some significance if the people questioned had enough knowledge to answer intelligently. But for people who generally didn't have the remotest idea whether you were selling it, giving it away, whom it was going to, what use it was being put to, whether it was going behind the Iron Curtain, or what, I frankly don't understand how anybody could make any use of it and I would just be interested in knowing your reason.
>
> *Mr. Ryan.* On the assumption—I suppose this is in part, Mr. Chairman, because people do act on these kinds of beliefs, these kinds of conclusions.
>
> *Mr. Hardy.* I hope the State Department doesn't act on that kind of information.[15]

Congress has imposed no formal restrictions on the use of opinion polls by the State Department, but Congressional criti-

---

14 See "State Department Public Opinion Polls," *House Report*, No. 1166, p. 11.
15 *Hearings* before the House International Operations Subcommittee, *op. cit.*, p. 117.

cism of the Department's polling operation has made it more difficult to continue these activities. Indeed, the Department's decision to terminate its contracts with polling agencies in April 1957 was made during the Congressional hearings discussed above. Although it would be an error to conclude that the Department stopped its efforts to survey public attitudes systematically because of Congressional criticism, it was probably a contributing factor.

PART II

Participants

Chapter 4

Characteristics of Position
Holders

THE PUBLIC DIMENSION of American foreign policy involves the
actions and reactions of four key groups: State Department
policy officers, State Department information officers, foreign
affairs reporters, and leaders of nongovernmental organizations.
By providing information to the public, each of these groups
helps to form public *opinion;* by providing and considering
public views on foreign affairs, each of these groups also contributes to making foreign *policy.* Since the activities or role of
each group in the *opinion-policy* process is dependent at least
in part on the activities or role of the other three groups, these
interdependent roles may be viewed as a political system.

In the language of role analysis, each of these groups occupies a position in the political system which concerns the
opinion-policy process. The term "position" refers to the location of an individual or set of individuals in such a system although it is difficult to separate the idea of location from the
relationships which define it.[1] Nevertheless, the purpose of this
chapter is to describe the incumbents of positions in a system
of interaction and not specifically to describe the relations be-

1 Neal Gross, Ward S. Mason, and Alexander W. McEachern, *Explorations in
Role Analysis: Studies of the School Superintendency Role* (New York: John
Wiley and Sons, 1958), p. 48.

51

tween them. These position holders will be described first in terms of the characteristics of the office or position they occupy and then in terms of their individual characteristics.

POSITIONAL CHARACTERISTICS

The participants in this study occupy one of four positions in the system governing the opinion-policy process. Each group of position holders performs actions distinct from counter position holders. Yet, there are also important differences among each group of position holders in the tasks they perform. The activities of various position holders are discussed below.

State Department Policy Officers

The policy officers in this study all share some responsibility for the conduct of American diplomacy, but the character and scope of contemporary foreign policy requires them to become engaged in a wide range of issue-areas. The activities of policy officers vary along two dimensions. First, these officers deal with a variety of area and functional specialties. Second, these officers contribute to varying phases of the foreign policy decision-making process.

Area Specialists. One group of policy officers in the State Department is responsible for conducting the bilateral relations between the United States and other foreign governments. These officers are ostensibly concerned with all aspects of these relations: political, security, economic, public affairs, educational and cultural affairs, and so on. They are organized into five geographic or regional bureaus: Bureau of African Affairs, Bureau of East Asian and Pacific Affairs, Bureau of European Affairs, Bureau of Inter-American Affairs, and the Bureau of Near Eastern and South Asian Affairs.

The responsibilities of the officials in these geographic bureaus vary according to the level at which they operate. There are one or more country desk officers for each country. These officers are the focal point within the State Department and the government for United States relations with each country. They are responsible for maintaining and supervising the communications between the government in Washington and the United States embassy in that country. They also handle relations between the government and the foreign mission of that country in the United States. Since they are perhaps the only persons in the government who read all of the incoming and outgoing messages between the two countries, these area desk officers are the principal resource people in the government on their particular country.

These officers do not have the authority either to make decisions or to initiate communications themselves. They must constantly refer problems for decision to others: their immediate superiors, decision-makers in other bureaus and subunits in the Department, and decision-makers in other federal agencies. Since they are often the first to become aware of foreign policy problems, these desk officers often help their superiors identify some of the problems with which they must deal. Moreover, they are frequently asked to write the initial drafts of policy statements by their superiors. Country officers, however, influence policy only as a consistent element.

Country officers report directly to a Country Director. The Country Director is a newly created position; its occupant usually has jurisdiction over U.S. relations with several countries, although there is a Country Director for each of the larger states. Unlike the country officer, the Country Director has the authority to send messages abroad and to make policy recommendations to his superiors. He also has a major responsibility for coordinating policy within the State Department and the government.

Country Directors are, in turn, responsible to the Assistant Secretary who heads their respective regional bureaus. Regional Assistant Secretaries have a general mandate to make day-to-day decisions on matters within their jurisdiction. In many cases, this is a negative power since they are reviewing the recommendations of area desk officers and Country Directors. Yet, they have a responsibility: for forming regional policy recommendations; for coordinating policy on an interagency basis; and for planning ahead on key regional problems. Since some of the most difficult foreign policy problems feature the conflicting interests of various regions, Assistant Secretaries are expected to resolve as many issues as possible lest they all come to the Secretary of State or others in the Secretariat for decision.

Functional Specialists. It is not possible to approach international problems solely from the standpoint of our relations with a particular country or region; it is also necessary to ensure that there is some consistency among the various components of American policy on a worldwide basis. The responsibility for conducting various elements of foreign policy on a worldwide basis is the task of another group of policy officers in the State Department. These officers bring knowledge of particular instruments of policy to bear on international problems. They are organized into a number of functional bureaus, such as the Bureau of Economic Affairs, the Bureau of International Organization Affairs, the Bureau of Education and Cultural Affairs, the Bureau of Security and Consular Affairs, the Bureau of Intelligence and Research, and of course the Bureau of Public Affairs, as well as a number of separate offices for the Legal Advisor, the Director of International Scientific and Technological Affairs, and so on.

These functional bureaus are less powerful and have less clear-cut jurisdiction than their regional counterparts. They usually receive jurisdiction over a problem area in their field of specialty only when it must be approached from a worldwide perspective and none of the regional bureaus can legitimately claim to make these decisions themselves because it involves the interests of several regional bureaus. Even then, functional bureaus must work very closely with those in the regional bureaus.

The responsibilities of officials in these functional bureaus also vary according to the level at which they operate. There is usually a Division Chief in charge of each program or activity assigned to one of these bureaus. This officer has responsibility for carrying out the existing policy and keeping superiors informed of problems requiring special attention. As in the case of country officers, these officials are the primary source people in the Department on their specialty.

Division Chiefs report directly to Office Directors who supervise the activities of several related programs. These Office Directors make day-to-day decisions and have an ongoing responsibility to recommend new policies to their superiors. These officers also have responsibility for coordinating the activities of their office with other bureaus in the Department as well as other federal agencies.

Office Directors are responsible to the Assistant Secretaries of the bureaus, who serve as the principal advisors in their specialty to the Secretary of State. They have a mandate to make decisions in their area and if possible to resolve differences between their bureau and other bureaus. Assistant Secretaries also have responsibility to plan and coordinate their activities with their counterparts in other government agencies.

The Secretariat. The problem of coordinating the action of the Department becomes most severe at the higher levels in the Department because the officers involved represent such different perspectives. Some look at policy from the standpoint of a given region, others from its impact on the use of a particular instrument. Top level policy officers have the difficult task of making the final determination of policy in these cases. In addition, top level officials must provide some of the housekeeping and other services required by the Department. Operational officers seldom have the opportunity to plan ahead, and so officers at this level engage in the planning function.

Positional Variables. The public affairs activities of policy officials vary according to the office or position they hold in the State Department. Because of the character of the positions they hold, these policy officers encounter various types of public affairs problems. Because of the character of the positions they occupy, these policy officers also have varying amounts of discretion in the opinion-policy process. These positional variables are discussed below.

In the first place, public affairs activities may be a function of various policy specialties. Policy officers who deal with country, regional, or other area problems may encounter a different set of public affairs problems from those who deal with aspects of policy which cut across geographical boundaries. One measure for this variable is the distinction between regional and functional bureaus. Another measure for this variable is career service. The elite corps of Foreign Service Officers (FSOs) in the State Department tend to approach problems on a geographic basis because they serve most of their career as representatives to particular countries and because they traditionally seek and secure positions in regional bureaus when they are in Washington. Policy officers in the Foreign Service Reserve, the Foreign Service Career Reserve (USIA), and the Civil Service often specialize in some aspect of foreign policy. They are less likely than FSOs to hold positions in regional bureaus. They are also less likely than FSOs to serve abroad.

In the second place, public affairs is a more important aspect of policy making in some positions than in other positions. International organizations, especially the United Nations and many of the specialized agencies associated with it, for example, have nurtured a close tie with the American public, and this is an important aspect of the responsibilities of officers in this bureau. On the other hand, officers in the Bureau of Intelligence and Research until 1960 were not even supposed to discuss policies with reporters and other representatives of the public. The measure for this variable is the number of information officers in each of the bureaus. In December 1965, there were three or more information officers in the bureaus of African Affairs, Inter-American Affairs, International Organization Affairs, and East Asian and Pacific Affairs. There were two or fewer information officers in the bureaus of Educational and Cultural Affairs, Economic Affairs, European Affairs, Near Eastern and South Asian Affairs, and so on.[2] Another possible measure for this variable is the type of appointment. Public affairs is probably more important to those with political appointments.

In the third place, the policy issues encountered by some position holders are more sensitive than they are for other position holders. Officers in the Bureau of Near Eastern and South Asian Affairs, for example, find it exceedingly difficult to carry

[2] See list of "Public Affairs Advisers in the Department of State, ACDA, and AID" prepared by the Bureau of Public Affairs, Department of State, dated December 20, 1965.

out a full-fledged information program because of the intense hostility between Arabs and Jews in the Middle East and because of the influential Jewish community in this country. On the other hand, the Bureau of Inter-American Affairs handles our relations with countries which are essentially friendly to the United States. Although the sample of policy officers was not originally designed to reflect these differences among them, it may be possible to distinguish between officers in regional bureaus on the basis of the friendly or hostile tone of United States relations with the countries for which they are responsible.

In the fourth place, the incumbents of some positions have more decision latitude than others. Some officers have a general mandate to make policy at least on day-to-day problems which arise in their area of responsibility. Other officials affect policy only as a persistent element in the policy-making process. The measure of this variable is the level at which an official operates in the Department. Assistant Secretaries as well as the relatively new category of Country Directors in the regional bureaus and Office Directors in functional bureaus have policy-making authority. In contrast, desk officers in regional bureaus and Division Chiefs in functional bureaus seldom have the authority to make policy on their own. Another measure for the authority and status of officers in the State Department is rank in their respective career services. With the exception of the Civil Service where officers acquire their rank from the position they occupy, members of other career services in the Department acquire rank independently of the position they occupy in the Department. Officers holding lower ranks are occasionally found at work in the Secretariat and higher-ranking officials are occasionally assigned to lower-level tasks, especially for short periods.

Finally, officers vary for whatever the reasons in their familiarity with the activities of counter position holders. Some officers have more frequent contacts than their colleagues with counter position holders. In order to measure this factor, each officer was asked to estimate how frequently he had contacts with counter position holders. Officers who met a counter position holder at least once a week were said to have frequent contact; those who met a counter position holder at least once a month had occasional contact; and those who met a counter position holder at least once a year were said seldom to have contact.

State Department Information Officers

The information officers in this study are all engaged in the development and maintenance of a two-way flow of communications between the Department of State and the public. The activities of these officers vary, depending both upon their location in the Department and upon the clientele they serve. Information officers are generally located either in the Secretariat, the Bureau of Public Affairs, or the Offices of Public Affairs Advisors and similar offices in each of the regional and functional bureaus.

The Secretariat. Perhaps, the best known information activity in the State Department is the spot news operation which is located in the Office of Press Relations in the Office of The Secretary.[3] The information officers in this Office are the principal channel of authoritative statements on current American foreign policy. When the Department wants to make news, these officers make statements to the press and arrange for press conferences. They also serve as sources for official confirmation, denial, or comment on diplomatic news originating outside the Department.

The activities of these press officers are centered around the noon briefing which is held in the Department every day. The noon briefing divides the press officers' work into roughly two parts. Prior to the noon briefing, the press officer tries to anticipate press inquiries and get appropriate responses to them. After the noon briefing, he answers individual queries on the basis of the guidance he has received for the noon briefing and attempts to follow-up some of the loose ends, if any, resulting from the exchange between the Department spokesman and reporters.

In the course of preparing for the daily noon briefing and the

[3] From July 1953 to July 1969 the Office of News, now Office of Press Relations, was located in the Bureau of Public Affairs. See *Foreign Affairs Manual Circular*, No. 531, July 24, 1969.

occasional press conferences of the Secretary and other top officials, information specialists prepare summaries of important news developments, answer hundreds of individual inquiries, and issue press releases. In addition to the briefing books prepared for formal press conferences, information officers are also called upon to serve as press officers at various international conferences or trouble spots around the world.

Reporters are also interested in the analysis and interpretation which Department officials may give to them on a not-for-attribution basis, and the press occasionally arranges for key officials to meet with reporters as a group for this purpose. Moreover, press officers themselves are often called upon to interpret Department policies and external events for reporters when they have kept abreast of developments.

The Bureau of Public Affairs. So much attention is given to the spot news operation that it is easy to overlook the fact that most information activities are channelled through the Bureau of Public Affairs or "P" area. Information officers in the Bureau's Office of Policy Guidance, Office of Media Services, Office of Public Services, and Historical Office are largely responsible for meeting the needs of the public for basic information and materials on foreign affairs.[4]

The personnel of the Office of Policy Guidance coordinate public affairs guidance on foreign policy within the Department and between the Department, the White House, and other agencies of the Government. For example, this staff coordinates policy guidance provided to the U.S. Information Agency and reviews and provides guidance on public statements involving foreign policy by government officials. Officers on this staff also prepare some analyses of American opinion on selected foreign policy issues and develop plans for informing the public about U.S. foreign policy.

The officers in the Office of Media Services try to take advantage of the trend toward independent public affairs programming by local TV and radio stations across the country by providing them with sound tapes, films, broadcast participants,

---

[4] Historical officers are not included in the population of information officers in this study.

and other assistance on request. They also encourage and assist weekly newspapers and magazines, which do not regularly cover foreign affairs, to print an occasional article on American foreign policy. In addition, they stimulate media efforts by holding national and regional foreign policy briefing conferences for editors and broadcasters. In recent years, they have also worked to foster and support better world affairs education in our schools, particularly secondary schools, by producing publications, recordings, films and filmstrips suitable for classroom use by teachers and students.

Information officers in the General Publications Division of this office prepare the *Department of State Bulletin*. Beginning in 1948, the Department supplemented the material in the *Bulletin* by developing a number of pocketsized pamphlets on American foreign policy, such as Fact Sheet, Background, and Foreign Affairs Outline. Each of these series was designed to deal with current opinion situations. The Department also puts out a number of very inexpensive "Background Notes" on various foreign countries. A new classroom series of publications, called "Issues in United States Foreign Policy," is designed to introduce the student, and the general lay public, to the key factors involved in difficult international questions without arguing the case for any given policy toward those questions.

The Department also attempts to reach the public directly through the Office of Public Services. The organization liaison officers of this office work closely with leaders of nongovernmental organizations with an interest in foreign affairs. These liaison officers attempt to facilitate the flow of information between these organizations and the State Department. In addition to supplying these organizations with information, the liaison officers help the organizations plan their own information-education programs in foreign affairs.

These officers also attempt to reach organization members directly. Beginning in June 1945, the Department sponsored an annual national conference for nongovernmental organizations at the State Department and, with the exception of several years during the Eisenhower Administration, these conferences have been held ever since. Moreover, the Office has encouraged Department officers to accept outside speaking and conference engagements as a means of bringing Department views directly to the attention of the public. In recent years the Department has not only increased the number of speaking engagements accepted by Department officers, but it has also sponsored a growing number of national, regional, and even community foreign policy briefing conferences throughout the country.

In addition to servicing the requests of groups for information and speakers, the information officers in this Office provide a channel for public views within the Department. Information officers in the Division of Public Correspondence systematically read and answer the public correspondence dealing with foreign policy sent to the President, the Secretary of State, and other government officials. Some of these letters along with the Department responses are regularly circulated in a newspaper column prepared by the Department called "Diplomatic Pouch."

Moreover, information officers seek to provide those segments of the public which require historical documentation access to some of the most important papers behind American foreign policy. The basic record of foreign relations is contained in the distinguished *Foreign Relations* series which has been published since 1861. This series contains the most important official documents of American foreign policy. Since this series runs nearly twenty-five years behind, however, the Historical Office also annually publishes current unclassified documentary material in *American Foreign Policy: Current Documents* so that important statements, treaties, and other materials will be readily available to the public.

Since only the more important documents can be published in the *Foreign Relations* series, the Department permits nonofficial research in its files in accordance with regulations which are administered by the Historical Office. As of January 1969, the regulations provided for three periods with respect to access to records for nonofficial research purposes: open, closed, and restricted. The open period is the period up to 30 years from the current year (at present, through 1938). The closed period is the period in advance of the publication of the *Foreign Relations* volumes (1945 to date). Between the open and closed periods is the restricted period, which at present extends from 1939 through 1944. On many topics the Department grants qualified researchers who are United States citizens access to records of the restricted period upon approval of their application and subject to the review of their notes. The foreign policy records for the open period may be consulted in the National Archives without a requirement of Department of State permission.[5]

Offices of Public Affairs Advisors. As the official outlet for general public explanations of American foreign policy, the above-mentioned information officers are very dependent upon geographical and functional specialists for information and policy guidance. In order to build a more effective working relationship between these information officers and the geographical and functional specialists, the Bureau of Public Affairs once sponsored a number of inter-departmental "Public Affairs Policy and Program Committees."[6] Each of these committees was made up of representatives of the operating units of the Bureau as well as the specialists concerned with a given policy. While the Bureau attempted to cope with the burgeoning demands for information in the Department by organizing and training its staff on a geographical and functional basis, the geographical and functional bureaus gradually began to recruit their own information specialists.

The emergence of information specialists in the regional and functional bureaus of the Department received institutional expression in the reorganization of 1949. At that time two new regional bureaus were established in the Department, and each regional bureau was provided with the specialized staff required to meet its responsibilities. The information specialists in the regional and later functional bureaus gradually assumed a growing number of information tasks, and they became the chief link between information officers in the Office of Press Relations,

---

5 *Federal Register,* Vol. 33, No. 93, May 11, 1968, p. 7078 (*Code of Federal Regulations,* Title 22, Part 6); *Foreign Affairs Manual,* Vol. 5, Section 480, Appendix A.

6 These committees were established by Mr. Francis Russell in 1946, and they were continued until he left the Office of Public Affairs in 1952. See memorandum on "U.S. Public Information Policy Papers" dated 1950 in the Cochrane, Friedman, and Seamans files, the Department of State.

the Bureau of Public Affairs, and these other areas of the Department.

Each Assistant Secretary of State or higher level official now has an officer who devotes his time to public affairs. These officers are directly responsible to their immediate boss. In some areas there is only one such officer; in other areas, such as Inter-American Affairs, there are half a dozen officers.

The information specialists in the regional and most functional bureau are called Public Affairs Advisors (PAAs). Although they are not an official source of information in the Department, they are actively involved in preparing the statements which are released through the Office of Press Relations, the Bureau of Public Affairs, and the United States Information Agency. They have also become heavily involved in the unofficial explanation and interpretation of policies in their area or specialty.

Positional Variables. The activities of information officers vary according to the office or position they hold in the State Department. Because of the character of the position they hold, some of these information officers are more directly responsible than their colleagues for serving the needs of particular counter position holders; and they also have more decision latitude than their colleagues in the opinion-policy process. These positional variables are discussed below.

First, information officers vary in their responsibilities for serving the needs of particular counter position holders and consequently in their awareness of the needs of these counter position holders. One measure for this variable is the location of an information officer in the State Department. On the one hand, Public Affairs Advisors and other information specialists in the regional and functional bureaus are particularly conscious of policy needs because they report directly to policy officers. On the other hand, most information officers in the "P" area are particularly conscious of press needs as well as the needs of nongovernmental organizations because they have the primary responsibility in the State Department for serving these needs. Other measures for this variable are frequency of contact with counter position holders and type of career service.

Second, information officers vary in the amount of discretion or authority they may exercise in the opinion-policy process. One measure for this variable is the level at which an information officer operates in the State Department. Information officers in the "P" area who hold the title of Deputy Assistant Secretary or higher, and information officers located elsewhere in the Department who hold the title of Deputy Public Affairs Advisor or higher are more likely than their colleagues to have the responsibility for raising with policy officials the need for putting out more information. Another measure for this variable is type of appointment. Information officers holding political appointments are expected to engage in politics on behalf of the administration and the Department; information officers holding other career appointments are supposed to limit themselves strictly to information rather than to propaganda activities.

Foreign Affairs Reporters

The foreign affairs reporters in this study are the men who gather the news from the State Department and other foreign affairs sources and convey it to their respective news organizations and the public. Although these individuals are all engaged in the same basic activities, their responsibilities vary from one news organization to the next. The activities of the reporters with various news organizations are discussed separately. It is possible to differentiate between these news organizations on several dimensions, and these variables are discussed at the end of this section.

Wire Services. The basic press coverage of the State Department is provided by two American wire services, Associated Press (AP) and United Press International (UPI).[7] Virtually all of the other news organizations in this country as well as many foreign news organizations rely upon these two wire services for on-the-spot coverage of the State Department. Since these two wire services are competing with one another for subscribers over such a wide geographic area, the competition between

---

7 Two foreign wire services also cover Department news, Reuters (British) and Agence France Presse (French).

them for spot news is both intense and continuous. In order to get the news out while it is still news, reporters for each of the wire services work as an effective team, jumping in to help each other cover the breaking stories.

Each of the wire services has a staff headed by an experienced diplomatic reporter with over 25 years of experience, and each occupies a corner of the cubicle-filled press room available to reporters in the Department. Both AP and UPI have formally divided their staff into two parts, one to write stories of primary interest to the domestic public and the other to write stories for foreign audiences since both organizations service the international as well as the domestic press. Four of the six AP reporters cover the Department for news of interest to audiences abroad; the chief and one reporter cover the Department for the domestic audience. The ten members of the UPI staff cover the Department in much the same way except that those who deal with news of interest to audiences abroad do not operate out of the press room in the Department but out of the UPI offices in downtown Washington.

The wire services are largely concerned with spot news; they only occasionally make news themselves. Since they service all the other news media, a wire reporter may write up to 10 stories a day. These stories vary from the routine (the announcement of arrangements for a foreign visitor or a Department appointee) to the important (the report of a development in basic policy). Although the wire reporter usually covers fast breaking news, he may also become involved in the analysis and interpretation of policies and events. Indeed, many spot news stories must be followed up first with a story dealing with the significance of the event and later with a story which attempts to place this event in a much broader perspective.

Television and Radio. The wire service reporters must compete increasingly with radio and television reporters in the fast news field. Whenever the electronic media can anticipate a story, they can provide instantaneous coverage, something which the wire services are incapable of doing. But State Department news seldom can be anticipated long enough in advance to make it feasible for the industry to offer this kind of coverage day in and day out. Consequently, the electronic reporters usually cover the Department in much the same way as newspaper reporters: they call in or write up a summary of their story for a program director who budgets a certain amount of airtime for their story on a future program. Most TV and radio reporters have a minimum of 45 seconds and a maximum of 2 minutes of airtime for their stories. The 2-minute period is usually only available on television during one of the half-hour news programs in the evening.

Although the TV-radio reporter has the greatest comparative advantage over other reporters in the fast news field, he must also engage heavily in analysis in order to make the news meaningful in the space available. The pressure for analysis in the electronic news is increased by the need to sell a story to producers who have had limited experience as reporters themselves. There is a danger that the TV and radio reporter will make his story more newsworthy than it really is in order to get on the air, if only because his producer may not buy anything else. Some TV people fight fiercely to get on the air because of a fee system which provides a $50 bonus for each TV appearance and $25 for each radio newscast placed on the air.

In addition to spot news broadcasts, most electronic reporters can look forward to several special hour or half-hour shows of their own during the year. These feature programs give the reporter an opportunity to handle important diplomatic problems at length. Whether their subject lends itself to pictorial coverage or not, these reporters have an excellent medium for covering diplomatic developments when they are given sufficient time on the air.

National Daily Newspapers. A third type of reporter covering the Department represents national newspapers. While it is difficult to find a list of national papers which will satisfy everyone, reporters from the *New York Times,* the *Baltimore Sun,* the *Washington Post,* the *Washington Star,* and the *Los Angeles Times* are included in this category. The reporters from these newspapers either are full-time diplomatic correspondents with the State Department or have foreign affairs as their beat.

The reporters representing these newspapers may be distinguished from their counterparts in local and regional papers because in each case their papers provide enough space so that these reporters can cover a story at length. Moreover, the reporting staff is usually large enough so that they can muster a number of people with some experience in diplomatic reporting to cover a complicated story without dropping everything else. These reporters not only have the time to develop sources throughout the Department but also frequently cover the embassies in Washington, the Hill, and other government departments in an effort to ferret out a foreign affairs story.

These reporters do not write a story every day. They are usually working on a number of possible stories at any given time, and no more than 2 or 3 stories a week are likely to appear under their by-line. The forte of these reporters is the interpretive story which attempts to develop all the facets of a situation. In many cases the story is designed to present the ideas of the best minds the reporter has consulted on a given problem.

Regional and Local Papers. In addition to the diplomatic reporters with the large national newspapers, there are a large number of reporters who more or less frequently cover foreign affairs news for their local or regional papers. A few of these correspondents are regulars at the State Department either because of the importance of their paper, their long experience in covering the Department, or some combination of the two. Most of them represent small Washington bureaus of 2 to 4 persons. Some of them work for newspaper chains which provide some interpretive pieces for a number of local and regional papers.

The distinctive thing about these reporters is that they do not cover the State Department as their beat. They seldom attend the Department noon briefings, and their sources in the Department are always limited. In most cases the reporters involved are White House Correspondents who only come to State when a big story is breaking, especially one that involves the President in some way. These reporters depend heavily upon the wire services to keep them informed of developments at the Department. They seldom have time to develop sources among the embassies in Washington. Lacking the time to dig out all of the nuances surrounding policy, they frequently write stories which provide tidbits of information, analogies or historical materials not covered in the wire service reports. These reporters are also involved in interpretation of events although they often lack both sufficient time and detailed information necessary to engage in analysis.

News Services. There are now a number of news services which provide material for local and regional newspapers across the country. These news services supplement the wire services. Unlike the wire service reporter, however, the news service reporter usually prepares his material for the editorial page. Indeed, the growth of news services points up the difficulty which local editors have had in writing on the many complicated and often technical national and foreign issues of interest to their readers. The reporters for these news services try to supplement the front page news with features, backgrounders, and situationers for the inside pages of the newspaper. These reporters usually have more opportunity to specialize and more time to prepare their stories than other newspaper reporters.

General News Magazines. Another type of reporter covering the Department is the one representing the general news magazine such as *Time, Newsweek, U.S. News, Life, Look,* and so on. The chief value of the weekly news magazine is in placing events which occurred during the previous week in perspective, and in presenting this summary of what happened during the week in capsule form to those who could not keep up with the daily reports in the press or who did not have adequate daily coverage of these developments in their local papers.

One of the distinctive characteristics of these news media is that they are even slower than the daily press. Reporters representing some of the general magazines such as *Look* must write their material 3 to 6 weeks in advance, and even reporters for the weekly news magazines have to write material at least 3 or 4 days ahead. This means that they must either avoid details which will prove incorrect by the time the magazine is published or they must play the dangerous game of anticipating events. In most cases they settle for a combination of the two. They emphasize the details that they are sure of and write around those which they are not. They also exercise their sixth sense to anticipate at what stage the news will be at the point when their magazine reaches the public so that they will not seem out-of-touch with current developments.

Another distinctive characteristic of general news magazines is the concept of "group journalism." Although all of the reporters discussed have an editor, producer, or audience for whom they must write, the magazine reporter probably has even less control than others over the final product. In the case of both *Time* and *Newsweek,* the reporters covering the Department send their copy to New York where a staff of writers put their material together with what is coming in from other news bureaus around the world. Reporters have to develop a good working relationship with the New York writers to ensure that these writers do not distort the facts they report in order to make the story more readable. *Newsweek* provides an additional protection for the reporter by sending a copy of the resulting story back to him for a quick check for accuracy before the material goes to the printers. *U.S. News* can provide even better protection to the reporter since its editorial offices are in Washington, and the reporter's initials are required at each stage in the development of the story. Other magazines such as *Look* are not group operations, and the reporter maintains control of his story although he may have to compete constantly with a photographer over space.

Trade and Ethnic Press. Reporters for trade magazines or the ethnic press differ from other reporters in two important respects. In the first place, they are more likely than other reporters to be concerned with reporting developments in a particular specialty because they usually write for a well-defined audience. They try to keep this audience informed of developments in their special area of interest that are not covered by the regular daily papers. Reporters for *Aviation Week,* for example, are constantly looking for new facts or developments in the aerospace field; reporters for *Nation's Business* are looking for stories with a business angle; and reporters for *Afro-American* are looking for stories of special interest to the black community, such as events in Africa.

In the second place, these reporters usually have more time than other reporters to work on their stories. In some cases they will have several months to develop a story; they will almost always have several days at least to prepare their material. Because of the additional opportunities they have to develop stories, these reporters feel that their articles contain information and not just facts. Since they write so few stories, they can often exercise much discretion in their choice of subjects.

Syndicated Columnists. It is customary to distinguish the syndicated columnist from other reporters on the basis of the fact that he is freer than other reporters to express his own opinions. Columnists supposedly engage in the personal analysis or interpretation of events rather than objective reporting. Although columnists generally may have more time or greater opportunity to interpret events than other reporters, this distinction is probably overdrawn. Most of the good columnists try to incorporate at least one new fact in their columns. As one well-known columnist put it, "I assume that everything that is reported is either badly reported or only partially reported."

Unlike other reporters, however, the columnist is allowed (indeed, he is encouraged) to develop a close personal relationship with his readers. Unlike other reporters, columnists usually envisage the President and other top government officials as one of the audiences for whom they consciously write their stories. Consequently, the columnist is not only interested in clarifying the meaning of events for the public but also in suggesting new policy initiatives to decision-makers. Moreover, since he is often talking to the leaders of an Administration as well as to the public, the columnist often relies more heavily than other reporters on sources both inside and outside the establishment who are critical of Administration policy.

Positional Variables. The activities of reporters vary from one news organization to the next. Because of the characteristics of various media of communication, some news organizations provide reporters with more of an opportunity than other news organizations to engage in interpretive reporting. Because of the personnel policies of various news organizations, reporters who work for them are more likely than reporters who work for other news organizations to become part of the establishment. These positional variables are discussed below.

In the first place, some news organizations offer reporters better opportunities to engage in interpretive reporting than others. One measure for this variable is the character of the news medium itself. News media such as the wire services and radio and television place an emphasis on transmitting on-the-spot news to wide audiences. Small newspapers, newspaper chains, or the ethnic press, lack either the interest or resources to provide very complete coverage of foreign affairs. Still other news media, such as the general news magazines, large newspapers, news services, trade magazines, and syndicated columnists, seek to supplement spot news with in-depth coverage of foreign affairs. The news organizations which emphasize spot news coverage or provide scant time and space for foreign affairs coverage generally provide their reporters with less opportunity than other news organizations to engage in interpretive reporting because they do not offer as much time either to develop interpretive stories or to present these in-depth stories in the media. Another measure for the amount of interpretation performed by reporters in various news organizations is the amount of time the news organization allows the reporter to devote either to the State Department or to the realm of foreign affairs. Some news organizations assign reporters to a State Department or foreign affairs beat exclusively. Others require their reporters to cover news developments all over the capital city. Reporters who devote full-time to foreign affairs are believed to be more likely than their colleagues to engage in interpretive reporting since they have the opportunity to develop ample sources within the State Department, other government agencies, foreign embassies, and so on. A final measure of this variable is frequency of contact with counter position holders.

In the second place, some news organizations ensure that their reporters are more likely than those from other news organizations to become part of the establishment by stationing reporters permanently on the State Department beat. Other organizations rotate reporters from one beat to another relatively frequently. Still other agencies, such as the *New York Times,* keep their diplomatic reporters on the same beat but often ask them to cover domestic stories. The measure for this variable is years of experience on the State Department or foreign affairs beat.

Leaders of Nongovernmental Organizations

There is a fantastic variety of nongovernmental organizations in this country, and a surprising number of them have an interest in foreign affairs. Nongovernmental organizations with a significant interest in foreign affairs usually make one person on their staff responsible for the international aspects of their program, and this individual performs some common tasks. Among other things, he is expected to keep the organization informed on the international subjects of special interest to it, to advise the organization on foreign affairs matters requiring group action and, if necessary or desirable, to bring the concerns of the organization to the attention of the proper authorities.

The international staff of these organizations share a similar position only in this minimal sense; their other duties differ widely as the formal titles of the positions they hold readily suggest. Some of these positions bear titles which point up the international concerns of the organization: Director of the Foreign Affairs Department, Associate General Secretary in charge of Peace and World Order, Manager of the International Group, Program Coordinator for Foreign Affairs, and so on. Other positions bear titles which suggest the functions performed rather than the subjects dealt with, such as Head of the Office of Public Relations, Director of Research, and Political Action Director.

In view of the diverse character of the international concerns of various nongovernmental organizations, it is necessary to describe the activities of the NGO leaders for each type of organization separately. At the end of this section some variables which cut across this typology will be discussed.

Business Groups. American business is international in scope. Most large companies not only engage in foreign commerce but also conduct worldwide operations. The First National City Bank of New York, for example, had 189 foreign establishments in 59 countries in 1966; in the same year, the Kaiser Industries Corporation included 64 corporate entities with plants and facilities in twenty foreign countries. Even small companies often rely upon foreign markets for a significant part of their business. The sensitivity of American business to foreign affairs is reflected regularly in the rise and fall of prices on the stock market in accordance with foreign prospects and dangers. Large business organizations are independent and vocal. They receive most of the information they need to operate from their own representatives and affiliates abroad, and they hire their own lobbyists to represent them in Washington. In most instances these large companies limit themselves strictly to their own economic interests; they do not want the responsibility for making American foreign policy. Nevertheless, these companies do join forces under the banner of one or more of the many business organizations to which they belong whenever it is in their interest to do so. There are scores of organizations which represent the interests of the large companies: The International Economic Policy Association, the National Foreign Trade Council, the Banker's Association for Foreign Trade, and so on. Large companies do not rely mainly upon more inclusive business organizations, such as the National Association of Manufacturers or the U.S. Chamber of Commerce, to represent them in the foreign field.

Small companies receive communications about overseas business from the general news media, from their specialized trade associations such as the American Retail Federation, and from the U.S. Chamber of Commerce. The Chamber maintains liaison with all departments of government whose activities affect foreign trade and commerce and provides this information to large as well as small business organizations. The principal source of its information is the Bureau of International Programs of the Department of Commerce, which is the domestic outlet for U.S. government information on foreign business conditions. This information is usually collected as part of the Comprehensive Reporting Program conducted by the State Department for agencies which do not have separate reporting systems overseas.

Business organizations have been so independent in their representation to the government that it was not until 1966 that the Department of State created an official contact point for the business community in Washington. To the extent that it is meaningful to speak of a business community, that community's interests are represented by the more inclusive business organizations. The U.S. Chamber of Commerce, for example, is one of the few business organizations which seeks to influence the government on broad foreign policy questions. With an international staff of about eight persons, the Chamber attempts to keep abreast of developments in foreign policy which may affect the business community and to bring the influence of the business community to bear on these problems.

Labor Groups. Labor also has an important stake in foreign affairs now that business is international in scope. Labor leaders have learned that they cannot effectively represent their members at the bargaining table unless they have a thorough knowledge of both business and labor conditions abroad. The principal fear of most labor leaders is that goods produced by cheap foreign labor will either force American wages down or force American workers out of their jobs. In order to prevent this, American labor organizations have become very active in the Free Trade Union Movement abroad. In addition, many labor organizations have naturally become involved in international affairs because of the high proportion of recent immigrants in their ranks. Of course, the American labor movement has also been spurred to undertake operations abroad for basic humanitarian reasons. As a result of these factors, American labor organizations are strongly committed to internationalism, and many of the large groups belong to several international labor organizations.

Most labor groups are associated with foreign and international labor organizations, and they rely heavily upon these affiliates for information on labor conditions abroad. An astonishing number of these organizations also send representatives and conduct programs abroad which gives them first hand information about the international labor movement. Of course, these labor organizations also maintain contacts with United States' officials who are concerned with international labor, especially those in the Bureau of International Labor Affairs in the Department of Labor and the office of the Special Assistant to the Secretary of State for Labor Affairs in the Department of State. The latter official has coordinating responsibilities for the Labor Attache Corps which operates overseas, as well as the labor advisers in various bureaus of the State Department in Washington.

Whereas the typical business organization tends to rely on its own sources of information and channels of influence, most labor organizations affiliated with the AFL-CIO feel that it is essential for them to have a central voice in foreign affairs. Consequently, they rely heavily upon the International Affairs Department of the AFL-CIO to represent them in international labor affairs. With a staff of about a dozen professional people, the International Affairs Department not only provides information to affiliated unions but also advises the policy making organs of the AFL-CIO of matters on which labor should take a position. Although the policies adopted by the AFL-CIO are not binding on affiliated unions, they usually receive wide spread support.

Once the AFL-CIO has decided upon a policy, it is then the task of the International Affairs Department to press this policy upon the relevant departments of the government. Of course, President Meany plays a primary role in bringing labor's influence to bear on United States' officials since he has ready access to them and regularly serves on important advisory committees. Although the AFL-CIO is intent upon representing a united labor front, it is curiously unwilling to undertake joint statements or common strategies with other types of organizations.

Farm Groups. Farm organizations also take an interest in American foreign policy. Like labor, farm groups are large membership organizations with a self-interest stake in foreign affairs. Farm organizations are particularly interested in agricultural production and marketing. Since many farmers are second or third generation immigrants, they also feel a relationship with nationality groups abroad. As the government has become more and more involved in improving food production abroad, farm organizations have become directly involved in Agency for International Development (AID) and other agency programs. For example, the International Assistance Corporation of the National Farmer's Union conducts agricultural technical assistance programs in fourteen foreign countries. In addition, farm organizations are heavily engaged in exchanges of personnel and ideas with farmers in other countries, and they participate actively in international food and agricultural organizations.

Farm organizations have few foreign affairs personnel on their staff, and unlike labor, the competition among farm organizations usually prevents them from working together. The primary channel for the foreign policy views of farm organizations in the government is the Department of Agriculture which has its own Foreign Agricultural Service. Farm organizations also have easy access to officials who deal with those aspects of foreign policy with which they are most concerned in the State Department and related agencies.

Professional Groups. A variety of professional organizations have an interest in foreign policies which affect their special interests. For example, the National Education Association is primarily concerned with American educational and cultural relations with other countries; the American Bar Association has an interest in international and comparative law; and the Federation of American Scientists takes an interest in issues which have a scientific component: nuclear weapons, disarmament, loyalty and security problems, and so on.

The membership of these organizations is likely to include persons both inside and outside the government who have real expertise in their international specialty. These organizations thus have access to much authoritative information on their foreign affairs specialty. Moreover, the experts in these organizations usually have close ties with their counterparts abroad, and the professional organization as a whole is usually quite active in various international organizations in their special field: the World Confederation of Teachers' Association, International Bar Association, and so on.

Within their areas of special interest these professional organizations have numerous resources for influencing the government. As indicated above, they usually have direct access to key position holders in the government. Moreover, these organizations frequently have formal representation on advisory bodies set up to provide a participant role for these groups in areas of special interest. Many organizations actually conduct government programs. The National Education Association, for example, has a large contract with AID for the Teacher's Corps. However, professional groups seldom use their special position to influence the government on more general policy questions. Thus, the American Bar Association took the official position that it was legal for the United States to be in Vietnam, but refrained from making any other statement on the war. The Federation of American Scientists also decided not to speak out on Vietnam although many of its members are critics of Administration policies.

Religious Groups. Many religious organizations are transnational groups, and consequently they have a longstanding interest in international affairs. Most of these international churches participate in the international conferences of their denomination, but historically the main interest of American religious organizations abroad has been humanitarian. Christian missions overseas have conducted educational programs, foreign relief services, and aid to refugee programs as well as spreading the gospel. More recently, church groups have taken an interest in exchange programs, international development, and international organization.

Church organizations which conduct overseas programs have information and expertise in these areas, usually humanitarian and relief activities. Most of these groups also can and do tap lay experts on other international problems of concern to them. But few church groups have developed a professional staff to collect information on various foreign problems and to bring religious viewpoints regularly to bear on foreign policy decisions. Religious organizations rely extensively upon United Nations and other international sources of information although they do maintain varying degrees of contact with U.S. government sources.

On issues which affect their overseas programs and activities, church groups have ready access to policy officials throughout the government. Moreover, the prestige of their leadership usually ensures that these groups will have access to top decision-makers on general foreign policy questions. When John Foster Dulles was Secretary of State, for example, leaders of the National Council of Churches could call him directly from New York. In order to make their views felt, however, most religious leaders feel that they must demonstrate some consensus among the religious community. The National Council of Churches tries to represent a large number of Protestant churches at the national level, and whenever possible this group acts in concert with Catholic and Jewish groups. As the Vietnam issue demonstrates, however, these religious groups are seldom able to achieve any real consensus on the moral viewpoint.

Veterans Groups. Veterans organizations such as the American Legion and the Veterans of Foreign Wars are composed of men who served in the armed forces during periods of hostility. These groups feel that they have a stake in foreign and national security affairs, and they often have branches or affiliate groups overseas. In contrast to labor or farm organizations, for example, the rank and file member of veterans organizations does not have to be sold on the importance of foreign affairs. The policy positions of these organizations take the form of resolutions passed at their national convention. Local posts usually originate most of the resolutions, and the membership imposes some definite limits upon the leadership. However, the national leadership, particularly the national policy committees, exercise considerable discretion over the wording of resolutions since they determine which resolutions that come to them from local posts will be presented to the convention delegates.

They have ready access to policy officials in the Department both because of the size of the groups they represent and because of the fact that their membership is so critical of the Department. Although veterans organizations have access to decision-makers, National Commanders usually lack the personal experience and staff resources necessary to maximize their influence in the State Department. Moreover, veterans organizations seldom join with other groups on common causes because they are so jealous of their sovereignty.

Ethnic Groups. A nation of immigrants also has a number of organizations which are concerned with American foreign policies toward nationality groups. In recent years the number of refugee group organizations has expanded. Although these groups are typically concerned with one nation's problems, the range of their concerns is sometimes much broader. Because of the persecution of Jews throughout the world, for example, the American Jewish Committee protests the violation of basic human rights wherever they occur and whomever they involve. Of course, the Committee has a special interest in the continued viability of Israel. Other groups such as the American Friends of the Middle East are attempting to educate people both at home and abroad on Arab culture.

Many of these groups hire lobbyists to represent their interests in the executive and legislative branches of the government. The American Jewish Committee, which is headquartered in New York, has a Washington representative who maintains liaison with public officials. Interestingly, the American Friends of the Middle East also started out as an action group, but when it discovered that it was making little headway in its efforts to change Congressional and public opinion, it dropped its action program in favor of a long-range education program. The American Friends of the Middle East does not officially submit its views to the State Department because there is so much suspicion in the Arab world of United States policies that the organization would be accused by Arabs of being an arm of the State Department. This group does have contacts with officials in the Department on an individual basis, however.

Public Affairs Groups. There is also an increasing number of organizations whose main purpose is to bring the influence of informed groups to bear on public policy questions. These groups are usually relatively small, middle-class, professional, liberal organizations which get their start because of public interest in a single issue area and broaden their perspective as the connection between issue-areas becomes more apparent. The National Committee for a SANE Nuclear Policy was organized in support of a nuclear test ban and then quickly broadened its foreign policy interests to other areas. Other examples of public affairs groups would be the Americans for Democratic Action, the Friends Committee on National Legislation, and the League of Women Voters.

These groups have good access to government offices, including the State Department. They either include among their members second or third echelon officials in the government or have the respect of these officials because of their reputation for public leadership, basic study programs, or strong grass-roots support. These organizations often have a small but highly professional staff, and they are particularly active in organizing other groups on problems of common concern. The Friends Committee for National Legislation, for example, provides a Disarmament Information Service for interested organizations.

Women's Groups. There are a wide range of women's groups with a concern for international affairs. Those women's groups whose chief interest lies in the area of world affairs can usually be classified as peace groups. Their aim is to abolish the causes of war and oppose the military aspects of foreign policy. One such organization is the Women's International League for Peace and Freedom which was organized at the Hague in 1915. One of the most recent such groups is Women's Strike for Peace which was begun by a housewife (who claims that she is not a political "hobbiest") because of anxieties over nuclear testing in the early 1960s. These groups do not always find it easy to get a hearing in the Department, but they are persistent enough to get their views heard.

In addition there are a number of women's groups which, like men's service groups, feel that they must have an international program in order to be relevant to their membership and to keep up with groups of the same type which have such programs. The character of these programs and their relations with the State Department depend largely on the nature of group membership. Organizations such as the American Association of University Women take an active and informed part in organization activities on foreign affairs. Even organizations such as the General Federation of Women's Clubs has an international committee which prepares resolutions for the consideration of delegates at the national convention.

Positional Variables. The activities of NGO leaders concerned with the State Department and foreign affairs vary from one organization to another. Because of the characteristics of various nongovernmental organizations, some of these leaders are more likely than others: to devote full time to international affairs; to rely upon the State Department for information; to make economic demands upon the Department; and to share the general policy orientation of the Department. These positional variables are discussed below.

In the first place, organizations vary in the extent of their commitment to international affairs. One measure for this variable is whether an organization has any of its personnel permanently stationed abroad. Another measure for this variable is the number of staff people in the organization who deal with foreign affairs. Organizations with at least one full-time individual responsible for foreign affairs on their staff are distinguished from organizations which have no full-time foreign affairs staff members.

In the second place, these organizations vary in the extent to which they rely upon the State Department for information on foreign affairs. One measure for this variable is the importance which they attribute to the State Department as a source of information. Each NGO leader was asked what sources of information on foreign affairs he relied upon. Those who rely primarily upon the State Department are distinguished from those who do not. Another measure of this variable is frequency of contact with Department officers. Each NGO leader was asked how frequently he had contacts with Department information and policy officers. Those who say they contact counter position holders at least once a month are distinguished from those who do not.

In the third place, some nongovernmental organizations are more likely than others to press specific economic demands on the Department. The measure for this variable is the distinction between economic and other organizations. Occupational and professional organizations are more likely than other organizations to represent the economic demands of their members.

In the fourth place, organizations vary in their foreign policy orientation. Some organizations are generally hostile to the State Department as an institution and to important elements of its policies. Other organizations are supportive. One measure of this variable is the public posture of the organization on foreign affairs. Organizations which advocate basic changes in American policy are deemed hostile. This would include peace groups on the one hand and organizations which advocate a more militant stand on the other hand.

In the fifth place, organizations vary in the size of their membership. Some organizations claim hundreds of thousands of individual members. Other organizations either have very small memberships or have no individual membership at all, such as business corporations and umbrella groups. The measure for this variable is the size and character of the group's membership.

PERSONAL CHARACTERISTICS

In order to describe the participants in the opinion-policy process, it is necessary to view them as individuals as well as position holders. As individuals occupying similar positions, they naturally share certain characteristics; but they also have characteristics which differentiate them from one another. What kind of individuals occupy these positions? How do counter position holders perceive them? These two questions are discussed separately.

Characteristics of Position Holders

The incumbents of a given position should share a number of personal characteristics both because similar criteria are used in selecting them for the position and because many of the same values are stressed for all those holding the position. What characteristics do individuals in each of these positions share? How do they differ from counter position holders? How do individuals in each position differ from one another?

State Department Policy Officers. A majority of policy officers in this study are members of the Foreign Service of the United States. They are recruited on the basis of competitive written examinations and personal interviews. When they enter the Foreign Service, they join an elite corps of public servants with an exceptionally high *esprit de corps.* These officers serve a majority of their public service in foreign posts, and this is actually a source of camaraderie among them as they share many of the same experiences abroad. Moreover, they traditionally hold the most influential positions in the Department when they are on home assignment, and so other policy officers naturally identify with the Foreign Service even if they have been recruited by and trained in the State Department rather than the Foreign Service.

Most of these officers share a long apprenticeship in the State Department or the Foreign Service before reaching their present position. Whether they serve at home or abroad, they belong to the same organization, and they not only share some of the glamor and excitement which comes from being involved in important foreign policy decisions, they also have shared the long hours, the routine, and the frustration of State Department work. They are linked by an informal network of communications which makes them privy to the personal side of diplomacy. These officials identify strongly with the State Department as an institution, and most of them are outspoken supporters of Department policies as well.

One of the most striking things about policy officers as individuals is their uniformly high level of formal education. The policy officers in this study have a mean of 5.8 years of formal schooling beyond high school. Virtually all of them possess a bachelor's degree, and two-thirds of them have earned advanced degrees, including five with the Ph.D. Moreover, three-fourths of them attended undergraduate college in the Northeastern part of the country and, if one classifies a pre-law course as social science, almost all of them majored in one of the social sciences in college.

State Department Information Officers. Information officers are recruited mainly on the basis of special education and previous experience as counter position holders. Some information officers are policy officers on temporary assignment to public affairs positions. Others are former reporters, publicists, organization leaders, or scholars. Since these officers are engaged in public affairs either on a temporary assignment or as a second career, it is not surprising that they have as a group served a mean of less than nine years in information posts.

In view of the fact that information officers are both recruited at an older age and from such varied sources, it is not surprising that in many ways these officers form a more diverse group than policy officers. First, the amount of formal education is more varied among information than policy officers. Information officers have a mean of 4.7 years of formal education beyond high school. Four-fifths of these officers hold the bachelor's degree, and two-fifths hold advanced degrees, including one

Ph.D. Information officers are as likely to have majored in one of the humanities or journalism as one of the social sciences, including pre-law.

Despite these differences they are linked together by informal as well as formal channels of communication within the State Department. Although in most cases they have not spent their entire career in the Department, these officers identify closely with the State Department as an institution as well as the policies it undertakes.

Foreign Affairs Reporters. Diplomatic reporters are recruited by various news organizations. Although each organization has its own recruitment policy, some general trends are discernible. Prior to World War II and even in the immediate post-war years, most reporters were drawn from schools of journalism. They were recruited as general reporters and selected at a later point to cover foreign affairs. In recent years individuals have been hired explicitly to cover foreign affairs and have usually prepared themselves for this assignment by majoring in international affairs or one of the other social sciences in college.

These changes in recruitment patterns help to explain the varied educational backgrounds of reporters. On the whole, reporters in this study are quite well educated. All but six of them have the bachelor's degree, and ten possess advanced degrees, including three with the Ph.D for a mean of 4.5 years of formal education beyond high school. There is no relationship between age and level of education. However, the younger reporters are more likely than their older colleagues to be among the half which attended college in the Northeast, particularly at Ivy League universities. They are also more likely than their older colleagues to be among the half which majored in one of the social sciences, most frequently political science. Younger reporters are less likely than their older colleagues to have majored in English or journalism.

Despite the varying sources of recruitment and the fact that they represent a variety of news media, the reporters covering foreign affairs constitute a distinct group in Washington. With few exceptions they are experienced reporters, and they regard the foreign affairs beat as a prestigious one. Some of these reporters have been covering diplomacy so long that they have identified very closely with Department. They encounter each other regularly—and read each other's output. Some have experience covering foreign affairs abroad, although this is less common among younger reporters.

Leaders of Nongovernmental Organizations. Those who are responsible for the international concerns of various nongovernmental organizations are recruited from a wide variety of sources. Some of these individuals are recruited from within the organization itself and have no special training in international affairs. Others are recruited from the academic or legal profession, depending on the needs of the organization. NGO leaders constitute a less tightly knit group than reporters and Department officers, although there are a number of information and other committees to which many of these individuals belong in an effort to coordinate their actions in areas of common interest.

As a group, NGO leaders are well-educated, having a mean of over six years of formal schooling since high school. Over half of the NGO leaders in this study have advanced academic degrees, including seven with the Ph.D. Approximately half of them majored in one of the social sciences in college.

Individual Variables. There are also important variations among the individuals occupying each position. Some of these variables are identified below.

In the first place, there are generational differences among individuals in each of these positions. The individuals being recruited into each of these positions today are not the same kind of individuals recruited two decades ago. Moreover, the activities being performed by old-timers are not the same activities being performed by newcomers. There are two measures for this variable: age and years of professional experience.

In the second place, there are variations among these individuals in their familiarity with the specific needs of counter position holders. Some of these individuals have an intimate knowledge of a counter position; others do not. One measure for this variable is simply the distinction between those who have prior experience as incumbents of a counter position and those who do not. Another measure is frequency of contact with counter position holders.

In the third place, these individuals have varying educational backgrounds. Some of the individuals in each position have more formal training than others. The measures for this variable are the amount and type of formal education. Individuals who have one or more advanced degrees are distinguished from those who do not. Also individuals who majored in one of the social sciences in college are distinguished from those who did not.

In the fourth place, it is felt that position holders vary in their general competence. Some individuals in a position are better able than others to cope with intricate problems. No measure is available for this variable except in the case of some policy officers. Among policy officers in the Foreign Service of the United States, the rate of promotion in the Foreign Service serves as a measure for competence of policy officers.[8]

Stereotyped Images of Counter Position Holders

The individual characteristics of position holders may be less important than the characteristics which are attributed to them by counter position holders. Most readers are familiar, for example, with the image of the closed-mouth Foreign Service Officer, the officious press agent, the prying reporter, and the influence-peddling lobbyist; indeed, the efforts of individuals in these positions to establish their own reputations indicate that the position holders themselves attach some importance to the stereotyped image. What personal qualities and performance characteristics do these groups attribute to each other?

In order to obtain some empirical data on this question, each respondent was asked to rate counter position holders on a scale running from a low of 1 to a high of 5 on the following qualities: intelligent, informed, skillful, responsible, and helpful. The results appear in Tables 4.1-4.4. They suggest that the respondents generally have a high regard for the personal qualities and performance characteristics of counter position holders. This conclusion must be tempered, however, by the knowledge that many respondents, according to their own state-

8 The average promotion rate for FSOs by grade is presented by John E. Harr in *The Anatomy of the Foreign Service—A Statistical Profile*, Foreign Affairs Personnel Study No. 4 (Carnegie Endowment for International Peace, 1965).

ments, are rating only those individuals with whom they have regular dealings and that they have a higher regard for these individuals than they do for others in the same position.

An analysis of the results in Tables 4.1 through 4.4 can provide at least two types of findings. First, it indicates how each group rates incumbents of a counter position on various personal qualities and performance characteristics. Second, it indicates how ratings by and for various groups compare with each other. These findings are discussed below.

Policy Officers. Policy officers receive high ratings from all groups; they receive especially high ratings from information officers, who feel that they are more intelligent, informed, and responsible than any other group. An analysis of the data in Table 4.1 indicates, however, that at least among information officers and reporters, policy officers are considered more intelligent, informed, and responsible than skillful and helpful.

Table 4.1 How Various Groups Rate Policy Officers on Five Qualities

	RATINGS						
	LOWEST				HIGHEST	NO	
GROUPS	1	2	3	4	5	RESPONSE	N
Information officers							
Intelligent	0	0	2	9	21	8	40
Informed	0	0	1	8	23	8	40
Skillful	0	1	4	17	9	9	40
Responsible	0	0	1	6	25	8	40
Helpful	0	1	6	16	9	8	40
Reporters							
Intelligent	0	0	1	15	13	11	40
Informed	0	0	1	15	13	11	40
Skillful	0	2	11	13	3	11	40
Responsible	0	0	2	11	16	11	40
Helpful	0	4	15	8	2	11	40
NGO leaders							
Intelligent	0	0	3	8	14	11	36
Informed	0	1	4	6	14	11	36
Skillful	0	0	4	14	7	11	36
Responsible	0	0	3	9	12	12	36
Helpful	0	2	7	9	7	11	36

There are also some interesting differences between information officers, reporters, and NGO leaders in their ratings of policy officers on each of these qualities. First, reporters are less likely than information officers to characterize policy officers as well informed. Second, reporters are less likely than either information officers or NGO leaders to characterize policy officers as helpful.

Information officers rate policy officers higher than they rate other groups on the qualities of intelligent, informed, and responsible; they do not regard policy officers as any more skillful or helpful than other groups. This finding suggests some problems in the personal relations between information and policy officers in the State Department, for respondents generally interpret "skillful" to mean ability to deal effectively with the focal group. Information officers apparently feel that policy officers do not handle their relations with them very well and are not as helpful to them as they should be. This gives credence to the belief that information officers are treated as second class citizens in the State Department.

Reporters are less likely than other groups to rate policy officers high on the quality of helpful. How is this finding to be explained? One possible explanation is that reporters feel that policy officers are not as well informed as they should be on topics about which reporters need information. Another explanation is that reporters believe that policy officers are too stingy in sharing their information and opinions with reporters. In this case, a policy officer is unhelpful if he appears to be less honest and forthcoming with reporters than they feel he can be under the circumstances. Both of these explanations underscore the dependence of reporters upon policy officers for information.

Information Officers. An analysis of the data in Table 4.2 indicates that there are no significant differences among other groups in their ratings for information officers on these five qualities. In comparison with other groups, information officers are sometimes rated differently. Policy officers rate information officers no higher than they rate other groups on the qualities of intelligent, informed, or skillful; but they regard information officers as more responsible than reporters and more helpful than either reporters or NGO leaders.

Table 4.2 How Various Groups Rate Information Officers on Five Qualities

	RATINGS						
	LOWEST				HIGHEST	NO	
GROUPS	1	2	3	4	5	RESPONSE	N
Policy officers							
Intelligent	0	0	8	23	4	5	40
Informed	0	0	15	14	6	5	40
Skillful	0	2	10	17	6	5	40
Responsible	0	1	5	17	12	5	40
Helpful	0	1	9	12	13	5	40
Reporters							
Intelligent	0	2	6	14	13	5	40
Informed	0	2	7	15	11	5	40
Skillful	0	6	12	13	4	5	40
Responsible	0	1	4	14	16	5	40
Helpful	1	5	7	16	6	5	40
NGO leaders							
Intelligent	0	1	7	10	6	12	36
Informed	0	1	7	7	9	12	36
Skillful	0	3	8	7	6	12	36
Responsible	0	0	6	8	9	13	36
Helpful	0	2	5	11	6	12	36

Moreover, reporters rate information officers higher than they rate policy officers on the quality of helpful even though they do not rate information officers any higher than policy officers on other qualities. The verbal comments of reporters suggest that the explanation for this finding is that reporters do not expect information officers to provide them with the same kind of information they expect from policy officers. It is only because reporters feel that information officers have less access to and less discretion in the release of information than policy officers that they regard information officers as more helpful than policy officers. Reporters find information officers more intelligent and responsible than skillful and helpful, and more informed than skillful.

Reporters. An analysis of the data in Table 4.3 indicates that all groups except policy officers rate reporters higher on the quality of intelligent than on the qualities of responsible and helpful. Policy officers are more likely than other position holders to rate reporters low on the qualities of intelligent and skillful, and they are more likely than information officers to rate reporters low on the quality of helpful. Why do counter position holders, particularly policy officers, find reporters so unhelpful?

Table 4.3 How Various Groups Rate Reporters on Five Qualities

	RATINGS						
	LOWEST				HIGHEST	NO	
GROUPS	1	2	3	4	5	RESPONSE	N
Policy officers							
Intelligent	0	0	12	16	5	7	40
Informed	0	2	12	15	4	7	40
Skillful	0	2	14	14	2	8	40
Responsible	0	3	16	13	1	7	40
Helpful	1	2	17	9	0	9	40
Information officers							
Intelligent	0	0	2	19	13	6	40
Informed	0	0	6	18	8	8	40
Skillful	0	0	7	13	12	8	40
Responsible	0	1	10	16	5	8	40
Helpful	0	2	10	14	5	9	40
NGO leaders							
Intelligent	0	0	0	13	11	12	36
Informed	0	0	5	12	7	12	36
Skillful	0	1	3	13	7	12	36
Responsible	0	2	6	13	3	12	36
Helpful	0	4	8	9	3	12	36

There are few officers who would seriously argue that the job of the press is to be helpful to the Department. Yet this attitude seems to underlie much of the criticism of the press in the Department. On the basis of the verbal responses of officials, a low rating on helpful reflects a general fear that the press will embarrass the Department either by reporting the wrong things or by failing to report the right things from the officer's point of view. The perception of the press as unhelpful is closely tied to the second and more serious charge that reporters are irresponsible. Reporters are regarded as irresponsible by information and policy officers on the personal level if they violate the confidence of an officer: "The worst thing is for a reporter to quote a Department officer when he asks not to be quoted." Reporters are regarded as irresponsible on the impersonal level when they distort events in order to make better copy.

There are essentially two explanations for the feeling among Department officers that the press distorts the news. In the first place, the problem of distortion occurs because newsmen are "essentially superficial." After all, reporters cannot become experts in all of the numerous fields they cover in the Department, and their ignorance naturally leads to oversimplification and error. In the second place, the problem of distortion arises from differences in judgment between officers and reporters. These differences in judgment arise in part from the fact that officers and reporters naturally interpret happenings in terms of their own needs. On the one hand,

> the man who is at the center of policy control inevitably knows a lot more about his own view and the facts available to the government than the press, especially at the beginning. And, because of the nature of his job, he has a view of the outcome. If something else is suggested, he thinks it's distortion.

On the other hand, the man who is creating news is "more interested in disaster and trouble than things that are going well," and he distorts policies and events accordingly. The more serious disagreements among officers and reporters involve questions of judgment. And, as one prominent correspondent contends, "What is the truth is often the critical question at issue, and during the short period of time—which is the only relevant period of time, it is often impossible to say what the truth is."

NGO leaders probably rate reporters low on the qualities of responsible and helpful because they are dissatisfied with the content of the information they receive from the press and with the way in which the press handles NGO news. Verbal comments by some NGO leaders suggest that the reporters who cover the organization world do not know organization politics and create difficulties for NGO leaders within their own organizations.

NGO Leaders. An analysis of the data in Table 4.4 indicates that there are significant differences among counter position holders in their image of NGO leaders. On the one hand, reporters are more likely than other groups to regard NGO leaders as irresponsible. On the other hand, information officers are more likely than other groups to regard NGO leaders as helpful.

Table 4.4 How Various Groups Rate NGO Leaders on Five Qualities

	RATINGS						
	LOWEST				HIGHEST	NO	
GROUPS	1	2	3	4	5	RESPONSE	N
Policy officers							
Intelligent	0	1	6	17	6	10	40
Informed	0	6	9	12	3	10	40
Skillful	0	2	14	10	4	10	40
Responsible	0	3	8	17	3	9	40
Helpful	0	4	16	9	2	10	40
Information officers							
Intelligent	0	1	5	14	6	13	40
Informed	0	2	12	10	1	15	40
Skillful	1	0	12	8	2	17	40
Responsible	0	0	6	16	1	17	40
Helpful	0	0	8	13	2	17	40
Reporters							
Intelligent	0	1	6	13	4	16	40
Informed	0	2	13	6	3	16	40
Skillful	1	7	11	5	1	16	40
Responsible	2	1	14	5	2	16	40
Helpful	1	2	12	3	5	17	40

A further analysis of reporters' ratings of NGO leaders provides the following results: reporters find NGO leaders more intelligent than informed, skillful, responsible, or helpful; they rate NGO leaders lower than they rate policy officers on the qualities of intelligent and skillful; they rate NGO leaders lower than they rate either information or policy officers on the qualities of informed and responsible. Why do reporters regard NGO leaders as uninformed and irresponsible?

Reporters probably find NGO leaders less informed than other groups because NGO leaders are less likely than other groups to keep up with the day-to-day events which are the trademark of reporters. NGO leaders probably know more than reporters about basic government policies in their area of interest. Reporters probably find NGO leaders less responsible than other groups because they perceive NGO leaders as prophets of special interests. According to reporters, NGO leaders are always trying to get them to carry organization messages to the public. To the reporter who is trying to write objective or balanced stories, NGO leaders are irresponsible because they want the general public to accept the group's special interests as the public interest.

A further analysis of Department officers' ratings of NGO leaders reveals the following findings: policy officers rate NGO leaders higher on the quality of intelligent than on the qualities of skillful and helpful; policy officers rate NGO leaders higher on the quality of responsible than on the quality of helpful; information officers rate NGO leaders higher on the qualities of intelligent and responsible than on the qualities of informed and skillful. Indeed, information officers rate NGO leaders lower than they rate other groups on the qualities of informed and skillful. Why do policy officers tend to find NGO leaders unhelpful while information officers find them helpful?

The varying images of NGO leaders among Department officers can be explained by the fact that information and policy officers perform different functions in the State Department, and consequently they either come into contact with different NGO leaders or the same NGO leaders on different missions. Policy officers find NGO leaders as well informed as other position holders because the NGO leaders whom they encounter either have specific requests for information or intend to influence Department policy. Moreover, policy officers are likely to regard NGO leaders as unhelpful because they make things difficult for policy officers by putting pressure where it may undermine present or proposed future policies.

Information officers regard NGO leaders as less informed than other groups because the NGO leaders whom they encounter are usually requesting general information on foreign affairs. Information officers are more likely than policy officers and reporters to regard NGO leaders as helpful because they perceive the organizations which these leaders represent as generally helpful to the Department in disseminating information to the public.

In this chapter the characteristics of each set of position holders have been described separately. Although inter- and intra-group differences among these position holders have been discussed in some detail, there has been little effort to show how these four groups are related to one another in the opinion-policy process. This is the purpose of the next chapter.

Chapter 5

Expectations and Attitudes

INCUMBENTS OF THE same position in a political system develop standards by which they evaluate their own performance as well as the performance of counter position holders. According to role theory, these evaluative standards or expectations are significant because human beings act with reference to them.[1] In view of the difficulty in obtaining detailed and accurate information about the day-to-day activities of position holders in the opinion-policy process, these role expectations and attitudes can add significantly to our understanding of the relations between these position holders. This chapter deals with the role expectations and attitudes of policy officers, information officers, reporters, and NGO leaders.

The instrument for measuring their role expectations and attitudes contains eight items on role expectations for each of the four positions and ten questions about the requirements for secrecy and publicity.[2] In each case the respondent is requested to indicate whether he feels that incumbents of the focal position absolutely must, preferably should, may or may not, preferably should not, or absolutely must not perform a particular activity. If the respondent replies may or may not, he is then asked whether he feels that incumbents of the focal position

[1] Neal Gross, Ward J. Mason, and Alexander W. McEachern, *Explorations in Role Analysis: Studies of the School Superintendency Role* (New York: John Wiley and Sons, 1958), p. 3.
[2] See Appendix A.

should perform this activity unless the situation precludes it, or should not perform this activity unless the situation requires it. Thus, the response to each item can be recorded somewhere on a continuum which measures both direction and intensity. The expectation can be either accepted or rejected; it can be regarded as mandatory, preferential, or permissive.[3]

In constructing questions on role expectations for the incumbents of these four positions, it is assumed that each group of position holders plays a distinctive role in the opinion-policy process. It is further assumed that the role expectations for each group vary depending on whether they are engaged in the opinion-forming process or the policy-making process. Information officers and reporters are more closely associated with the opinion-forming process than the policy-making process, for example.[4] Moreover, it is assumed that some role expectations for a group are more discretionary and political than others. Previous studies of role expectations for information officers and reporters indicate that these groups hold both neutral and political role expectations and that neutral role expectations are more generally accepted than discretionary and political ones.[5] In order to test these hypotheses, questions which purport to measure attitudes along each of these dimensions are included in the instrument.

In constructing questions which reflect group expectations for the information output of the State Department, it is assumed that respondents will perceive a need to balance the requirements for publicity in the public opinion-forming process against the requirements for secrecy in the foreign policy-making process.[6] Of course, with respect to any particular decision on information policy individuals may choose either to release or to withhold an item of information, but it is expected that individuals will arrive at such decisions only after having considered the needs of both the public and policy and

[3] Gross, *op. cit.*, p. 58.
[4] Dan D. Nimmo, *Newsgathering in Washington* (New York: Atherton Press, 1962), Chapter II.
[5] *Ibid.*, Chapter III. See also Bernard C. Cohen, *The Press and Foreign Policy* (Princeton, N.J.: Princeton University Press, 1963), Chapter II.
[6] Nimmo, *op. cit.*, pp. 194-195.

not with respect to any single principle. In order to test this hypothesis, each respondent was asked how compelling he finds five reasons for releasing information and five reasons for withholding information.

The purpose of this chapter is to describe the role expectations and attitudes for each group in the opinion-policy process and to identify some of the attitudinal variables which can be employed in subsequent analysis of the relations among these position holders. In the first two sections of this chapter, the gross results of the instrument on role expectations and attitudes will be described with the assistance of the verbal comments made by respondents while answering the questions. In the third section, factor analytic techniques will be employed to test the hypotheses generated above and to identify the attitudinal factors which emerge from the role expectation and attitude instrument.

EXPECTATIONS

In this section the role of policy officers, information officers, reporters, and NGO leaders will be examined both with reference to the focal group's own expectations and with reference to expectations of counter position holders for the focal group. The discussion will revolve around the answers to the following questions: What expectations do the incumbents of each position hold for their own role in the opinion-policy process? What role expectations do counter position holders have for them? What differences in role expectations are there among these groups?

State Department Policy Officers

The policy officers in the State Department play a key role in the opinion-policy process. As the only group which participates regularly in the policy-making process, these officers are usually expected to become experts in some policy area because they have continuous access to official and unofficial sources of information on this aspect of foreign affairs. They control, at least in part, what portion of this information is made available to the public. Likewise, they determine, at least in part, what access other groups have to the foreign policy-making process. What are the role expectations for policy officers in the opinion-policy process? The responses to questions on the policy officers' role appear in Table 5.1.

Table 5.1 Attitudes Toward Policy Officers' Role in Opinion
Formation

TO WHAT EXTENT DO YOU FEEL THAT POLICY OFFICERS SHOULD OR SHOULD NOT	ABSO-LUTELY MUST 1	PREFER-ABLY SHOULD 2	MAY OR MAY NOT 3*		5†	PREFER-ABLY SHOULD NOT 6	ABSO-LUTELY MUST NOT 7	NO RE-SPONSE	N
			3*	4	5†				
#11—Play a leading role in opinion-making in this country?									
Policy officers	20	12	2	0	4	1	0	1	40
Information officers	12	18	3	2	1	0	1	3	40
Reporters	9	15	5	0	2	2	0	7	40
NGO leaders	10	10	2	2	1	3	1	7	36
#12—Take time off to meet with reporters and pressure group leaders?									
Policy officers	17	14	3	0	4	1	1	0	40
Information officers	18	14	5	0	0	2	0	1	40
Reporters	21	12	0	0	1	0	0	6	40
NGO leaders	13	15	0	0	0	0	0	8	36
#13—Interpret U.S. national interests and the interests of foreign countries to domestic groups?									
Policy officers	16	15	4	1	2	1	0	1	40
Information officers	15	16	4	0	0	0	1	4	40
Reporters	10	23	0	0	0	0	1	6	40
NGO leaders	9	18	0	0	0	0	0	9	36
#14—Inform information officers of policy deliberations prior to decisions?									
Policy officers	16	18	4	0	1	0	1	0	40
Information officers	17	12	5	1	2	0	1	2	40

TO WHAT EXTENT DO YOU FEEL THAT POLICY OFFICERS SHOULD OR SHOULD NOT	ABSO-LUTELY MUST 1	PREFER-ABLY SHOULD 2	MAY OR MAY NOT 3*	4	5†	PREFER-ABLY SHOULD NOT 6	ABSO-LUTELY MUST NOT 7	NO RE-SPONSE	N
Reporters	16	15	3	0	0	0	0	6	40
NGO leaders	5	13	5	1	1	1	0	10	36

#15—Determine what information is released to the public?

Policy officers	18	6	5	0	1	7	3	0	40
Information officers	3	15	3	1	7	2	7	2	40
Reporters	5	10	2	0	1	10	6	6	40
NGO leaders	6	8	2	2	3	4	2	9	36

#16—Take public opinion into account in the formation of foreign policy?

Policy officers	16	15	3	2	2	1	0	1	40
Information officers	20	11	4	0	1	1	1	2	40
Reporters	13	10	4	0	2	3	3	5	40
NGO leaders	14	11	2	0	1	1	0	7	36

#17—Solicit the views of pressure groups on policies affecting their special interests?

Policy officers	9	16	6	1	4	2	2	0	40
Information officers	12	16	2	0	7	2	0	1	40
Reporters	7	13	6	1	1	5	1	6	40
NGO leaders	11	15	2	0	0	0	1	7	36

#18—Solicit the views of nongovernmental experts on policies in their field of specialization?

Policy officers	11	25	1	0	0	2	1	0	40
Information officers	17	14	4	1	2	0	0	2	40
Reporters	15	16	1	0	1	1	0	6	40
NGO leaders	14	12	0	0	0	0	0	10	36

* 3—Should unless the situation precludes it.
† 5—Should not unless the situation requires it.

The Formation of Public Opinion. The data indicate that most policy officers accept the idea that policy officials, especially at higher levels in the State Department, should play a leading role in opinion-making in this country (Question 11), that they should take time off to meet with reporters and pressure group leaders (Question 12), and that they should interpret the national interest of the United States and the interests of foreign countries to domestic groups (Question 13). The data also show that most members of other groups agree.

Despite the general acceptance of the policy officer's role in opinion formation by all groups, most policy officers do not regard public affairs as a very critical part of their job. For many of them, the information function is incidental to their policy-making role. "We play a leading role in opinion formation in this country," explains one policy official, "because we make policy and public opinion reacts to it." This preoccupation with policy-making affects the policy officer's role in domestic public affairs in two essential ways. First, it means that most of these officials play a passive role in opinion formation. Second, it means that when policy officers do become involved in information activities, they are primarily interested in the effect of public information on foreign policy.

The passive involvement of many policy officers in the public affairs of the State Department is particularly serious for information officers. After all, they depend primarily upon policy officers for information and opinions to guide them in their dealings with the press and other groups. What responsibility do policy officers accept for keeping these information officers informed? The data show that most policy officers feel that they should inform information officers of policy deliberations prior to decisions (Question 14), and most members of other groups agree. When a policy officer says that he keeps information officers informed, however, he usually means either that information officers in his area have access to many of the same overseas cables as he does, or that an information officer attends all of the regular staff meetings in his bureau.

Moreover, policy officers vary considerably in regard to the kind of access to information they believe that information officers should have. Some officials believe that information officers should have a nodding acquaintance with everything. Others are of the opinion that information officers should just be informed of decisions likely to become of interest to the public. Still others feel that they should be informed only after information has begun to leak out. Although many policy officers claim that they keep information officers abreast of developments in their area of responsibility, a number of them acknowledge that it is really impractical to do so.

The instrumental view which many policy officers have of public affairs makes them very jealous of their prerogatives in the information field. What decisions are policy officers willing to share with information officers? Most policy officers seem to feel that they should determine what information is released to the public (Question 15). Other groups are more likely than policy officers to think that this is a responsibility which policy officials should share with information officers. As one of the few policy officers who perceived this activity as a joint responsibility explains, "Actually it is a team operation. The substantive officer knows the subject best. The information officer is more apt to know how this information will affect the press and the public. He controls the mechanics."

The Formation of Foreign Policy. The data show that most policy officers feel that they should take public opinion into account in the formation of foreign policy (Question 16). Although all other groups accept this role segment for policy officers, information officers are more likely than other groups to feel that policy officers should undertake this activity. Policy officers who feel that this role segment is mandatory suggest three reasons for considering domestic public attitudes in policymaking. First, they indicate that they cannot carry out many policies without the support of Congress and the public. Second, they feel that policy jells too hard, and anything which causes the Department to check its views is helpful. Third, they believe that public opinion information aids the Department in interpreting its policies to the public.

Many policy officers feel that public opinion should only be taken into account at the political levels in the Department or the White House. These officials invariably regard public opinion as a restraining influence on policy, and they feel that if lower level officers have their attention focused on public views rather than the best policy, they may discard alternatives before their superiors have a chance to evaluate them simply because they think certain things would not wash politically. A number of these policy officers recognize, however, that lower-level officers have to be attuned to ideas on the outside if they are not going to advocate a stream of impracticalities.

The data also indicate that a majority of policy officers feel that they should solicit the views of pressure groups on policies affecting their special interests (Question 17). The data reveal that although a majority of those in other groups agree, policy officers and reporters feel less intensely than information officers and NGO leaders about this role segment. Many policy officers profess that it is important for them to have detailed knowledge of public problems but that it really is not necessary to solicit the views of various pressure groups because NGO leaders keep them informed.

There are a number of reasons why policy officers may not be anxious to solicit group views. First, they consider such groups biased and unreliable sources of information: "We have some prejudice against such information. It would be biased information. They are not trained observers." Second, there is feeling that many groups have not put any serious thought into real problems: "It's kind of disappointing in terms of getting anything useful . . . They are not giving it any hard thought." Third, policy officers are constantly aware that if they were to initiate such discussions they would have to give out new factual information, and this might be disadvantageous.

Moreover, the data indicate most respondents in all four groups agree that policy officers should solicit the views of non-governmental experts in their field of specialization (Question 18). Although NGO leaders feel more intensely than other groups about this role segment, policy officers acknowledge that academic views are helpful to them. One officer, who is especially well qualified to discuss this point, feels that academics contribute: (1) historical material and background, (2) ideas and analysis, and (3) current interpretation. The place where consultations with the academic community break down, according to this official, is where one tries to get academics to focus on specific policy issues. One reason for this may be that it is difficult for outsiders to see nuances of policy when they do not follow things on a day-to-day basis.

Many policy officers seem to feel that they get most of the material they can use from academics indirectly by reading the professional journals. Nevertheless, the Department has become increasingly active in consulting academic experts in the universities and foundations. A few officers discount the contributions which these gentlemen can make either on the grounds that there are no scholars working in their field or that they, not the academics, are the real experts.

State Department Information Officers

Information officers may be regarded as middlemen between Department policy officers on the one hand and foreign affairs reporters and leaders of nongovernmental organizations on the other hand. They help the State Department to explain its policies to the public and to interpret public attitudes toward Department policies. Although information officers owe their primary allegiance to their superiors in the Department, most of them are highly conscious of their responsibility to the public. As one information officer put it, "We play the role of those in the Department who are responsible for informing the public. We are working for the public." What part do State Department information officers play in the opinion-policy process? The responses to questions on the information officer's role appear in Table 5.2.

The Formation of Public Opinion. The data show all groups agreeing that information officers should handle routine information activities for the State Department (Question 19). Most information officers feel that it is their job to handle individual inquiries from the press and other groups. They recognize the importance of this function: "We are the front for the Department and our receptivity establishes the Department's reputation." Nevertheless, a few information officers do not regard this role segment as an important part of the information officer's job. These officers accept this task only because questions arise that need to be answered and no one else is available to do it; they maintain that information officers seldom have

Table 5.2 Attitudes Toward Information Officers' Role in Opinion Formation

TO WHAT EXTENT DO YOU FEEL THAT INFORMATION OFFICERS SHOULD OR SHOULD NOT	ABSO- LUTELY MUST 1	PREFER- ABLY SHOULD 2	MAY OR MAY NOT 3*	4	5†	PREFER- ABLY SHOULD NOT 6	ABSO- LUTELY MUST NOT 7	NO RE- SPONSE	N
#19—Handle routine information activities for the State Department?									
Policy officers	18	14	3	1	1	2	0	1	40
Information officers	20	18	1	0	0	1	0	0	40
Reporters	18	16	1	0	0	0	0	5	40
NGO leaders	16	8	1	0	2	1	0	8	36
#20—Advise policy-makers on information policies?									
Policy officers	30	7	1	0	1	0	0	1	40
Information officers	34	4	1	0	1	0	0	0	40
Reporters	18	15	1	0	0	1	0	5	40
NGO leaders	13	10	3	0	0	0	0	10	36
#21—Interpret the facts underlying policy for the public?									
Policy officers	15	12	3	0	3	6	0	1	40
Information officers	19	10	3	0	3	4	1	0	40
Reporters	14	15	2	0	1	1	2	5	40
NGO leaders	8	7	3	1	4	1	4	8	36
#22—Exercise discretion in timing the release of information to the public?									
Policy officers	15	16	3	1	1	2	0	2	40
Information officers	23	11	1	1	2	2	1	0	40
Reporters	7	16	5	0	0	4	1	7	40
NGO leaders	4	8	3	3	2	6	1	9	36

#23—Keep the public informed on policy deliberations prior to the time that formal policy statements are released?

TO WHAT EXTENT DO YOU FEEL THAT INFORMATION OFFICERS SHOULD OR SHOULD NOT	ABSOLUTELY MUST 1	PREFERABLY SHOULD 2	MAY OR MAY NOT			PREFERABLY SHOULD NOT 6	ABSOLUTELY MUST NOT 7	NO RESPONSE	N
			3*	4	5†				
Policy officers	1	5	10	0	1	0	3	1	21
Information officers	4	3	5	0	3	0	2	0	17
Reporters	4	7	5	0	1	1	1	2	21
NGO leaders	1	4	5	0	1	0	0	9	20
#24—Apply pressure within the Department for a more liberal information policy?									
Policy officers	14	11	6	1	0	7	0	1	40
Information officers	16	12	6	0	5	1	0	0	40
Reporters	18	13	2	0	1	1	0	5	40
NGO leaders	7	10	2	2	4	1	1	9	36
#25—Systematically analyze general public opinion of foreign affairs?									
Policy officers	18	14	6	0	0	1	0	1	40
Information officers	16	9	6	0	7	1	1	0	40
Reporters	7	20	3	0	2	2	1	5	40
NGO leaders	16	7	2	1	0	0	0	10	36
#26—Participate actively in policy-making?									
Policy officers	13	16	4	1	3	0	2	1	40
Information officers	16	13	3	1	4	1	2	0	40
Reporters	9	12	2	0	3	4	5	5	40
NGO leaders	4	8	4	1	4	2	5	8	36

* 3—Should unless the situation precludes it.
† 5—Should not unless the situation requires it.

enough detailed information to answer such inquiries satisfactorily.

The data further indicate that all groups feel that information officers should advise policy-makers on information policies (Question 20). Although Department officers are more likely than reporters and NGO leaders to have this role expectation for information officers, at least one information officer acknowledges that that does not mean that he gets the opportunity to do it. Moreover, the verbal responses of Department officers to this question clearly indicate that this advice is restricted largely to recommendations on the most effective way to disseminate information. Apparently, this is one of the few areas that policy officers credit information officers with knowing more than they do.

Many information officers feel that they are more than a conduit between State Department policy officers and the public. These officers assume a more discretionary and political role for themselves in fighting bureaucratic secrecy and timidity in the Department and, conversely, in preventing the premature disclosure of information by the press and other groups. Since they feel responsible for getting an appropriate balance in the information output of the Department, these officers regard themselves as aggressive and honest brokers between policy officials and the press.

Thus, the data show a majority of those in all groups believing that information officers should not only provide the public with facts, but interpret the facts underlying policy for the public (Question 21). As one prominent information officer puts it, "I do both—equally divided. The open part of the job is to be a conduit. In my private conversations, I am interpreting and explaining." Most information officers feel that it is very important for them to be in a position to provide a reasonable explanation of what Department policy is, what the Department is trying to do, and why the Department is trying to do it.

Although a majority of the members of all groups agree that information officers should exercise discretion in timing the release of information to the public, the data indicate that information officers are more likely than reporters and NGO leaders to prescribe this activity (Question 22). Some information officers claim that this role segment is not terribly important because timing is largely determined by events. This may help to explain why reporters are not really so opposed to giving information officers some discretion in timing the release of information.

According to the data, there is a lack of agreement among members of all four groups on the question of whether or not information officers should keep the public informed of policy deliberations prior to the time that formal policy statements are released (Question 23).[7] Some information officers feel that this discretion is essential if the Department is going to avoid a great deal of post-facto information activities.

The data also indicate that almost all reporters, as well as most members of other groups, feel that information officers should apply pressure within the Department for a more liberal information policy (Question 24). As one information officer put it, "I'm often an advocate of the press in the Department. More correctly, I'm a reporter inside the Department. I try to get answers from other Department officers." Another information officer insists, "Most of us feel this is part of our function. We must open up as many channels as possible. I've proposed more frequent open conferences and backgrounders for Assistant Secretaries."

The Formation of Foreign Policy. The groups who carry the Department's message to the public are not indifferent to the content of Department policies. Although a majority in all groups agree that information officers should systematically analyze general public opinion on foreign policy for the Department (Question 25), many information officers, especially those in higher level positions, regard an understanding of public opinion as something which is incidental to carrying out their other responsibilities. On the whole, information officers are not disturbed by the unscientific approach of the Department to public opinion studies.

The data also indicate that majorities in all groups expect information officers to participate actively in policy-making in the Department, although NGO leaders are less likely than information officers to share this role expectation for information officers. In practice, most information officers recognize that their influence in the policy-making councils of the Department is both limited and individual. Information officers can contribute

---

7 Only approximately half of the respondents are recorded here as answering this question because the pre-test failed to reveal the fact that the initial wording of the question was not appropriate for measuring the attitudinal dimension for which the question was asked. The initial wording was "Should information officers *reveal* information on policy deliberations prior to the time that formal policy statements are released?"

to policy in two ways. First, they can influence policy by helping to determine how policy is articulated. Second, information officers who work at higher levels in the Department can offer their views on important policy questions. It is important to realize that these information officials may not feel that it is legitimate for them to comment on anything which does not bear directly upon the public affairs aspect of policy.

Foreign Affairs Reporters

Reporters who regularly cover the State Department and foreign affairs play a key role in the opinion-policy process. They substantially aid Department officers in communicating foreign events and policies to the general public. They also provide information about foreign affairs to those in the State Department and the government. Moreover, they provide information on public perception of foreign events and policies to Department officers. What specific functions do these reporters perform in the opinion-policy process? The responses to questions on the reporter's role appear in Table 5.3.

The Formation of Public Opinion. The data indicate a high degree of consensus among all groups on the reporter's role as a neutral purveyor of facts (Question 31). This aspect of the reporter's role places great emphasis on objectivity. Virtually all reporters agree that they should write stories without regard for the editorial views of their news organizations (Question 27). Few reporters acknowledge that the editors or managers of their news organization influence their stories: "I can't think of a single story where the editorial policy has concerned me at all. I would say that the tendency of the reporter is to lean against the prevailing wind, and this is true even within the news organization." Although most reporters contend that they leave this out of their thinking altogether, a few reporters acknowledge that the top management of their news organization does set broad policy guidelines for them.

Additional evidence of the desire of reporters to resist the pressures exerted by their news organizations may be found in the relations between television reporters and the producers of network news programs. Most reporters for the electronic media are on a fee system which provides them with a cash bonus for each time they are selected to appear on a news program. The competition among reporters for time on news shows places great pressure upon them to make their stories seem more newsworthy than they really are. Reporters claim that they resist these pressures in order to live up to the expectations of others for objective reporting: "I don't want to harden a story because many government officials listen to these broadcasts, and inaccurate stories dry up your sources." One prominent television reporter says that he is constantly at odds with the producers of the evening news program of his network because "I refuse to give them the headline—to sell a story. I try to give the producer the complete story, not just one in capsule form."

This penchant for objectivity also leads reporters to incorporate statements of Department policy into their stories (Question 28), although the verbal responses of reporters to this question suggest that many of them feel no obligation to report everything that the Department releases, especially if the Department's statements do not include any new information or do not seem very important to reporters. Policy officers and NGO leaders are more likely than reporters to feel that they have an obligation to carry such information. This may reflect the feeling among many policy officers and NGO leaders that the press does not report all that it should on foreign affairs.

The idea of objective reporting also leads majorities in all groups to the conclusion that reporters should verify information obtained from unofficial sources within the Department before publication in any form (Question 29). Although most reporters accept the need to verify the information they receive, they disagree over the extent to which it is practical to do so and how it should be done. Most experienced reporters feel that it is always possible to get some degree of sureness about information, although the process of verification is never complete. A few find it so difficult to verify their stories that they do so only when they can: "Time is so short, I don't have time to check material, so I just write it." Some reporters claim that they check out dubious stories with information officers; others apparently avoid this practice. As one reporter explains, "If I am dubious about a lead, I check it out. I don't go back to information people to see if it's right, however. If a reporter

Table 5.3 Attitudes Toward Reporters' Role in Opinion Formation

TO WHAT EXTENT DO YOU FEEL THAT REPORTERS SHOULD OR SHOULD NOT	ABSO-LUTELY MUST 1	PREFER-ABLY SHOULD 2	MAY OR 3*	MAY NOT 4	5†	PREFER-ABLY SHOULD NOT 6	ABSO-LUTELY MUST NOT 7	NO RE-SPONSE	N
#27—Write without regard for the editorial views of their news organization									
Policy officers	26	6	0	0	3	1	0	4	40
Information officers	24	5	3	3	1	1	0	3	40
Reporters	29	6	1	0	0	1	0	3	40
NGO leaders	15	4	2	1	1	2	0	11	36
#28—Incorporate statements of Department policy in their material whether they agree or disagree with it									
Policy officers	6	18	5	3	4	1	2	1	40
Information officers	4	14	6	9	2	1	2	2	40
Reporters	4	10	5	0	6	8	5	2	40
NGO leaders	1	11	4	3	2	4	1	10	36
#29—Verify information obtained from unauthorized sources in the Department before publication in any form									
Policy officers	27	6	2	1	0	0	0	4	40
Information officers	16	18	1	0	3	0	0	2	40
Reporters	19	8	5	0	2	1	2	3	40
NGO leaders	14	9	0	1	2	0	0	10	36
#30—Work through Department information officers									
Policy officers	11	20	1	0	1	1	1	5	40
Information officers	13	20	1	3	2	0	0	1	40
Reporters	19	8	5	0	2	1	2	3	40
NGO leaders	14	9	0	1	2	0	0	10	36

#31—Report the facts avoiding any interpretation whatever?

TO WHAT EXTENT DO YOU FEEL THAT REPORTERS SHOULD OR SHOULD NOT	ABSOLUTELY MUST 1	PREFERABLY SHOULD 2	MAY OR MAY NOT		PREFERABLY SHOULD NOT 6	ABSOLUTELY MUST NOT 7	NO RESPONSE	N
			3*	4	5†				
Policy officers	8	18	3	0	0	5	0	6	40
Information officers	5	20	3	1	1	8	1	1	40
Reporters	13	16	1	0	0	5	3	2	40
NGO leaders	9	12	2	0	0	4	1	8	36

#32—Interpret the facts for the public?

Policy officers	13	17	3	0	2	2	2	1	40
Information officers	16	16	4	0	1	2	0	1	40
Reporters	19	15	3	0	0	0	1	2	40
NGO leaders	6	12	1	1	3	2	3	8	36

33—Bring public views and needs to the attention of Department officers?

Policy officers	9	19	5	0	0	4	2	1	40
Information officers	15	17	2	0	2	2	1	1	40
Reporters	2	13	3	0	3	11	6	2	40
NGO leaders	7	12	4	0	2	1	1	9	36

#34—Attempt to influence policy officers?

Policy officers	5	7	3	2	2	10	9	2	40
Information officers	1	8	3	7	3	5	12	1	40
Reporters	2	4	0	1	6	10	14	3	40
NGO leaders	2	3	2	2	4	9	5	9	36

* 3—Should unless the situation precludes it.
† 5—Should not unless the situation requires it.

goes back to his source or an information officer, then he is really imposing censorship on himself. I simply try the story out with someone else with similar responsibilities and authority." Information officers are less likely than policy officers to expect reporters to verify such information.

Although some reporters may not find it prudent to check out dubious stories with Department information officers, the data indicates that almost all respondents feel that reporters should work through Department information officers (Question 30). Many reporters rely upon information officers, but this does not mean that these reporters deal exclusively with information officers.

Foreign affairs reporters are also conscious of the ways in which they enter into the manufacturing of news. The data show that although most members of all four groups feel that reporters should report facts without any interpretation whatever (Question 31), cross-tabulations show that many of these same individuals feel that reporters should interpret the facts for the public (Question 32). Apparently, the majority of respondents in each group prefer a combination of factual and interpretive stories and news analysis. The data suggest, however, that NGO leaders are more suspicious than other groups of the interpretive role of reporters. This may reflect the organization world's displeasure with the way their own stories are treated by the press.

A distinction should probably be made here between two kinds of interpretation: (1) personal opinion and (2) reporting selective facts and opinions. Most foreign affairs reporters say that they are very cautious about interjecting their own opinions into their stories. They make a sharp distinction between news analysis and editorializing. As one reporter puts it, "In the field of diplomacy, words are not facts. In almost every instance we have to put what we get into everyday words. Then we must ask ourselves, why was this said? What is it meant to achieve? We can do this without interjecting our own opinions."

The primary purpose of interpretation is to point up the significance of a story and to make it more meaningful. Most reporters attempt to place the news in perspective by relating it to a pattern of development: present, past, and future. One reporter explains what he means by interpretive reporting as follows: "Report requisite background, historical context, contradictions, ambiguities; distinguish between protocol and substance; explain motivations where possible; set forth opposing internal and external points of view; explain, explain, explain . . . ."

Reporters readily express their own views toward interpretive reporting, but the interviews suggest that these opinions probably do not provide a very reliable basis for classifying individual reporters along this dimension. There are several reasons for this. First, the term "interpretation" covers a variety of actions. Second, the evidence suggests that there may be little correspondence between what reporters say they do and what they actually do, especially in view of the difficulty in establishing objective standards for evaluation. Third, the extent to which a reporter engages in interpretation depends, to some extent, on the kind of story he is covering, and he is not always free to make that choice himself.

The Formation of Foreign Policy. The primary task of reporters is to relate current information to the public; however, reporters are not indifferent to the issues and events which they report. They frequently have wide experience in foreign affairs and strong opinions on current foreign policies. Moreover, they often regard themselves as a two-way link between the government and the public. In view of the ready access of reporters to Department policy officers, it is important to ask what roles reporters play in the formation of foreign policy.

The data indicate that policy-making roles so often attributed to reporters by others are not widely and firmly accepted by reporters themselves. Although a majority of counter position holders believe that reporters should bring public views and needs to the attention of Department officers, reporters themselves are almost evenly divided on this role segment (Question 33). The following responses by reporters reveal the opposing currents of thought among them on their role as articulators of public opinion: "Yes, our job is not simply to report the mood of the government, but also the mood of the public . . . ; no, I know the government position, I don't know what the masses feel." Part of the problem here is that most individuals fail to make a distinction between the reporter and his media. The media may provide other groups with considerable opinion information, but the foreign affairs reporter does not usually perceive himself as performing this task.

The data also show a majority in all groups rejecting the proposition that reporters should attempt to influence policy officers (Question 34). Reporters are even more reluctant than counter position holders to accept this function, although a number of reporters acknowledge that they get into long private conversations about policy with these officials. Reporters regard these opportunities to influence policy officials as a by-product of their work rather than an inherent part of their job.

Be this as it may, one of the enduring attractions of the reportorial trade is the involvement of reporters in important affairs of state. Reporters consciously or unconsciously feel that they can influence Department policy in several ways. First, they may influence policy indirectly by playing a leading role in determining how events abroad are perceived by the public. Second, they may serve as catalytic agents by bringing some of the views which are being expressed in private among lower-level officials to the attention of higher-level officials. Third, they may influence policy directly by the questions they ask of policy officers. Fourth, they have been known to serve as intermediaries between foreign emissaries and government officials. The latter role was played by John Scali, ABC's Diplomatic Correspondent in Washington, during the Cuban missile crisis in 1962.

Leaders of Nongovernmental Organizations

Nongovernmental organizations play a critical role in the formation of public opinion on foreign policy questions. They provide local forums for the discussion of public issues, and many of the citizens in this country who have an interest in international affairs participate in these programs. These organizations also play a significant role in the policy-making process. They keep the Department informed of the impact of its policies upon the special interests and attitudes of major segments of the domestic public. What role do those with the primary staff responsibility for these organization programs in international affairs play in the opinion-policy process? The responses to questions on the role of these group leaders appear in Table 5.4.

The Formation of Public Opinion. Few of the leaders of nongovernmental organizations interviewed in this study serve as members of the governing boards of national committees which have the formal power to make organization policy. Most of them hold staff positions which allow them to participate only indirectly in the formation of organization policies. Indeed, a few deny that they have any influence at all on the policy positions formed by their organization: "I don't determine any _____ policies. As a staff official, it would be improper." However, many of these NGO leaders give advice to their organization's governing board or national committee. In this advisory role, these NGO leaders conduct background studies, prepare agenda, and make recommendations which often give them a decisive role in organization policy. As one NGO leader explains, "Ninety-five percent of the foreign policy of the _____ is shaped here. The Committee acts on our advice."

Although most of these NGO leaders participate only indirectly in making organization policy, the policy-making bodies of these organizations meet so infrequently that staff officers have to be given some discretion in the application of broad policy guidelines to changing conditions. The data show that almost all NGO leaders feel that they must have discretion in applying organization policies to current situations (Question 35). Most Department policy officers, information officers, and reporters accept this role segment for leaders of nongovernmental organizations.

Most NGO leaders also believe that they should consult the membership prior to the adoption of basic organization policies (Question 36), but data suggest that there is less agreement among NGO leaders than members of other groups on this point. Moreover, when NGO leaders say they consult the membership, they are more likely than the members of other groups to mean an executive board, an occasional conference, or the local leadership rather than the general membership. For example, one NGO leader said, "Yes, you need some participation of the membership. We have a convention every four years, a conference each year. Moreover, we have a number of seminars at which we discuss problems. We try to guide these conferences. The initiative among the rank and file is about the same as the general public." At the same time, there are a few organizations, such as the U.S. Chamber of Commerce, which occasionally poll their members before taking a stand on key public issues.

The data further indicate that although a majority of NGO leaders feel that they should propose adjustments of the organization's special interest in favor of national and possibly foreign

Table 5.4   Attitudes Toward NGO Leaders' Role in Opinion
            Formation

TO WHAT EXTENT DO YOU FEEL THAT NGO LEADERS SHOULD OR SHOULD NOT	ABSO-LUTELY MUST 1	PREFER-ABLY SHOULD 2	MAY OR MAY NOT 3*	4	5†	PREFER-ABLY SHOULD NOT 6	ABSO-LUTELY MUST NOT 7	NO RE-SPONSE	N
#35—Exercise their own discretion in applying organization policies to current situations?									
Policy officers	3	21	1	2	3	2	2	6	40
Information officers	5	16	5	4	2	1	0	7	40
Reporters	2	13	4	4	2	3	0	12	40
NGO leaders	27	3	3	0	2	0	0	1	36
#36—Consult the membership prior to the adoption of basic organization policies?									
Policy officers	11	18	1	0	1	3	1	5	40
Information officers	15	15	1	2	0	0	0	7	40
Reporters	10	13	4	1	0	0	0	12	40
NGO leaders	14	10	5	0	3.	0	3	1	36
#37—Propose adjustments of the organization's special interests in favor of national and possibly foreign interests?									
Policy officers	15	15	2	1	0	2	0	5	40
Information officers	7	19	5	0	1	1	0	7	40
Reporters	5	19	2	1	2	0	0	11	40
NGO leaders	11	6	4	3	7	1	0	4	36
#38—Prepare material of special interest for release in the organizational media?									
Policy officers	9	22	3	0	0	0	0	6	40
Information officers	9	19	2	0	1	0	0	9	40
Reporters	7	17	2	1	0	1	0	12	40
NGO leaders	24	7	2	0	0	1	1	1	36

#39—Mobilize support

TO WHAT EXTENT DO YOU FEEL THAT NGO LEADERS SHOULD OR SHOULD NOT	ABSO- LUTELY MUST 1	PREFER- ABLY SHOULD 2	MAY OR MAY NOT 3*	4	5†	PREFER- ABLY SHOULD NOT 6	ABSO- LUTELY MUST NOT 7	NO RE- SPONSE	N
within the organization for policies adopted by the leadership?									
Policy officers	9	20	3	0	1	0	0	7	40
Information officers	3	22	0	0	1	2	1	11	40
Reporters	7	17	2	1	1	0	0	12	40
NGO leaders	22	8	1	0	2	1	0	2	36
#40—Help to educate the general public on foreign affairs?									
Policy officers	19	13	3	0	0	1	0	4	40
Information officers	16	13	2	1	1	0	1	6	40
Reporters	11	12	4	1	0	1	1	10	40
NGO leaders	19	8	3	0	2	0	3	1	36
#41—Bring pressure to bear on members of Congress to support organization policies?									
Policy officers	13	16	4	0	1	0	1	5	40
Information officers	7	20	4	0	1	0	1	7	40
Reporters	6	15	0	2	2	3	0	12	40
NGO leaders	29	3	3	0	0	1	0	0	36
#42—Submit organization views directly to policy officers in the State Department?									
Policy officers	11	13	4	0	3	2	2	5	40
Information officers	6	22	2	2	1	0	0	7	40
Reporters	4	15	6	1	1	3	0	10	40
NGO leaders	22	3	3	0	7	1	0	0	36

* 3—Should unless the situation precludes it.
† 5—Should not unless the situation requires it.

interests (Question 37), this view is more likely to be taken by policy officers than reporters and information officers. Most organizations identify their interest with the national interest although many perceive at least a theoretical need to pare down the natural thrust of their organization's position in the general interest. For instance, one NGO leader states, "We believe in free trade. However, sometimes this hurts American industry so we support measures to indemnify these workers and industries from foreign competition. We must make pragmatic changes as problems come up."

In addition to playing a leading role in formulating organization policies, most NGO leaders also play an active role in selling these policies to the membership and to the general public. The data show that NGO leaders are more likely than other groups to feel that they *must* prepare material of special interest for release in the organization media (Question 38). Virtually all of these organizations have regular newsletters, magazines, or newspapers which provide a medium for internal communications, and many of these NGO leaders have regular or occasional columns or stories which appear in these outlets.

Moreover, the data indicate that NGO leaders are more likely than other groups to feel that they *must* mobilize support within the organization for policies adopted by the leadership (Question 39). Most leaders claim that these efforts are quite low key because organization policies are basically representative of the membership. A few NGO leaders indicate that they have gone off on a limb on a policy and are hard at work to create a climate of acceptance within their organization for their stand.

Most nongovernmental organizations stress educational programs among their own members, but many of these organizations also attempt to educate the general public. Almost all of the respondents feel that NGO leaders should help to educate the general public on foreign affairs (Question 40). The types of general education programs undertaken by these organizations are almost as diverse as the organizations themselves. Some groups engage in mailings; others sponsor news broadcasts and public affairs programs; still others try to get their stories carried in the mass media. Most organizations employ a combination of all of these methods.

The Formation of Foreign Policy. Many nongovernmental organizations feel that they have a stake in American foreign policy, and the leaders of these organizations are agreed that policy officers in the State Department should solicit their views, particularly when policy may affect their special interests (Question 17, Table 5.1). The question is at what point in the policy-making process should NGO leaders try to bring their influence to bear on foreign policy?

Since many nongovernmental organizations are particularly well organized to influence foreign policy in the legislature, it is not surprising that virtually all NGO leaders feel that it is part of their job to bring pressure to bear on members of Congress to support organization policies (Question 41). Most members of other groups agree. Within certain limits even non-profit, non-lobbying groups feel that it is their prerogative to make their views known to the people's representatives.

Leaders of nongovernmental organizations are also more likely than other groups to feel that NGO leaders should submit organization views directly to policy officers in the State Department (Question 42). Nevertheless, the verbal responses of a number of NGO leaders suggest that they are reluctant to press their views on the Department. It is not uncommon, even for organizations which supposedly have regular relations with the Department, for NGO leaders to contact the Department only in emergency situations or on specific problems with which they have a special interest. The data also indicate that some policy officers are opposed to direct representations by groups in the Department. The reluctance of organization leaders to exert their influence in the Department as well as the apparent resistance of some policy officers to group influences will be discussed further in Chapter 8.

Patterns of Group Role Expectations

The data in Tables 5.1-5.4 show a high proportion of respondents in all groups, except leaders of nongovernmental organizations, willing to discuss specific role segments of counter position holders. This suggests that these respondents are familiar with the tasks performed by these position holders and have no difficulty perceiving them as holders of a single position. Moreover, the uniformity of responses to most questions on role expectations for these four groups indicates that there is general agreement on the role performed by each of these groups. Indeed, the uniformity of role expectations for each of these position holders suggests that the role of each group is regarded as legitimate by counter position holders.

General agreement on many of these role expectations should not obscure the fact that there is less agreement in some areas than in others. The incumbents of a focal position, for example, appear to be less sure of the role which they should play in bringing public opinion to bear on foreign policy than they are of the role that they should play in the formation of public opinion on foreign affairs.[8] This may reflect the doubt in the minds of many respondents about the part that should be played by domestic factors in foreign policy decisions.

There also appears to be less agreement within and among groups on role expectations which may be classified as discretionary and political than there is on other role expectations. There is seemingly less consensus among respondents on the discretionary roles of information officers than there is on their neutral roles.[9] Moreover, counter position holders are more likely than the focal group to reject these discretionary and political role expectations. Uniform responses to certain role expectations may disguise substantive differences if each group accepts this role segment for different reasons. Information and policy officers, for example, accept a leading role for policy officers in opinion-making in this country (Question 11) because the Department needs public support. Reporters and NGO leaders, who are often suspicious of Department efforts to gain public support for its policies, accept this role expectation because they are so dependent upon the Department for information themselves.

Since each group may accept role orientations of others which are a source of some tension, these role expectations do not give a very complete picture of the relations between these groups. This picture can be supplemented by examining the attitudes of each of these groups toward some outcome of the political system they form. In the next section, therefore, the attitudes of these four groups toward the requirements for re-

8 At least 20 percent reject the role in Questions 17, 33, 34, and 42.
9 At least 20 percent reject the role in Questions 21, 24, and 26.

leasing and withholding State Department information is discussed.

ATTITUDES

All of these groups expect counter position holders to play a role in the formation of public opinion in this country, but each group has a somewhat different stake in the public opinion-forming process. Department officers must seek public support within limits set by the needs of effective foreign policy. Reporters and NGO leaders usually want as open a public dialogue as possible on Department policies for the enlightenment of the general public. It is commonly assumed that Department officers will find the reasons for secrecy more compelling than reporters or leaders of nongovernmental organizations, and that the leaders of nongovernmental organizations and reporters will find the reasons for publicity more compelling than Department officers. What are the attitudes of each of these groups toward the conflicting needs of secrecy and publicity? The responses to the ten questions on releasing and withholding information appear in Tables 5.5 and 5.6.

Table 5.5   Attitudes Toward the Releasing of Information

TO WHAT EXTENT DO YOU FEEL THAT THE STATE DEPARTMENT SHOULD OR SHOULD NOT	ABSO-LUTELY MUST 1	PREFER-ABLY SHOULD 2	MAY OR MAY NOT 3*	4	5†	PREFER-ABLY SHOULD NOT 6	ABSO-LUTELY MUST NOT 7	NO RE-SPONSE	N
#1—Release information because the public has a right-to-know?									
Policy officers	3	10	24	1	1	1	0	0	40
Information officers	12	8	19	0	0	0	0	1	40
Reporters	16	9	13	1	0	0	0	1	40
NGO leaders	14	8	9	0	0	1	0	4	36
#2—Release information because it may improve public understanding of existing programs and policies?									

TO WHAT EXTENT DO YOU FEEL THAT THE STATE DEPARTMENT SHOULD OR SHOULD NOT	ABSO-LUTELY MUST 1	PREFER-ABLY SHOULD 2	MAY OR MAY NOT 3*	4	5†	PREFER-ABLY SHOULD NOT 6	ABSO-LUTELY MUST NOT 7	NO RE-SPONSE	N
Policy officers	27	12	1	0	0	0	0	0	40
Information officers	30	6	2	0	0	0	0	2	40
Reporters	23	15	0	1	0	0	0	1	40
NGO leaders	18	11	3	0	0	0	0	4	36

#3—Release information because it may strengthen this government's negotiating position?

Policy officers	8	24	7	1	0	0	0	0	40
Information officers	5	27	4	0	1	1	1	1	40
Reporters	2	29	3	1	2	2	0	1	40
NGO leaders	6	17	6	1	1	0	0	5	36

#4—Release information because it may reduce the number of misleading speculations which are being made in public?

Policy officers	9	23	6	1	1	0	0	0	40
Information officers	16	14	7	1	0	0	0	2	40
Reporters	15	19	3	1	0	1	0	1	40
NGO leaders	9	16	4	1	2	0	0	4	36

#5—Release information because it may promote domestic political support for Department policies?

Policy officers	3	24	3	0	6	4	0	0	40
Information officers	3	20	4	0	5	5	1	1	40
Reporters	1	21	5	1	3	6	2	1	40
NGO leaders	3	12	4	2	2	8	1	4	36

* 3—Should unless the situation precludes it.
† 5—Should not unless the situation requires it.

Releasing Information

Contrary to expectations, reporters and NGO leaders are not

much more inclined to accept reasons for releasing information than Department officers. The high degree of acceptance of publicity by all four groups suggests that at least in theory there does not have to be a specific reason for releasing information because the value of an informed public is accepted by all respondents. Nevertheless, the basic reason accepted by all groups for releasing information is to improve public understanding of existing programs and policies (Question 2). This reason is more readily accepted by all groups than the prescription that the public has a right-to-know, because members of all four groups perceive limits to this right (Question 1). Although reporters feel more intensely about the public's right-to-know than Department officers, many of them admit that it is terribly difficult to pin down this concept. More than one reporter suggest that the public's right-to-know is a principle dear to editors and publishers who do not know what there is to know.

All groups feel that it is legitimate for the Department to release information for instrumental reasons, i.e., to strengthen the government's negotiating position (Question 3), to reduce the number of misleading speculations which are being made in public (Question 4), and to promote domestic public support for Department policies (Question 5). However, there is a lack of consensus among these groups on which of these reasons is most compelling. Policy officers are more likely than reporters to emphasize negotiations. In verbal responses to these questions, Department officers show that they regard the instrumental use of publicity as very problematical. They feel that, even if the Department has a definite purpose for releasing information, publicity may well not have the intended effect.

Withholding Information

The data in Table 5.6 show that there are significant differences between NGO leaders and reporters on the one hand and Department officers on the other hand on reasons for withholding information. As expected, Department officers, especially policy officers, find the reasons for secrecy more compelling than NGO leaders and reporters. Although all groups agree that information should be withheld for reasons of national

Table 5.6   Attitudes Toward the Withholding of Information

TO WHAT EXTENT DO YOU FEEL THAT THE STATE DEPARTMENT SHOULD OR SHOULD NOT	ABSO- LUTELY MUST 1	PREFER- ABLY SHOULD 2	MAY OR MAY NOT			PREFER- ABLY SHOULD NOT 6	ABSO- LUTELY MUST NOT 7	NO RE- SPONSE	N
			3*	4	5†				
#6—Withhold information because it may endanger national security?									
Policy officers	33	5	1	0	0	0	1	0	40
Information officers	34	3	0	0	1	0	0	2	40
Reporters	16	11	9	1	2	0	0	1	40
NGO leaders	14	6	5	3	3	0	1	4	36
#7—Temporarily withhold information because it may require explanatory material not yet available?									
Policy officers	4	22	10	1	0	3	0	0	40
Information officers	5	21	4	1	4	3	0	2	40
Reporters	2	12	5	3	9	4	4	1	40
NGO leaders	4	12	6	3	4	2	0	5	36
#8—Withhold information because it may embarrass friendly governments and their leaders?									
Policy officers	9	17	9	1	3	1	0	0	40
Information officers	2	15	11	2	6	1	0	2	40
Reporters	2	7	7	4	12	7	1	0	40
NGO leaders	1	5	6	3	14	3	0	4	36
#9—Withhold information because it may expose differences of opinion within the State Department and the government?									
Policy officers	5	9	6	1	12	7	0	0	40
Information officers	1	7	7	0	10	10	3	2	40
Reporters	0	5	4	3	6	8	12	2	40
NGO leaders	1	1	2	3	5	12	8	4	36

#10—Withhold informa-

TO WHAT EXTENT DO YOU FEEL THAT THE STATE DEPARTMENT SHOULD OR SHOULD NOT	ABSO- LUTELY MUST 1	PREFER- ABLY SHOULD 2	MAY OR MAY NOT			PREFER- ABLY SHOULD NOT 6	ABSO- LUTELY MUST NOT 7	NO RE- SPONSE	N
			3*	4	5†				
tion because it may dis- credit the State Depart- ment and the Adminis- tration in power?									
Policy officers	1	4	8	0	11	13	3	0	40
Information officers	1	2	4	2	12	15	3	1	40
Reporters	0	4	2	3	5	14	11	1	40
NGO leaders	1	0	3	3	3	17	5	4	36

* 3—Should unless the situation precludes it.
† 5—Should not unless the situation requires it.

security (Question 6), NGO leaders and reporters feel that the principle suffers from the same definitional problems that all groups perceive in the public's right-to-know.

Department officers generally feel that it makes sense to with- hold information temporarily in order to provide additional explanatory material, and most members of other groups agree (Question 7). As one officer put it, "Our purpose is not to make headlines. There is much to be said for completeness and dignity in government operations unless there is a special need for speed or timing." However, reporters, who are less likely than other groups to accept this reason, are suspicious of the real reasons for which such information might be withheld.

The data indicate that Department policy officers are more willing than other groups to withhold information which they feel may embarrass friendly governments and their leaders (Question 8). Although information officers generally accept this reason as legitimate, they feel that the burden of proof should rest with the policy officer who favors secrecy. The verbal re- sponses of information officers suggest that the mere fact that it causes discomfort is not enough; one must show how it will damage official relations with another country. A surprising number of reporters and NGO leaders are willing to go along with this reason up to a point, but they generally feel that Department officers are overly cautious in this respect. As one NGO leader remarks, "The Department regards all the governments they deal with as friendly governments." The attitudes of a few reporters who claim to disregard this factor completely may in part justify the protective attitudes of many Department officers.

Department officers are more willing than reporters or NGO leaders to withhold information because it may expose differences of opinion within the Department and the government (Question 9). Nevertheless, policy officers are almost evenly divided on this question. On the one hand, a number of them believe that their mandate is opposite the press and that from their standpoint at least it is usually best not to get into public relations until problems are ironed out. On the other hand, a number of them feel that the whole question of dissent must be encouraged. These views are also reflected in the opinions of information officers although they introduce a greater awareness of the needs of the public and the press. As one information officer said, "We distill our wisdom from our division; it is dishonest to prevent the public from knowing that this occurs." Reporters generally view this reason for withholding information as a self-serving device, and in practice they claim that this kind of information is easy to get. NGO leaders appear even more opposed to this practice than reporters. As one such leader states, "There is much too little of that. The public ought to have a better picture of the fact that policies are being reviewed in the Department. AID people are unhappy about the escalation of the Vietnam War. This never comes out."

Policy officers are also more willing than reporters and NGO leaders to withhold information because it may embarrass the State Department and the Administration in power (Question 10). The verbal responses of Department officers suggest that they feel this is a significant consideration, but long run credibility is more important. The majority position appears to be that if the release of information just discredits the Department and the government domestically, it is not valid to withhold it because the press is going to find it out anyway, but if the release of information may discredit the government abroad, the Department must serve the U.S. policy interest. NGO leaders and reporters tend to make the former interpretation rather than the latter, and they regard this justification as not legitimate but understandable. Reporters indicate that this is the toughest kind of information to get in the Department.

The Pattern of Responses

All groups seem to prefer publicity to secrecy, although the need to withhold information because it may endanger national security is generally accepted by all groups and although the need to release information because the public has a right-to-know is not intensely felt by most groups. Thus, all groups are more willing to release than to withhold information for each of the following reasons:

1. Because it may improve public understanding (Questions 2 and 7).
2. Because it may affect our relations with other countries (Questions 3 and 8).[10]
3. Because it may serve policy interests at home (Questions 4 and 9).
4. Because it may increase or maintain domestic political support for the Department and the government (Questions 5 and 10).

Publicity is more acceptable than secrecy to all groups because this is a democratic country, and an informed citizenry is regarded as a prerequisite for a democratic foreign policy.

This preference for publicity over secrecy should not obscure other patterns which emerge in the responses of groups to these questions, however. On the whole all groups believe that efforts to improve public understanding are the most compelling reasons for releasing information and second only to national security reasons for withholding information (Questions 2, 4, and 7). In sharp contrast, all groups find efforts to serve domestic political ends one of the least acceptable reasons for either releasing or withholding information (Questions 5 and 10). Finally, all groups feel it is legitimate for the government to withhold or release information as the conduct of American diplomacy requires it, but NGO leaders and reporters are less

---

10 Policy officers are no more or less likely to release than to withhold information because it may affect our relations with other countries.

likely than information and policy officers to accept foreign considerations as the most significant factor to be taken into account in deciding to release or withhold information (Questions 6 and 9).[11]

FACTOR ANALYSIS

Six dimensions have been hypothesized in the role expectations and attitudes of participants in the opinion-policy process. They are: (1) the role of a policy officer, (2) the role of an information officer, (3) the role of a reporter, (4) the role of an NGO leader, (5) an attitude toward publicity, and (6) an attitude toward secrecy. In addition, it has been hypothesized that there is some differentiation in the role expectations for each group, both with respect to the process in which they are engaged and with respect to the amount of discretion each exercises. An examination of both the gross pattern of group responses to individual questions and the verbal comments of individuals answering these questions seems to confirm the existence of these attitudinal dimensions. Before it is possible to claim that certain questions measure an individual's expectations or attitudes on one of these dimensions, it is necessary to analyze the patterned responses of individuals in each of these groups to all 42 questions. Only if there is some pattern to the responses of individuals to certain questions is it possible to maintain that these responses represent a single attitudinal dimension or factor.

Factor analysis can be used to test empirically for the existence of the hypothesized dimensions. The factor analytic procedure employed here consisted of an initial principal axis solution on the intercorrelations among the 42 items.[12] Six factors were extracted by this procedure since there were six hypothesized initially. These six factors were then rotated by the Varimax

11 Information officers as well as reporters and NGO leaders are less likely than policy officers to accept the withholding of information because it may embarrass friendly governments and their leaders.
12 William W. Cooley and Paul R. Lohnes, *Multivariate Procedures for the Behavioral Sciences* (New York: John Wiley and Sons, 1962), Chapter VIII.

procedure.[13] If the six factors which emerge can be identified as the ones hypothesized, then there is some empirical evidence to support these hypotheses and some empirical bases for claiming that certain questions on the instrument measure a given factor. The questions or items included under each of the six factors which emerged from this procedure appear in Table 5.7.[14] The items which most clearly define each factor are ranked

Table 5.7   Rotated Factor Loadings for the Items on Role Expectations and Attitudes

Factor I: Role Expectations of Policy Officers

ITEM	FACTOR LOADING
Policy officers should solicit the views of nongovernmental experts on policies in their field of specialization (Question 18).	67
Policy officers should interpret U.S. national interests and the interests of foreign countries to domestic groups (Question 13).	65
Policy officers should solicit the views of interest groups on policies affecting their special interests (Question 17).	61
Policy officers should take public opinion into account in the formation of foreign policy (Question 16).	58
Policy officers should take time off to meet with newsmen and interest-group leaders (Question 12).	48
Reporters should attempt to influence policy officers (Question 34).	44
Policy officers should determine what information is released to the public (Question 15).	41
Policy officers should play a leading role in opinion-making in this country (Question 11).	39
Information officers should systematically analyze general public opinion on foreign affairs (Question 25).	31

Factor II: Information as an Instrument of Policy

ITEM	FACTOR LOADING
The State Department should withhold information because it	

13 H. F. Kaiser "The Varimax Criterion for Analytic Rotation in Factor Analysis," *Psychometrika*, Volume XXIII, 1958, pp. 187-200.

14 All six factors had eigenvalues over 1.5 and together they accounted for 44 percent of the total variance. This was a reasonable proportion of variance to expect since single items do not usually have very high reliabilities and consequently do not have substantial common factor variance.

130 PARTICIPANTS

may embarrass friendly governments and their leaders (Question 8). **74**

The State Department should withhold information because it may expose differences of opinion within the Department and the government (Question 9). **69**

The State Department should withhold information because it may endanger the national security (Question 6). **65**

The State Department should withhold information because it may discredit the State Department and the Administration in power (Question 10). **64**

The State Department should temporarily withhold information because it may require explanatory material not yet available (Question 7). **64**

The State Department should release information because it may strengthen this government's negotiating position (Question 3). **56**

The State Department should release information because it may promote domestic political support for Department policies (Question 5). **37**

Factor III: Role Expectations of NGO Leaders

ITEM	FACTOR LOADING
NGO leaders should prepare material of special interest for release in the organization media (Question 38).	79
NGO leaders should mobilize support within the organization for policies adopted by the leadership (Question 39).	76
NGO leaders should bring pressure to bear on members of Congress to support organization policies (Question 41).	72
NGO leaders should help to educate the general public on foreign affairs (Question 40).	65
NGO leaders should exercise their own discretion in applying organization policies to current situations (Question 35).	57
NGO leaders should submit organization views directly to policy officers in the State Department (Question 42).	53
NGO leaders should consult the membership prior to the adoption of basic organization policies (Question 36).	52
NGO leaders should propose adjustments of the organization's special interests in favor of national and possibly foreign interests (Question 37).	44

Factor IV: Role Expectations of Information Officers

ITEM	FACTOR LOADING
Information officers should participate actively in policy making (Question 26).	73

Information officers should interpret the facts underlying policy for the public (Question 21).	69
Information officers should apply pressure within the Department for a more liberal information policy (Question 24).	64
Information officers should advise policy officers on information policies (Question 20).	63
Information officers should exercise discretion in timing the release of information to the public (Question 22).	62
Information officers should keep the public informed on policy deliberations prior to the time that formal policy statements are released (Question 23).	44
Policy officers should inform information officers of policy deliberations prior to decisions (Question 14).	37

Factor V: Role Expectations of Reporters

ITEM	FACTOR LOADING
Reporters should verify information obtained from unauthorized sources in the Department before publication in any form (Question 29).	54
Reporters should report the facts avoiding any interpretation whatsoever (Question 31).	52
Reporters should bring public views and needs to the attention of Department officers (Question 33).	52
Reporters should incorporate statements of Department policy in their material whether they agree or disagree with it (Question 28).	49
Reporters should work through Department information officers (Question 30).	47
Reporters should write without regard for the editorial views of their news organization (Question 27).	44

Factor VI: Information as a Prerequisite of Democracy

ITEM	FACTOR LOADING
The State Department should release information because it may reduce the number of misleading speculations which are being made in public (Question 4).	59
The State Department should release information because it may improve public understanding of existing programs and policies (Question 2).	57
The State Department should release information because the public has a right-to-know (Question 1).	56
Reporters should interpret the facts for the public (Question 32).	52
Information officers should handle routine information activities for the State Department (Question 19).	37

according to the size of their factor loadings, indicating their relative strength.

Factor I represents role expectations for policy officers in the opinion-policy process. It includes: (1) the extent to which policy officers should seek the views of domestic groups and individuals on foreign policy, and (2) the extent to which policy officers should interpret foreign developments to domestic opinion leaders. A high score on this factor indicates that an individual expects policy officers to become actively engaged in public affairs; a low score depicts an expectation that policy officers should not become engrossed in public affairs activities. It is assumed that the more discretionary and political role expectations of policy officers are active, not passive.

Factor II portrays the attitudes of individuals toward the State Department's use of information as an instrument of policy. It involves: (1) withholding information for diplomatic reasons, (2) withholding information for domestic political reasons, (3) releasing information for diplomatic reasons, and (4) releasing information for domestic political advantage. A high score on this factor suggests that an individual accepts the manipulation of information by the State Department; a low score indicates that an individual rejects the manipulation of foreign affairs information by the State Department.

Factor III depicts role expectations for NGO leaders in the opinion-policy process. It indicates that leaders of nongovernmental organizations should (1) conduct information programs for the membership and the general public, (2) play a role in the formation of organization policies, and (3) bring organization views to the attention of the government. A high score on this factor indicates that an individual expects NGO leaders to play a discretionary and political role in the opinion-policy process; a low score suggests an expectation that NGO leaders will not exercise very much discretion in the opinion-policy process.

Factor IV represents the discretionary and political role expectations for information officers in the opinion-policy process. It depicts the information officer as an aggressive broker between State Department policy officers on the one hand and foreign affairs reporters and NGOs on the other hand. It does not include the expectation that information officers will just handle routine information activities for the State Department. A high score on this factor indicates that the individual expects information officers to play a discretionary and political role in the opinion-policy process; a low score reveals an expectation that information officers will play a neutral role in the opinion-policy process.

Whereas Factor IV presents a discretionary and political role for information officers, Factor V portrays neutral role expectations for reporters in the opinion-policy process. It involves: (1) the neutral conveyance of facts from the State Department to the public and (2) the neutral transmission of public views and needs to the Department. It excludes the expectation that reporters should interpret facts or present their own opinions. A high score indicates that the individual expects reporters to play a neutral role in the opinion-policy process; a low score suggests an expectation for discretionary and political actions by reporters in the opinion-policy process.

Whereas Factor II portrays the use of information as an instrument of policy, Factor VI suggests the value of information activities generally for the democratic management of foreign affairs. It involves: (1) the release of information to promote an informed electorate, (2) the expectation that reporters should help to interpret facts for the public, and (3) the expectation that information officers should handle routine information activities for the State Department. A high score indicates that the individual feels there is a compelling need for public information on foreign affairs; a low score suggests that the individual feels that the need for public information is only one of several requirements which the State Department should take into account in releasing information.

The role factors which emerge from this analysis (Factors I, III, IV, and V) are the ones hypothesized. The attitudinal factors which emerge from this procedure are similar to the ones predicted. However, instead of a separate factor on secrecy and publicity, the analysis suggests that Factor II represents the informational requirements of policy and Factor VI portrays the informational requirements of the public.

As expected, the factors dealing with the role expectations of State Department information officers and foreign affairs reporters suggest a distinction between discretionary and neutral role segments. Factor IV includes the more discretionary and political roles of information officers; it excludes the expectation that information officers should handle routine information activities (Question 14). Factor V involves the neutral roles of reporters; it leaves out the expectation that information officers should interpret the facts for the public.

Contrary to expectations, there is no distinction between the role expectations of these groups in the opinion-forming process on the one hand or the policy-making process on the other hand. Role expectations in the policy-making process load as high on Factors I, III, IV, and V as role expectations in the opinion-forming process. Therefore, it appears that the participants in the opinion-policy process accept at least in theory the two-way flow of communications among them.

Different Role Expectations and Attitudes Among Groups

On the basis of earlier discussion, it is also hypothesized that there are some significant differences among these four groups in their role expectations and attitudes. NGO leaders are believed, for example, to be more anxious than other groups both for policy officers to pay attention to outside views (Factor I) and for reporters to adhere to the norm of objective reporting (Factor V). With respect to attitudinal differences on information policy, Department officers are expected to be more willing than other groups to accept information as an instrument of policy, although no significant differences are expected in the attitudes of groups toward the informational requirements of the public (Factor VI). What differences are there among these four groups in either their role expectations or attitudes?

In order to answer this question, factor scores were calculated for all individuals from the rotated factor structure. If there is a significant difference between the mean factor scores of each group on particular factors, the variation between groups is regarded as significant. The results appear in Table 5.8. They show a significant difference among the four groups on Factors I, II, V, and VI. There is no significant difference among these groups on Factors III and IV, although there may be important differences among members of each group on these factors.

Table 5.8 Differences in Mean Factor Scores by Group

FACTORS	GROUPS	POLICY OFFICERS	INFOR- MATION OFFICERS	RE- PORTERS	NGO LEADERS	LEVEL OF SIGNIFI- CANCE
I.	Role expectations of policy officers	—.31	—.18	—.13	.73	.005
II.	Information as an in- strument of policy	.48	.30	—.56	—.25	.005
III.	Role expectations of NGO leaders	.01	.08	.09	—.28	NS
IV.	Role expectations of information offiicers	.00	.03	.07	.17	NS
V.	Role expectations of reporters	.10	—.26	—.45	.61	.005
VI.	Information as a prerequisite as a democracy	—.42	.00	.46	—.14	.005

As expected, the data show that NGO leaders have different role expectations for policy officers and reporters than other groups.[15] NGO leaders are more willing than other groups to have policy officers play an active role in opinion-making and in taking public opinion into account in policy-making (Factor I). This is not surprising because NGO leaders probably have a greater stake than other groups in getting policy officers to take their views into account in making policy. NGO leaders are also more likely than information officers and reporters to expect reporters to be objective (Factor V). This may be explained by the fact that NGO leaders are so dependent upon the press both as a source and as a channel for information on foreign affairs. Policy officers are also more likely than reporters to expect the press to be objective in covering foreign affairs. Policy officers have an obvious stake in the caliber of foreign affairs coverage in the press.

[15] Duncan's multiple test was used to determine the existence of significant differences between each pair of mean factor scores. See D. B. Duncan, "Multiple Range Tests for Correlated and Heteroscedastic Means," *Biometrics,* Volume XIII, 1957, pp. 164-176.

The differences between groups in their role expectations may be a function of their familiarity with these position holders. One reason why NGO leaders may tend to be more likely than other groups to accept the role expectations of counter position holders is that they are less familiar than these other groups with variations in role behavior (Factors I, IV, and V). Conversely, the incumbents of each focal position may tend to be less likely than counter position holders to accept the factor measuring their role expectations because they are more aware than other groups of variations in role expectations and behavior (Factors I, III, and V).

As expected, there is a significant difference between these groups in their attitudes toward the informational requirements of policy. State Department officers are more likely than NGO leaders and reporters to approve the manipulation of information for diplomatic and domestic political reasons (Factor II). Contrary to expectations, reporters are more likely than either policy officers or NGO leaders to emphasize the information requirements of the public (Factor VI).

These two factors are extremely important, for they suggest that the conflict among these groups, especially between policy officers and reporters is based on the varying emphasis which these groups place on the requirements of democracy and foreign policy. On the one hand, Department officers, especially policy officers, are more conscious than reporters and NGOs of the requirements of policy. Consequently, they are more likely than these other groups to manipulate information for diplomatic and domestic political reasons. On the other hand, reporters place more emphasis than policy officers and NGO leaders on an informed electorate. Thus, they are more likely than policy officers and NGO leaders to stress the need for public information irrespective of other considerations.

Subsequent analysis of the intercorrelations among these six factors by group point up the relations between these role expectations and attitudes. Correlation analysis suggests that the role expectations and attitudes of policy officers and reporters may be conflicting. On the one hand, policy officers, who stress the informational requirements of policy (Factor II), do not expect reporters to be very objective (Factor V). On the other hand, reporters who accept the need for objective report-ing (Factor V), do not expect policy officers to be very forth-coming (Factor I).

This analysis also indicates that NGO expectations for policy officers and reporters is associated with their attitudes toward State Department information policies. NGO leaders who expect policy officers to be forthcoming and to listen to public views (Factor I) and who expect reporters to be objective (Factor V) accept State Department information policies (Factors II and VI). Conversely, NGO leaders who do not expect policy officers to be forthcoming or to listen to public views (Factor I), and who do not expect reporters to be objective (Factor V) reject Department information policies (Factors II and VI).

Finally, this analysis suggests that NGO leaders perceive a conflict between their role (Factor III) and the role of informa-tion officers (Factor IV) since these two factors are inversely re-lated for them. Information officers apparently perceive NGO leaders and reporters quite differently. On the one hand, in-formation officers, who accept the more discretionary and politi-cal role of NGO leaders (Factor III), expect reporters to be objective (Factor V). On the other hand, information officers who expect reporters to play a more discretionary and political role (Factor V) reject such a role for NGO leaders (Factor III). This indicates that at least insofar as information officers are concerned, reporters and NGO leaders also play conflicting roles in the opinion-policy process.

In this chapter role expectations for each group have been viewed from the perspective of all four groups. This provides an overview of the distinct, but mutually dependent, roles played by each group in the opinion-policy process as well as some of the conflicts between policy and opinion elites, especially in their attitudes toward the requirements for State Department informa-tion policies. Subsequent chapters provide some of the reasons for and sources of cooperation and conflict between these position holders.

PART III

Interactions

Chapter 6

State Department Information
Policies

THE PRIMARY responsibility of the State Department is to
conduct the foreign relations of the United States. The
Department also has a responsibility, however, to keep the
domestic public informed on foreign affairs and to keep itself
informed on domestic public opinion. When the demands of
policy and the public seem to be consistent, these two responsibilities are accepted without any particular difficulty. When
the demands of policy and the public appear to be in conflict,
the question arises: what is the extent of the Department's
obligation to inform the public and to listen to public views?

This chapter deals with the manner in which the State Department attempts to resolve this question, and the tension
which such efforts produce in the relations between information and policy officers. In the course of this chapter, additional
questions will be raised. What are the conflicts, if any, between
the needs of policy and the public? What role, if any, do information and policy officers play in resolving these conflicts?
To what extent do information and policy officers perceive
antagonism in their relations? Is this perceived antagonism associated with the conflicting needs of policy and the public?

For the purposes of this discussion, decisions on the Department's obligation to inform the public and to listen to public
views will be called information policies, and this term will be

141

defined broadly to encompass all of the ways in which a policy becomes known to the public. The primary concern, to be sure, is the way in which the Department articulates its policies for the public; but there is also concern with messages which are implicit in the actions taken by the Department and reported to the public by others. After all, "Effective press relations depend not immediately upon the individuals who implement it, but on realistic policies. Good men can make the best of good policy; whether press officer or correspondents, they cannot make good policy out of bad."[1]

In defining information policy in this way we are explicitly rejecting the deadly analogy of packaging which is so often used in relation to information activities. According to this analogy, information is something which is tacked on to a plan or action only when it is fully developed, just as a finished product is packaged for sale. This means that those who have the task of deciding how an event or plan of action will be explained in public simply discover what policy is and address themselves to the question of how this policy should be presented. The danger here is either that the actions undertaken cannot be given a proper face or that the aims implicit in the actions undertaken belie the official explanation of the policy. Unfortunately, there is today an interval in many peoples' minds between what the State Department does and what it says it does. This hiatus is known as the credibility gap.

THE CREDIBILITY GAP

The widespread suspicion that the State Department regularly misleads the public on foreign affairs stems from two sources. First, the credibility gap is brought about by the notion that so much information is withheld from the public for security or other reasons. Second, the credibility gap is fostered by the release of information which for one reason or another is unsuited for public consumption.

---

[1] "Behind the Vietnam Story," *Columbia Journalism Review,* Winter 1965, Vol. III, p. 18.

Problems of Secrecy

The lack of public confidence in State Department information policies may be explained in part by the atmosphere of secrecy which shrouds the conduct of diplomacy. The reasons for this secrecy are not difficult to enumerate. Like other departments and agencies of the government concerned with national security affairs, the State Department safeguards official information in the interests of the defense of the United States. Like most other large-scale organizations, the State Department also protects the internal flow of communications for administrative and other reasons. This secrecy creates in turn an atmosphere in which rumors and misleading speculations add to the suspicion and distrust of Department information activities.

Withholding Information for Security Reasons. The need to provide for the security of information often conflicts with the need to build public understanding and support for a policy. Department officers contend that 95 percent of the information which the public needs to understand Department policies is available to the public, but the remaining 5 percent (if these proportions are anywhere near correct) is often critical in terms of understanding. The apparent demands of policy may prevent the State Department from building the kind of support which is required for effective policy.

The problem of balancing the conflicting requirements of policy and public was well illustrated by the dilemma in which events in the Far East placed the State Department after World War II. On the one hand, the State Department was condemned for not preparing the American public for the inevitable displacement of the Nationalist regime by a Communist regime in 1949.[2] On the other hand, the Department came under heavy partisan attacks for failing to intervene effectively in behalf of the Chinese Nationalists during the civil war. In a paper en-

---

2 Polls taken by the National Opinion Research Center in the spring and fall of 1949 indicated that only 4 percent of the people felt that the situation in China was one of the major problems facing the nation. The State Department did not issue its volume on *United States Relations with China with Special Reference to the Period 1944-1949* until August 5, 1949. The Chinese Communist People's Republic was proclaimed on October 1, 1949.

titled "The Crisis of American Opinion and Foreign Policy,"
Gabriel Almond lamented the fact that public discussion of
Far Eastern policy was singularly shallow, and he reproached
the State Department for its failure to anticipate and prepare
the public for the serious and humiliating consequences to the
United States of its policy in the Far East.[3]

The Department's position on this matter was explained by
the Director of the Office of Public Affairs in a letter to Professor Almond:

> I think you pass somewhat hastily over the serious dilemma
> that the Department found itself in with respect to explain-
> ing the policies that we were following toward China. Gen-
> eral Marshall made the most strenuous efforts to try to bring
> Chiang Kai-shek to undertake the kinds of action which
> could have saved his regime, but without success. . . .
>
> It seemed clear then . . . that for the United States to have
> gone beyond the tremendous program of material assistance
> to the Nationalist regime and put American soldiers into
> the business of imposing the Kuomintang on an unwilling
> Chinese population would have been a greater disaster than
> anything that has taken place. And yet for the State Depart-
> ment to have announced its conviction that the Kuomintang
> was following policies which spelled its ultimate doom would
> have only hastened that doom, the last thing that we wanted
> to do.[4]

While the Department frankly admitted that a substantial part
of its public relations problem in this period stemmed from
the Far Eastern situation, it did not see how it could have
adopted a more open information policy under the circumstances.

In fact the State Department was not able to avoid the dangers
inherent in this situation, for this same officer recalled that
Secretary Acheson was compelled against his better judgment to
make a major statement on Far Eastern policy before the Na-

---

[3] Gabriel A. Almond, "The Crisis of American Opinion and Foreign Policy,"
unpublished, 1950.
[4] Letter dated February 1, 1951. Cochrane, Friedman and Seamon files in the
State Department.

tional Press Club on January 12, 1950.[5] Unfortunately, the Secretary's speech on that occasion conspicuously failed to include South Korea within the "defense perimeter" of the United States,[6] and Mr. Acheson has subsequently been accused of inviting Communist aggression in Korea. While it may never be known whether the Secretary's remarks actually contributed to the Communist decision to invade South Korea, the incident does illustrate both the need for and the danger of publicity.

The consequences of the Department's information policy on China cannot be measured solely in terms of the actions which it may have unwittingly fostered; however, it must also be assessed in terms of the actions which it may have obstructed. After all, widespread public dissatisfaction not only places greater pressure upon the Department to spell out its policy; it also inhibits the Department from taking actions which are likely to increase public indignation. Thus, during the critical period in November 1950 when Secretary of State Acheson and others in government feared that the Chinese Communists might launch an attack against the exposed columns of United Nations forces in North Korea, the Secretary did not bring his fears to the attention of the President. Richard Neustadt suggests that Acheson's failure to act in this instance is partially attributable to the heavy domestic criticism then falling upon the Secretary and his Department.[7]

The dilemma which arises from the conflicting demands of policy and the public becomes even more pressing when government officials claim a right to lie to the public if it is a question of national survival. There was widespread public comment as

[5] Interview, July 27, 1962.
[6] Secretary Acheson, "Crisis in Asia—An Examination of U.S. Policy," *The Department of State Bulletin*, January 23, 1950, pp. 115-116. "So far as the military security of other areas in the Pacific is concerned," Mr. Acheson said, "no person can guarantee these areas against military attack. Should such an attack occur. . . ," Secretary Acheson continued, "the initial reliance must be on the people attacked to resist it and then upon the commitments of the entire civilized world under the Charter of the United Nations. . . ." This is generally what took place 5 months later.
[7] Richard E. Neustadt, *Presidential Power: The Politics of Leadership* (New York: John Wiley and Sons, 1960), p. 145.

well as a congressional investigation into the information policies of the government during the Cuban missile crisis in 1962, in part at least because the then Assistant Secretary of Defense for Public Affairs, Arthur Sylvester, was said to claim such a right.[8] Although a number of Department officials in the State Department claim to be quite willing to mislead the public if it serves an important policy interest, the propensity for them to do so must decrease rapidly when they know that they are speaking on-the-record, for there are very few instances indeed in which official Department spokesmen have knowingly misled the public.

Nevertheless, even these spokesmen have unwittingly contributed to the notion that the Department purposively misleads the public as an instrument of foreign policy by carrying the false cover stories given to them by higher officials. In 1960 a Department spokesman, Link White, put out an erroneous cover story to explain the presence of a U-2 plane over Russia.[9] Less than a year later, a Department spokesman erroneously denied the role of this country in the Bay of Pigs invasion of Cuba.[10] Both instances unfortunately suggest that the intelligence community is playing such an important role in the conduct of our foreign relations that those with a primary responsibility for informing the American people on foreign affairs, State Department information officers, themselves are uninformed about what is really going on abroad.

Withholding Information for Administrative and Political Reasons. A large amount of State Department information is withheld for purely administrative reasons. The principal explanation given by Department officers for safeguarding the internal working papers of the Department is to protect the flow of written comment and opinion within the administration. On the one hand, it is argued that Department officers will not

---

[8] A full explanation of the context in which this language was used and circumstances in which this statement was made by Mr. Sylvester appears in Part I, "Government Information Plans and Policies," *Hearings* before the House Subcommittee on Government Information, 88th Congress, 1st Session, pp. 146-147, 149-151, and 168-169.

[9] *The New York Times,* May 6 and 7, 1960.

[10] *The New York Times,* April 18, 1961, p. 1.

be perfectly candid in their written reports or memoranda if they know that this information may later be used to discredit them in public. Although administrative privacy may be necessary in order to preserve the value of internal communications, it does not always protect the individual. Indeed, the privacy of Department communications may actually be used to discredit such individuals since doubts and suspicions raised against them cannot be effectively refuted in public. For example, in 1951 Harold Stassen accused Owen Lattimore and others, whom the State Department had consulted on China policy in October 1949, of urging the immediate recognition of Red China.[11] While the minutes of the conference attended by Stassen, Lattimore, and others did not support this interpretation, the Department did not feel it could release comments and opinions which it had solicited in private. As a result, Lattimore had to fend for himself until other participants agreed to release their portions of the transcript.

On the other hand, it is feared that isolated reports or memoranda would be mistaken or misrepresented as official policy rather than expressions of individual opinion. The State Department and other national security organizations are particularly anxious to keep disagreements between various bureaus or departments from erupting in public. For example, the policy guidance staff of the State Department, according to one staff member, has changed or deleted statements by military personnel on foreign affairs which revealed overtones of interservice rivalry. This staff member relates that the Directorate for Security Review in the Defense Department frequently requested the Guidance Staff to make changes or deletions when the Defense unit could not justify such alterations solely on the grounds of security clearance.

Of course, there is always the possibility that the Department is really withholding information simply because it might embarrass or discredit the Department in public. James Reston indicates that "there is a great reluctance to put out informa-

11 "The Institute of Pacific Relations," Part 3-5, *Hearings* before the Internal Security Subcommittee of the Senate Judiciary Committee, 82d Congress, 2d Session.

tion that doesn't fit the line."[12] While Department officers claim to recognize that it is important for the public to have all the facts, both good and bad, in order to exercise its democratic franchise intelligently, they argue that such information may prejudice the interests of the nation. This argument is not as fictitious as it appears. The security of the nation might occasionally be damaged if the State Department were seriously discredited.

Leaks. When information is withheld for the above reasons, it is classified according to the degree of protection it requires: "Top Secret," "Secret," "Confidential," and "Official Use Only." The tendency of government officials to overclassify information often produces its own antidote in the form of "leaks" to the public. A leak is an unauthorized disclosure of any item of official government information. Although the probability that such indiscretions will occur is seemingly increased with the growing number of persons having access to such information, all but one of the experienced press officers and reporters questioned on this point acknowledge that most leaks occur at the top echelons of the Department. This confirms the frequent allusion to the American ship of state as "a vessel leaking only at the top."[13]

There are two broad classifications of leaks—intentional and unintentional. Intentional leaks usually occur when a Department official wants to obtain Congressional and general public support or criticism for a matter pending in the Administration, or it may simply result from the frustration of a government official with the problem of clearing information whether within the administration itself or with allied states. On the other hand, unintentional leaks usually occur either when officials do not realize that unauthorized persons are eavesdropping or when they are not fully cognizant of all of the implications of what they are saying.

Unfortunately, the atmosphere of secrecy which often produces

[12] *Hearings* before the House Government Information Subcommittee, *op. cit.,* p. 75.
[13] John S. Dickey, "The Secretary and the American Public," ed. by Don K. Price, *The Secretary of State,* 1960, p. 152.

such leaks also makes it more likely that, when leaks do occur, they will contain partial and misleading information. Since such information usually makes the headlines, there is great internal as well as external pressure for more complete disclosure whenever a leak occurs. Professional diplomats will sometimes favor complete publicity rather than the publication of incorrect information through leakage. Certainly, Department information officers favor disclosure when part of a story has leaked out since it often brings the credibility of their information service into question. Former Assistant Secretary of State for Public Affairs Berding has argued that when a leak occurs, "the State Department should reach a realistic decision to disclose something of the negotiations under way."[14]

Although leaks may speed up the disclosure of information, it is doubtful if they really compensate for the overclassification of administrative and security information. In the first place, leaks are often "fortuitous accidents" which cannot be depended upon to inform the public. In the second place, they frequently misinform the public since they contain information which has not been coordinated within the Department. Professor Francis E. Rourke suggests that the error of leaks and the error of overclassification "will in fact be cumulative, and that defense policy will simultaneously suffer from both inadequate and excessive resort to the classification system."[15]

Problems of Publicity

The credibility gap is not simply the consequence of withholding information from the public; it also arises when the Department puts out the wrong kind of information. In order for the information released by the Department to be credible, it must be as truthful, complete, intelligible, and accurate as possible. The problems of ensuring that Department information meets these tests will be discussed below.

The Truthfulness of Information. Although the Department

14 Andrew Berding, *Foreign Affairs and You* (Garden City, N.Y.; Doubleday and Company, 1962), p. 157.
15 Francis E. Rourke, *Secrecy and Publicity: Dilemmas of Democracy* (Baltimore: The Johns Hopkins Press, 1961), p. 83.

is the principal source of foreign policy information for the American public, it is not the public's only source, and the Department must take into account the information already available to the public in preparing its releases. Thus, it is important for the Department not only to ensure that the information it releases is true insofar as it can determine the truth but also that this information can be accepted as the truth by the public.

One of the unenviable positions in which the Department sometimes finds itself is that of telling the public much less than they already know (or at least think they know). For example, it is difficult for most Americans to understand why the State Department refused to admit for so long that we were using bases in Thailand for air raids into North Vietnam and Laos. The Department refused to acknowledge this on the grounds that we had an agreement not to do so with the Thai government. In this case the Department probably erred in agreeing to respect the desires of the Thais to remain officially out of the conflict when it was apparent to everyone that they were providing direct assistance. The refusal to acknowledge matters which are bound to become general knowledge only serves to discredit the information activities of the Department. Even if no additional facts can be made available to the public, it is quite possible that the Department can suggest new interpretations of foreign policies and actions which will make Department information activities seem more truthful.

This need for interpretation was well illustrated during one of the first open clashes between the United States and the Soviet Union in the postwar period, the controversy over the admission of Argentina to the San Francisco Conference in the spring of 1945. At a meeting of the American Delegation shortly after the confrontation of the two great powers at the Plenary Session, the press officer of the Delegation reported that the background press conference which had been tentatively scheduled for the next day was being "held up because nothing was being produced to talk about." John Foster Dulles disagreed, maintaining that "it was terribly important to have background statements on today's news" because the events of the day "were a terrific shock to the people and foreshadowed alignments of the great powers."

At first, Secretary Stettinius felt that his speech at the Plenary Session of the Conference had contained about all that could be said at the time on the substance of the conflict between the United States and the Soviet Union. Others argued that any defense of our position would only exaggerate the differences and tend to increase the likelihood of further conflict. But Commander Harold Stassen argued convincingly that, quite aside from the specific point at issue, the public should be made to understand that "differences of viewpoint would be inevitable and that it was no tragedy to have these differences develop." Mr. Dulles further explained that "the whole question of the way differences are settled in international relations should be interpreted in order that they might not be misinterpreted."[16] The Secretary was apparently impressed by this argument, for he subsequently asked this member if he would make his statement on the air later that evening.

The Completeness of Information. The suspicion that the State Department only reports those facts which seem to support administration policies makes it exceedingly difficult to maintain the integrity of government information. There have been frequent attempts to bring into question the veracity and completeness of government releases and publications. For example, Bryton Barron, who was once employed by the Historical Office of the Department, launched an especially bitter campaign to discredit the compilation of documents relating to the wartime conferences, particularly the Yalta papers.[17] His charges have been thoroughly investigated both by the administration and by Congress, and there is no evidence of bias in the selection of these important documents.

The Department also comes under criticism for only presenting its own interpretation of the facts. This criticism seems wide of the mark. In a pluralistic country with private channels of communication, there is ample opportunity for the critics of the

---

16 Minutes of the 24th Meeting of U.S. Delegation, San Francisco, April 30, 1945.
17 See "Report to the Committee on Appropriations, United States House of Representatives on inquiry into allegations made by Mr. Bryton Barron regarding the Department of State," House Appropriations Subcommittee hearings for 1958, 85th Congress, 1st Session, pp. 938-980.

Department to present their own case. Moreover, the Department would surely be censured, and justly so, if it undertook the task of presenting these other views. These positions can best be explained by the critics themselves. The Department's responsibility is not to present all sides of every issue but to present the facts as it understands them and its policy in each situation.

The Clarity of Information. The credibility of Department information is also a function of its clarity. It is often imperative for someone to translate the formal language of diplomacy into clear and simple English before a statement is released to the public. Yet some policy officers are very reluctant to depart from the exact wording of an agreement. Several information officers stated that there was considerable resistance within the State Department and especially within the old Division of Publications itself in the 1940s to the notion of publishing popular material on American foreign policy as well as official documents.

The Accuracy of Information. Not only must Department information be clearly stated, it must also be free of erroneous statements and faulty interpretations. The need for the State Department to review the accuracy of not only its statements but those of other agencies in the foreign affairs field was demonstrated by the Senate Special Preparedness Subcommittee in its hearings on "Military Cold War Education and Speech Review Policies" in 1962.[18] In spite of the fact that some of the State Department reviewers had been over-zealous in making deletions in military speeches, with few exceptions "all of the military officers appearing before the subcommittee . . . agreed that none of the changes and alternations had prevented them from getting their message over to their listeners."[19] Far from demonstrating that the deletions made by the State Department were governed by a "no-win" foreign policy, the hearings mani-

[18] *Hearings* before the Special Preparedness Subcommittee of the Senate Armed Services Committee on "Military Cold War Education and Speech Review Policies," 87th Congress, 2d Session.
[19] Report by Special Preparedness Subcommittee of the Senate Armed Services Committee, 87th Congress, 2d Session, p. 14.

fested the need to cut down the plethora of misleading and inaccurate information being disseminated by the government, and especially the military establishment, on foreign affairs.[20]

As the preceding discussion suggests, the task of forming a credible information policy is not simply a matter of putting out as much information as possible. It is also terribly important what kind of information is released by the State Department and the government. Since these requirements of policy and the public are sometimes conflicting, the question of what kind of information is released depends to a large extent on who makes the decisions on information policies.

HOW DECISIONS ON INFORMATION POLICY ARE MADE

Information policy is the outcome of conscious or unconscious decisions on how foreign policy should be projected to the public. Decisions on information policy concern both information and policy officers. How are these decisions made? What influence do information and policy officers respectively have in these decisions? In order to deal with these and other questions, it is useful to have a model of decision-making in mind.

Harold Lasswell has suggested a model which identifies seven phases of the decision process: intelligence, recommendation, prescription, invocation, application, appraisal, and termination.[21] The intelligence phase involves gathering information which aids in the recognition of a problem as well as formulating alternatives to the problem. The recommending phase concerns the promotion of one or more alternatives. The prescrip-

20 *Hearings* before the Special Preparedness Subcommittee, *op. cit.*, "Supplement Containing Speech Changes with Reasons and Analysis," Part 7.
21 See Harold D. Lasswell, *The Decision Process: Seven Categories of Functional Analysis* (College Park, Maryland: Bureau of Government Research, University of Maryland, 1956). For applications, see Richard Arens and Harold D. Lasswell, *In Defense of Public Order: The Emerging Field of Sanction Law* (New York: Columbia University Press, 1961) and James A. Robinson, *Congress and Foreign Policy-Making: A Study in Legislative Influence and Initiative*, Rev. Ed. (Homewood, Ill.: The Dorsey Press, 1967), p. 210.

tion phase refers to the choice of an alternative. The invocation phase deals with the provisional application of this alternative, followed by the final application phase. The reappraisal phase concerns an evaluation of the prescribed alternative, and the termination phase marks the end of the prescription. There is a great deal of overlap between the intelligence and appraisal phases in the decision-making process; the appraisal of past and present information policies provides intelligence for the formation of new information policies. Which of these seven phases are more likely than not to be performed by information or policy officers?

Intelligence

Two sources of intelligence are relevant to decisions on information policy, opinion information and policy information. Opinion information refers to data on the substance of what the public is thinking, what the public wants to know, and what the public needs to know. Policy information means data on international relations and foreign policy; it concerns what there is to know about policy and how information may affect policy. Both sets of data help Department officers to identify the areas where information policy is needed and to suggest some ideas about what information policy decision should be made. In practice, however, the Department has relied mainly upon public demands for information to identify the areas in which decisions on information policy must be made. Even when the Department tries to foresee the need for information policy, it does so with the purpose of anticipating public demands for information.

Opinion Information. Department officers gain some awareness of what the American public is thinking about general foreign policy simply by being stationed in Washington, although many of these officers are conscious of the special climate of opinion that exists in the Capital. They receive impressions of public attitudes toward foreign affairs through their personal acquaintances or through exposure to various mass media of communication. A number of officers also have occasional contacts with foreign affairs reporters, leaders of pressure groups, and individual citizens in their official capacities at the State Department. Moreover, some officers undertake speaking engagements outside Washington which give them an opportunity to converse with private citizens about foreign policy.

All these sources of opinion information are highly impressionistic, and it is doubtful if any Foreign Service officer would base his report about the climate of opinion abroad on this kind of data. Yet Department officers lack any really systematic means of assessing domestic public attitudes. More will be said about this in discussing the appraisal of information policy. At this point one should simply note that those indicators of general public opinion now available in the Department are found in the offices of information officers. Some of these officers read and answer public correspondence, maintain frequent and regular contact with reporters and NGO leaders, and clip editorial and press comment about key foreign policy issues.

Of course, certain individuals and groups are quite vocal in making their demands known to Department officials. Many but not all of these groups have special interests which make it easy for Department officers to identify their stake in a given policy. These groups voice their demands by letter, by personal representations, and usually by a combination of both. Their demands are usually pitched as high in the Department as possible, although the lower level officials are often asked to draft a reply to or sit down and talk with these groups.

Although these representations occur at numerous and varied points within the Department, they are most consistently channeled through the official contact points for these groups and individuals in the State Department. Some of these contact points are scattered throughout the Department, such as the Office of the Special Assistant to the Secretary for Labor Affairs, but most of them are supervised by information officers either in the Bureau of Public Affairs or in the Offices of Public Affairs Advisers in other bureaus. Thus, information officers are generally more likely than policy officers to be informed about public demands for new information policies.

Policy Information. Information about international affairs and foreign policy is widely dispersed in the State Department.

The division of labor among Department officials has long since reached the point that no one officer is knowledgeable about all aspects of American foreign policy. There is simply too much information being produced for any one officer to scan. Moreover, individual officers lack the varied training and background necessary to understand developments in all fields of policy themselves. The policy officers holding lower-level positions in the Department are more likely than higher-level officials to have a detailed knowledge of events and actions in their particular area of specialty. The policy officers occupying higher-level positions are more likely than their lower-level colleagues to know the direction of Administration policies generally.

Information officers are very dependent upon policy officers at all levels in the Department for information which would help them anticipate the public's demand and need for information. Indeed, at one point information officers could scarcely perform this function at all since they were systematically denied access to policy information. This problem is well documented in the case of Henry Suydam, who became the Chief of the Division of Current Information in the Department in April 1921.[22] Suydam thought that one of the primary duties of the Division would be the faithful scanning of department correspondence for items that could be given to the press. He hoped to build an enlightened public opinion in support of American foreign policy with the information furnished by the other divisions of the Department. When he later discovered that he was to receive only a few unimportant telegrams and practically no dispatches whatever, he protested to his superiors that "the practice of withholding information within the Department from the Chief of this Division, whose designated function was to provide that information, appeared to be an anomalous procedure and inevitably placed both the Department and this Division in a false light."

Of course, Suydam realized that the problem of routing information to his Division was no mere question of mechanics,

[22] See various letters and memoranda between August 9 and October 3, 1921 in the files of the Office of Press Relations.

and he stated quite bluntly that there were a number of officers in the Department who had no adequate understanding of the work the Division was attempting to accomplish. In order to improve the flow of information to the Division, Suydam urged Secretary of State Hughes to issue a Department Order requesting all officers of the Department to keep the Division of Current Information informed as to any matters of fact or policy coming to their notice; instead, the Under Secretary simply instructed the message center to supply Suydam "with copies of all incoming telegrams except those which were given special distribution" such as "telegrams marked confidential or strictly confidential regarding policy and not facts." Suydam's retort that "the classes of correspondence designed for him were of value only as matters of record and of no value as news" was of little avail.

When Henry Suydam returned to the State Department in 1953 as Chief of the Division of News, his access to information improved considerably. A full set of cables is now sent to the Office of Press Relations and the Office of Assistant Secretary for Public Affairs each morning, and much of this information is supposedly available to other information officers on request. Moreover, information officers regularly sit in on the policy-making councils at their level and area in the Department. In this sense policy officers do keep information officers in higher level positions informed on policy deliberations prior to decisions (Question 14). However, there is still much information in the Department which does not reach Department information officers, particularly those occupying lower level positions in the Department. Indeed, some information is still given such limited distribution that the Department spokesman himself depends upon key officials to show him information on an informal basis so that he will know about the most sensitive subjects.

Moreover, it is usually not sufficient just to have access to information. The volume of intelligence is so great that information officers cannot digest all which is available to them. Like most policy officers, information officers also lack the sophisticated scientific and technical background which is often necessary in order to discern what developments in a certain field should receive public attention. On the other hand, it should be noted that information officers are one of the few groups within the Department, aside from the top officials themselves, who are in a position to become relatively well informed on all aspects of American foreign policy. Most policy officers are so engrossed in the problems of their own particular area or specialty that they have neither the time nor the incentive to keep well informed on current developments in all fields of diplomacy. But information officers must be prepared to discuss the whole range of foreign policy problems and issues with their clientele groups, so that if these groups demand a specific knowledge of policy, they can often provide a good first approximation of the truth about policy in a particular area.

Recommendation

Information officers maintain more varied, frequent, and regular contacts with representatives of the public than policy officers; they generally have a better understanding than policy officers of what Congress and the public want or need to know. Policy officers usually become quite expert in some aspect of American foreign relations; they are more likely than information officers to know what there is to know in their specific area or specialty. Both information and policy officers have a stake in information policy, and they are both likely to have definite ideas about how a particular policy should be handled in public. Which officer is usually responsible for proposing information policy?

Generally speaking, it is the job of information officers to propose or recommend information policies in the Department. Information officers are expected to prepare the initial drafts of information policy guidelines, press releases, proclamations, speeches, and other public statements. Few policy officers feel that they have time to prepare public speeches or releases, although most of them become engaged in these activities at one time or another. Thus, information officers are expected to assume the initiative both in preparing material for the public and in clearing this material with all of the relevant policy officers before it is released.

The part played by information officers in recommending the alternatives for information policy is not confined to the Department itself. State Department information officers actually prepare much of the information released by the President on foreign affairs. They regularly assist in the preparation of the briefing book which the President reads prior to each of his press conferences; they often write the initial drafts of Presidential speeches, statements or proclamations dealing with American foreign policy; and they answer most of his incoming correspondence on foreign affairs.[23]

The Department also performs some of these information activities for related agencies. For example, the Bureau of Public Affairs handles a number of information functions for the Arms Control and Disarmament Agency. Even when the Bureau has no specific function to perform for related agencies, however, it must still cover these areas as part of its overall responsibility for keeping the public informed on American foreign policy. Thus, when the Treasury Department failed to provide the basic pamphlet material needed on the "Balance of Payments" problem in 1961, the State Department filled the hiatus.[24]

In preparing material for release to the public, information officers are frequently performing a function which would not or could not be performed as well by others. Many information officers possess special skills, knowledge, or a knack for relating the work of the State Department to specific audiences. The well-known documentary publications of the Department, such as the *Foreign Relations* series, could not be kept up without the assistance of a special staff of trained historians. Organization liaison officers are in a position to offer useful advice on how to deal with a bewildering number of nongovernmental organizations.

Moreover, information officers must take the initiative if they are going to apply pressure within the Department for a more liberal information policy (Question 24). There is some inter-

23 See Robert Manning, "The Geometry of Informed Circles," *The Saturday Review*, May 13, 1961, pp. 63-64.
24 "U.S. Balance of Payments: Questions and Answers," Department of State Publication 7194, July 1961.

view and documentary evidence that information officers do perform this function. If Department actions precipitate unfavorable public and press reaction, for example, information officers approach policy officers with the request for the release of more information or further explanation or interpretation. There are definite limits to the amount of pressure these information officers can exert on policy officials, however. As one information officer puts it, "the general tendency of information officers is to want a liberal policy. The people he talks to know that this is his standard approach. There is a limit to how far he can go."

When information officers are properly informed and when they have the confidence of policy officials, they can play a very significant role in recommending information policy. Perhaps the best illustration of this function being performed by information officers occurred in late February of 1947 when Under Secretary of State Acheson requested Francis Russell, the Director of the Office of Public Affairs, to hold a meeting of the Subcommittee on Foreign Policy Information of the State-War-Navy Coordinating Committee which he chaired in order to draft an information policy paper on aid to Greece.[25] The concrete results of this Subcommittee meeting was a paper entitled "The Public Information Program on United States Aid to Greece" which suggested ways:

1. To make possible the formulation of intelligent opinions by the American people on the problems created by the present situation in Greece through the furnishing of full and frank information by the government.

2. To portray the world conflict between free and totalitarian or imposed forms of government.

3. To bring about an understanding by the American people of the world strategic situation.[26]

This information policy paper later "became the most significant document used in the drafting of the Truman Doctrine."[27]

[25] Joseph M. Jones, The Fifteen Weeks (New York: The Viking Press, 1955), p. 150.
[26] Ibid., p. 152.
[27] Ibid.

Prescription

Whereas information officers are expected to take the initiative in recommending information policies, policy officers usually expect to prescribe such policies. When information officers lack intelligence about policy, Department policy officers consciously or unconsciously determine the information policy of the government. Even when information officers have the required intelligence, most policy officers feel that it is their job to determine what information is released to the public because they are responsible for the conduct of foreign relations. Some Department officers, especially information officers, feel that these decisions should be made jointly (Question 15). In practice, information officers enter into the prescription phase of information policy decisions in two ways. First, they serve as coordinators of information policy among the relevant policy officers. Second, they occasionally appeal the information policy decisions of policy officials at one level to policy officials at the next higher level in the Department.

Coordinators of Information Policy. Information officers have a responsibility for clearing public information with all of the relevant policy makers. In practice this means that information officers must hand-carry the proposed release or statement to various policy officers for clearance. When policy officers in several different bureaus are involved, information officers complain that the resulting statement too often represents the "lowest common denominator" of what these policy officers are willing to release to the public.

Of course, information officers also serve as coordinators within the Department whenever other departments and agencies want to clear their statements on foreign affairs with the Department. For example, the policy guidance for the United States Information Agency is prepared by the Office of Policy Guidance in the Bureau of Public Affairs, which coordinates the guidelines furnished by each of the geographical and functional bureaus. This policy guidance is formally given to USIA representatives at the Public Affairs Advisers Meeting where information policy both for the noon briefing and for the daily overseas information broadcasts is established. According to the participants, there is a healthy interchange on the international and domestic ramifications of various information policies during this meeting.

Operating under a Presidential Directive issued in 1950, the Office of Policy Guidance also reviews the speeches and publications of other government departments and agencies on foreign affairs. Information officers serve largely as coordinators in the speech review process. It is the point to which other departments and agencies send speeches and other material for clearance by the State Department. The members of this staff identify the passages which may require Department comment, consult the public affairs advisers or desk officers in the area of the Department which would be most concerned, and then prepare a consolidated departmental reply to the originating agency. This office makes changes or deletions only when there is "a question of fact with regard to some past event, rather than present policy for which it already has ample guidance; when quotations are used which have been found to be 'not honest or real or actual quotations' or when it has standing instructions that no comment . . . should be made on this particular subject. . . ."[28]

Appeals of Information Policy Decisions. Information officers can appeal the information policy decisions of lower level officials to the next higher level. When differences of opinion over information policy emerge at the bureau level, the Assistant Secretary for Public Affairs always has the option of taking the matter to the Department Secretariat. The number of issues which the Assistant Secretary can afford to appeal are limited, however; information officers usually have to abide by the decisions made by the Assistant Secretaries in the regional and functional bureau most affected.

Invocation and Application

The timing of the release of information to the public is often critical in both public affairs and foreign affairs. Consequently, both information and policy officers feel that they should determine when to invoke the prescribed information policy. In practice, policy officers usually reserve the right to withhold information until certain policy restrictions are lifted. Then, informa-

[28] Phillip H. Burris, *Hearings* before the Special Preparedness Sub-committee, *op. cit.,* Part 2, p. 848.

tion officers are given an opportunity to exercise some discretion in timing the release of information to the public from a public relations standpoint if events do not force their hand.

Moreover, once policy officers have satisfied themselves that information policy is in the national interest, they rely extensively upon information officers to carry out that policy. Even in the case of major policy speeches and announcements which policy-makers deliver themselves, they usually have information officers lay the groundwork for their presentations. It is at this stage that information officers are most appreciated by their cohorts in the Department. For it is the information officer who can tell the official how a particular statement will be played in the morning papers, what stories will be competing with it for headlines, and how to get in touch with key reporters in a hurry. According to the interviews with both information and policy officers, this is the kind of advice that information officers are best qualified to offer and that most policy officers are willing to accept.

Of course, information officers are not always effective in carrying out government information policies, and the public is sometimes left to interpret the most important policies and events for itself. For example, the government's decision in the summer of 1960 to extend economic aid to Latin America, which later became known as the Alliance for Progress, was announced to the world by the White House in "a vaguely worded, rambling statement that left everyone in doubt as to what it meant."[29] The announcement even failed to suggest the magnitude of the new program. Moreover, "it was put out in the midst of a bitter quarrel with Fidel Castro, so that the press and the public naturally conjectured it was a reaction to Castro and not an affirmative action genuinely designed to help Latin America."[30]

Appraisal and Termination

Department officers evaluate the success or failure of their information policies in much the same way that they determine the need for new information policies; they assume that existing

29 Berding, op. cit., p. 65.
30 Ibid.

policies are satisfactory until they encounter specific problems or complaints. Since each set of officers is more likely to hear complaints from or encounter problems with those groups with which it works most closely, this appraisal usually reinforces the predispositions of these officers in the information policy-making process. In this section the concern is primarily with the assessment of Department information policies from the standpoint of public affairs, and so this phase of the decision process is performed largely by information officers. In addition to the informal and largely impressionistic sources of opinion information discussed above, information officers at one time or another have used various measures of public opinion toward the State Department and its policies: review of public correspondence, surveys of press comment, and public opinion studies.

Review of Public Correspondence. One measure of public understanding of American foreign policy is the number and character of the public correspondence received by the State Department. The Department's Public Correspondence Division reads and answers thousands of cards and letters on American foreign policy each month. These cards and letters are a valuable source of intelligence about public attitudes toward foreign affairs.

Public correspondence helps the Department to pinpoint the nature and scope of opposition or resistance to its policies because it comes largely from those who oppose Department policies. As a rule of thumb, information officers attempt to determine the source of opposition whenever they receive ten letters expressing the same view on the same issue in one week. Public correspondence is particularly useful in anticipating organized campaigns against various features of American policy abroad. For example, several information officers stated that the Division was able to anticipate by almost six months the nation-wide campaign to halt aid to Yugoslavia and other Soviet-bloc countries during the second session of the 87th Congress.

Although public correspondence may not provide a very accurate reflection of the quantitative distribution of opinion, it does portray the nation's foreign policy as it is understood by the public.[31] Public correspondence is invaluable as a guide for planning information policy on foreign policies since this correspondence sometimes shows how the public has misinterpreted a political event or in what way its perspective is too narrow.[32] Such information is also useful to top officials of the Department who are constantly trying to interpret their policies to the public; information officers indicate that top officials occasionally request a small sample of the letters received on a current issue.

Surveys of Press Comment. Although all officers receive a great deal of intelligence through the mass media, information officers attempt to make this intelligence available in a more usable form. For example, the information officers in several bureaus clip and circulate all of the newspaper articles of primary interest to policy officers in their area or specialty. Moreover, the Public Opinion Adviser to the Assistant Secretary for Public Affairs prepares special studies on American public opinion at the request of the Assistant Secretary and other top officials of the State Department. These studies are based primarily on the editorial comment in selected newspapers across the country.[33]

Although these special studies are no doubt helpful, they are the work of one man with little or no staff support. This stands in sharp contrast to what the Department was doing in this field some years ago. In 1947 the Public Opinion Studies Division with a staff of some 25 persons prepared comprehensive studies of public attitudes on American foreign policy by analyzing congressional statements, newspaper editorials and columns, organization statements, radio programs, and even public opinion polls. This staff prepared daily, weekly, and monthly opinion summaries as well as special reports on specific problem areas such as Europe, the Far East, and the United Nations.

Public Opinion Polls. When asked, many policy officers seem

31 Leila A. Sussmann, *Dear FDR: A Study of Political Letter-Writing* (Totawa, N.J.: The Bedminster Press, 1963), p. 73.
32 *Ibid.,* p. 175.
33 See H. Schuyler Foster, "Does Press Comment Represent Public Opinion?" Speech delivered at a session of the annual meeting of the American Association for Public Opinion Research on May 15, 1953.

to think that someone in the information area should also undertake more systematic studies of general public opinion (Question 25). Information officers in the Office of the Assistant Secretary for Public Affairs and the Office of Press Relations do not think this would be very helpful, however. Although information officers do not use opinion surveys, they shall be considered briefly here because they are generally conceded to be a more reliable index than any of those mentioned above for determining what the general public is thinking and because the Department has had contracts with private polling agencies in the past.

Public opinion polls are particularly valuable in correcting the erroneous impressions which Department officers get of public opinion on foreign affairs. There is a tendency for the officials working in the hypersensitive atmosphere of Washington to misjudge the real character of public opinion on foreign affairs. For example, there was a great deal of criticism of the United Nations during the Korean War, and these attacks were sufficiently numerous and serious to alarm officials.[34] Although other indexes of opinion did suggest some turning against the U.N.,[35] the polls continued to show strong public support for that organization.[36] "Even in February 1951, when approximately half of the people were dissatisfied with the way the U.N. was dealing with the Korean situation, an opinion survey by the National Opinion Research Center indicated that over three-fourths of the people believed the U.S. should continue to belong to the U.N."[37]

[34] Richard C. Snyder and Edgar S. Furniss, *American Foreign Policy: Formulation, Principles and Programs* (Princeton: Center of International Studies, 1954), p. 559. The authors suggest that policy officers were most concerned with public attitudes toward the U.N. in 1953, but this concern actually reached its peak somewhat earlier.

[35] H. Schuyler Foster, *Hearings* before the International Operations Subcommittee, *op. cit.*, pp. 162-163.

[36] See "Popular Opinion Trends Respecting the United Nations, 1945-51," Special Report on American Opinion, November 20, 1951, and "Gallup Poll Results Indicating American Attitudes on the U.N. (1951-1962)" in the files of the Public Opinion Studies Staff.

[37] *Ibid.*

Whatever value public opinion polls are to policy officers, they are an integral aspect of any public information program. After all, the Department is surely in a much better position to achieve public support if it has dependable information on the way its policies are being received by the public.[38] For instance, in the spring of 1947 the State Department used public opinion polls extensively in planning its information policy on the Truman Doctrine. Although a majority of the press and radio commentators favored President Truman's package of economic and military aid at an early stage, the polls taken by Gallup and by the National Opinion Research Center showed that

> the general public strongly supports financial and economic assistance to Greece and Turkey . . . but there is considerable reluctance to send military assistance either in the form of supplies or military advisers. The Gallup findings showed that a majority of nearly 5 to 3 opposed sending military advisers "to train the Greek army" and about the same was true in the case of Turkey . . . . According to the Denver poll, a two-to-one majority (of those with opinions) feel that sending military supplies will make war with Russia more likely.[39]

Realizing that a large portion of the public feared that military aid would cause tension, encourage fighting, or lead to war,[40] the Department considered it "advisable to play down military aid to Turkey and to present that aid, as could be done with truthfulness, in the context of Turkey's overall economic situation."[41]

In spite of the numerous ways in which public-opinion information can be utilized by the State Department, there has been a noticeable curtailment in the employment of public-

---

38 Angus Campbell, "The Uses of Interview Surveys in Federal Administration," *The Journal of Social Issues*, May 1946, p. 15.

39 "U.S. Public Opinion on President Truman's Proposals for Aid to Greece and Turkey (Developments between March 12 and March 27)," dated March 28, 1947 in the files of the Public Opinion Studies Staff.

40 Forty-five percent of the people polled by the National Opinion Research Center on April 21, 1947 felt that military aid to Greece would have this result.

41 See Joseph M. Jones, *op. cit.*, p. 162.

opinion analysis by Department officers. The first major cut in the Public Opinion Studies Staff occurred in 1953, and by 1957 the State Department had actually terminated all its contracts with private polling agencies—to the delight of some Congressmen.

A majority of information and policy officers feel that they become sufficiently well-informed about public reactions and understanding of their information policies simply as a by-product of their efforts to serve the press, maintain contact with nongovernmental organizations, and answer public correspondence. There is no conscious effort to evaluate public views on foreign affairs despite the varied sources of feedback available to the Department. Department officers depend almost entirely upon the public itself to draw public affairs problems to their attention; they make few independent studies of their own. Although the Department does little work in this field, information officers usually have a strong hand in the appraisal of information programs both because they have a more direct personal stake in their effectiveness and because they are in closer contact with the general public.

Information Policies on Spot News Items: An Illustration. The seven phases of the decision process are well illustrated by the spot news operation in the State Department. The *intelligence* function is largely performed by the Office of Press Relations where reporters exert pressure for the release of current information and press officers try to anticipate these demands. Each morning one of these press officers arrives at the Department early so that he can read the overnight cables and draft a list of questions with which he feels the Department must be prepared to deal that day. Once this list has been reviewed and perhaps amended by other press officers, specific assignments are made to the Public Affairs Advisers in the regional and functional bureaus concerned with each aspect of policy. These information officers in turn talk with the policy officers who have the required policy information.

Once they have been briefed by policy officers, these public affairs advisers are expected to take the initiative in drafting information policy guidelines for the press officer who will serve as the Department spokesman at the regular noon briefing. This *recommendation* must then be cleared with all of the policy officers who have a stake in the matter. Policy officers may accept, rewrite, or reject his proposals. Information officers may appeal these decisions to higher policy officials. When information officers achieve the *prescription* of the policy officers concerned, the Public Affairs Adviser in each area is ready to attend the Public Affairs Advisers Meeting at 11:00 each morning in the Office of Press Relations where information officers review the material prepared for the Department spokesman and decide how he should handle each item at the noon briefing, the *invocation*.

Following the noon briefing, the officers in the Office of Press Relations enter the *application* phase since they try to answer all subsequent press queries on the basis of the information policy prescriptions generated for the daily noon briefing. The *appraisal* of the Department's new information policies usually begins with the questions raised by reporters at the noon briefing. Later in the afternoon, the stories based on the briefing reach newspaper, television, and radio audiences. The information and policy officers concerned with each news item scrutinize these press stories and await repercussions, if any are expected, in order either to anticipate new demands for information or to order the *termination* of the present information policy.

RELATIONS BETWEEN INFORMATION AND POLICY OFFICER

Pattern of Discord and Collaboration

In many ways information and policy officers in the Department are bound together in a community of shared interests. They both owe their primary allegiance to the State Department, and they both have a stake in the success of the Department's policies and in the public image of the Department, recognizing as they do that the two are closely related. Their collaboration on information policy is thus fostered by the recognition that they share many of the same policy concerns. They also have much in common since they work in the same building and share the same rumors, discomforts, and pleasures.

Despite the many interests which information and policy officers have in common, there is evidence of a basic conflict of interests between them. Policy officers are primarily concerned with American policy overseas. Their attention is focused on the complex and fluid overseas environment in which American foreign policy must operate. Information officers are chiefly concerned with the effect which domestic criticism and suspicion may have on the operation of the Department. Their attention is focused on the need to speak and act in ways that will build public support for Department policies. When the needs of policy and the public seem to be in conflict, information and policy officers become embroiled in a competitive dialogue over the content of information policy.

In order to measure perceived antagonism among information and policy officers, each respondent was asked whether he would characterize the relations between information and policy officers as always cooperative, usually cooperative, compatible, usually antagonistic, or always antagonistic. The results appear in Table 6.1.

Table 6.1 Perceived Antagonism Among Information and Policy Officers

	AL-WAYS CO-OPER-ATIVE	USU-ALLY CO-OPER-ATIVE	MORE CO-OPER-ATIVE	BOTH CO-OPER-ATIVE AND ANTAG-ONISTIC	MORE ANTAG-ONISTIC	USUALLY ANTAG-ONISTIC	AL-WAYS ANTAG-ONISTIC	NO RE-SPONSE	N
Perceived antagonism among information officers toward policy officers	2	22	8	1	0	1	0	6	40
Perceived antagonism among policy officers toward information officers	2	27	3	2	1	1	0	4	40

The data in Table 6.1 show that most information and policy officers regard their relations as cooperative, although few regard

their relations with counter position holders as always cooperative. Information officers are apparently more conscious than
policy officers of the element of conflict in their relations. Despite the reluctance of information and policy officers to characterize their relations as antagonistic, the data also suggest that
some information and policy officials are more likely than others
to perceive antagonism in their relations. What accounts for
the incidence of perceived antagonism among these officials?

Correlates of Perceived Antagonism

Biographical Data. There are variations among information
and policy officers in age, amount of professional experience,
and amount of formal education; and these variables may be
related to perceived antagonism among them. If conflicts between Department officers are cumulative, age and professional
experience should be positively related to perceived antagonism
among them. If education has a moderating influence, it should
be negatively related to perceived antagonism.

The above assumptions suggest the following hypotheses:

1. Older individuals are more likely than their younger colleagues to perceive antagonism in their relation with counter
position holders.

2. Individuals with more professional experience are more
likely than their less experienced colleagues to perceive antagonism in their relations with counter position holders.

3. Individuals who have earned advanced academic degrees
are less likely than their colleagues to perceive antagonism in
their relation with counter position holders.

The results show that among higher level policy officers, older
policy officers are more likely than their younger colleagues to
perceive antagonism in their relation with information officers
although policy officers with more professional experience are
no more or less likely than their colleagues to perceive antagonism in their relation with information officers. Policy
officers with more formal education than their fellow officers are
no more or less likely than their colleagues to perceive antagonism in their relations with information officers. There is no

relationship between the age, professional experience, and formal education of information officers and perceived antagonism toward policy officers.

Data on Stereotyped Images. Information and policy officers have varying images of the personal qualities and performance characteristics of counter position holders. If information and policy officers are mutually dependent upon one another, officers who rate counter position holders lower on the qualities of (a) intelligent, (b) informed, (c) skillful, (d) responsible, and (e) helpful should be more likely than their colleagues to perceive antagonism in their relations with them.

The above assumption suggests the following hypothesis:

4. Individuals who rate counter position holders lower on the perceived characteristics of intelligent, informed, skillful, responsible, and helpful are more likely than their colleagues to perceive antagonism in their relations with them.

The results show that information officers who rate policy officers lower than their colleagues on the quality of skillful are more likely than their colleagues to perceive antagonism in their relations with policy officers. There is no relationship between the ratings of information and policy officers for each other on any of the other qualities and perceived antagonism for one another.

Positional Data. These officers occupy positions in the State Department which levy varying requirements on them. If the conflict between information and policy officers arises out of the different functions which these position holders play in the opinion-policy process, individuals who occupy positions which are more sensitive to these pressures should be more likely than individuals in other positions to perceive antagonism in their relations with counter position holders.

The above assumption suggests the following hypotheses:

5. Officers who hold political appointments are more likely than their colleagues to perceive antagonism in their relations with counter position holders.

6. Officers who hold positions of County Director, Office Di-

rector, Public Affairs Adviser and higher-level positions are more likely than their lower-level colleagues to perceive antagonism in their relations with counter position holders.

7. Foreign Service Officers in information and policy positions are more likely than officers in other career services to perceive antagonism in their relations with counter position holders.

8. Officers in frequent daily contact with counter position holders are more likely than their colleagues to perceive antagonism in their relations with them.

9. Information officers in the Bureau of Public Affairs are more likely than information specialists in other areas to perceive antagonism in their relations with policy officers.

10. Policy officers in regional bureaus are more likely than those in functional bureaus to perceive antagonism in their relations with information officers.

11. Policy officers who serve in bureaus which have more information officers are more likely than their colleagues to perceive antagonism in their relations with information officers.

The results indicate that although the relationship is not statistically significant, four of five policy officers with political appointments perceive some antagonism in their relations with information officers. Policy officers holding higher-level positions in the Department are more likely than their colleagues to perceive antagonism in their relations with information officers. There is no relationship among policy officers between type of career service, frequency of contact, type of policy specialty, or number of information officers in the bureau and perceived antagonism for information officers. Moreover, there is no relationship among information officers between any of the above variables and perceived antagonism for policy officers.

Data on Role Expectations. These officers also hold varying role expectations. If the more discretionary and political role expectations of information and policy officers diverge, factors reflecting these expectations should be associated with perceived antagonism among them. Moreover, if the conflict between information and policy officers is exacerbated by varying perceptions of the informational requirements of democracy and foreign policy, factors reflecting these attitudes should also be correlated with perceived antagonism among them.

The above assumptions suggest the following hypotheses:

12. Officers who accept the more discretionary and political segments of their own role are more likely than their colleagues to perceive antagonism in their relations with counter position holders.

13. Officers who reject the more discretionary and political role segments of counter position holders are more likely than those who accept these role segments to perceive antagonism in their relations with counter position holders.

14. Policy officers who stress the informational requirements of foreign policy (Factor II) and play down the informational requirements of democracy (Factor VI) are more likely than their colleagues to perceive antagonism in their relations with information officers.[42]

15. Information officers who play down the informational requirements of foreign policy (Factor II) and stress the informational requirements of democracy (Factor VI) are more likely than their colleagues to perceive antagonism in their relation with policy officers.[43]

The results suggest that officers who accept the more discretionary and political segments of their own role and reject the more discretionary and political roles of counter position holders are no more or less likely than their colleagues to perceive antagonism in their relation with counter position holders. Policy officers who are more likely than their colleagues to accept informational requirements of foreign policy are more likely than their colleagues to perceive antagonism in their relations with information officers; but information officers who reject the informational requirements of foreign policy are no more or less likely than their colleagues to perceive antagonism in their relations with policy officers. Information officers who are more likely than colleagues to stress the informational re-

[42] James L. McCamy, *Government Publicity* (Chicago: The University of Chicago Press, 1939), pp. 175-183.
[43] *Ibid.*

quirements of democracy are *more,* not less, likely to perceive antagonism for policy officers; however, there is no relation between policy officer attitudes toward the informational requirements of democracy and perceived antagonism for information officers.

Opinion Versus Policy-Making Needs?

The above findings indicate that perceived antagonism among information and policy officers is not cumulative. These findings also show that education does not moderate perceived antagonism among these two groups. Although the stereotyped images of information and policy officers are not consistently related to perceived antagonism, the data suggest that information officers are more dependent upon policy officers than *vice versa.* The data further indicate that information and policy officers play conflicting roles in the opinion-policy process. This conflict apparently stems from different evaluations of the requirements of information policy and not from the acceptance or rejection of certain role expectations. Moreover, the data show that these differences are felt more intensely by higher level officials in the Department where the most difficult problems of information policy must be resolved.

Perceived Antagonism Among Policy Officers for Information Officers. Virtually all of the Assistant Secretaries in the regional bureaus perceive antagonism in their relations with information officers. These officers are older and less well-educated than their colleagues. As political appointees, they also deal with information officers more frequently than their colleagues. Several officers at the level of Assistant Secretary claim that their public affairs adviser is in their office more frequently than any other officer.

Assistant Secretaries in the regional and even functional bureaus play a critical role in the formation of information policies. They not only have to settle the differences among their own subordinates on information policy; they are also expected to resolve most of the inter-bureau conflicts on information policy. After all, this is the last level at which questions of information policy can be resolved before they go to the Secretary or the Under Secretary. As political appointees, they have more discretionary and political expectations than information officers; as the principal decision-maker in their respective policy areas, they are very conscious of the needs of their own subordinates in the policy-making machine.

These officials are more likely than lower-level officers to view their relations with information officers in the context of conflicting policy and opinion needs. As one Assistant Secretary of State put it, "If an information officer is worth his salt, he is constantly pressing policy officers to release information because he is more sensitive than they are to information requirements. Most policy officers are bureaucrats who would prefer not to be bothered. The relations between information and policy officers will normally be competitive then since he is usually pressing to release more information than the policy officers want to release." To underscore this point, another Assistant Secretary jotted down a reminder to put a good recommendation in the file of an information officer who used to argue with him about every issue. The Assistant Secretary felt that the man would be very surprised that he thought well of him!

Cohen questions the extent to which information officers battle with desk officers on behalf of the freest possible exposure of information.[44] The data in this study suggest that while individual country officers are not fully conscious of pressure for the full disclosure of information by these officials, the Assistant Secretaries of the regional bureaus are very much aware of this pressure. Moreover, policy officers, regardless of level, who are more concerned with the informational requirements of foreign policy are more likely than their colleagues to perceive antagonism in their relations with information officers.

Perceived Antagonism Among Information Officers for Policy Officers. Somewhat paradoxically, information officers holding political appointments, information officers holding higher-level positions, and information officers who have more frequent contacts with policy officers are no more or less likely than their

[44] Bernard C. Cohen, *The Press and Foreign Policy* (Princeton, N.J.: Princeton University Press, 1963), p. 157.

colleagues to perceive antagonism in their relations with policy officers.

Why do the information officers who deal frequently with policy officers under conditions which policy officers deem competitive not perceive more antagonism in their relations with these officials? There is a strong possibility that they do, but they are reluctant to admit it because their effectiveness in the Department is so dependent on their acceptance by these officials.[45] If an information officer cannot obtain the confidence of the ranking officials in the Department, he cannot perform his function. Consequently, all of the top information officers insist that their relations with policy officers are cooperative.

However, the data show another source of perceived antagonism among information officers for policy officers. This is the feeling of many information officers, particularly those who deal with the slower media of communication, that their efforts are not appreciated within the Department. As one such officer put it, "This is no-man's land. I don't think people in the State Department really know we are here." This may help to explain why perceived antagonism among information officers for policy officers is positively associated with the feeling that policy officers lack skill. In this regard it is interesting to note that although information officers who are Foreign Service Officers claim that their relations with policy officers are cooperative, they are more likely than their colleagues to rate policy officers lower on the quality of skillful.

Whereas the data suggest that policy officers perceive antagonism in their relations with information officers because the latter often try to get the former to release more information than they would prefer to release, there is little direct evidence that information officers perceive antagonism in their relations with policy officers because the former are more likely than the

45 The principal problem which information officers confront within their own organization is the acceptance of the publicity function. See McCamy, *op. cit.*, pp. 209-210. Also see Nimmo, *op. cit.*, p. 63 and J. A. R. Pimlott, *Public Relations and American Democracy* (Princeton, N.J.: Princeton University Press, 1951), pp. 54-55.

latter to see the need for public information. Indeed, it is those information officers who are more hesitant than their colleagues in the acceptance of the informational requirements of the public, who are more likely than their colleagues to perceive antagonism in their relations with policy officers.

Chapter 7

The State Department
and the Press

THIS CHAPTER DEALS with elements of cooperation and antagonism between State Department officials and foreign affairs
reporters. The chapter may be envisaged in two parts. The first
part contains a general analysis of State Department-press relations based on the literature on the press and foreign policy as
well as interviews with Department officers and reporters. The
second part consists of an empirical study of the correlates of
antagonism among the officers and reporters interviewed in this
study. Although the main body of the chapter deals exclusively
with officer-reporter relations in Washington, a brief addendum
at the end of the chapter concerns the relations between American officials and reporters overseas.

COMMUNITY OF INTEREST

Historically, the State Department has relied primarily upon
private channels of communication to keep the public informed
on foreign affairs and to keep itself informed on public affairs.
Indeed, prior to World War II the press was practically the
only channel of communication between the State Department
and the public and, accordingly, most of the machinery set up
within the Department for public affairs was geared to service

179

this medium. Any study of the public relations of the State Department must be based on a thorough understanding of the relationship between the State Department and the privately-owned, mass media of communication: newspapers, magazines, radio, and television.

State Department Interests Served by the Press

The dependence of the State Department upon the press to disseminate foreign-policy information to the public and to obtain information on public affairs is largely explained by the fact that the privately-owned, mass media of communication share with the Department of State a community of interest in seeing that the American people are informed on foreign affairs and that the State Department is informed on public opinion.[1] Virtually all of the reporters in this study understand their main responsibility to be one of presenting the facts behind American foreign policy to the general public. Many of these reporters also feel that they represent the public interest in questioning Department officials.

These reporters provide the State Department with a powerful means of disseminating foreign policy information to the general public. It is estimated, for example, that four out of every five adults have access to one or more of the 1,750 daily newspapers in America,[2] and that the three popular news magazines, i.e., *Time, Newsweek,* and *U.S. News and World Report* alone reach as many as 10 percent of the adult population of the country.[3] Radio and television together also reach the vast majority of American adults including those who are least apt to pay much attention to foreign affairs in the printed media.[4] Whether the printed and electronic media are considered sep-

---

[1] Joseph W. Alsop, Jr., "Reporting Politics," in *The Press in Perspective,* ed. by Ralph D. Casey (Baton Rouge: Louisiana State University Press, 1963), p. 174.

[2] V. O. Key, *Public Opinion and American Democracy* (New York: Alfred A. Knopf, 1960), p. 375.

[3] Alfred O. Hero, *Mass Media and World Affairs,* Studies in Citizen Participation in International Relations, Volume IV, World Peace Foundation, 1959, p. 64.

[4] *Ibid.,* pp. 107-109.

arately or together, they constitute the most important channels of communication available to the State Department. As one high-ranking information officer put it, "The press is our principal means of getting information out of the building."

Except for the information specialists who serve other channels in the Offices of Public and Media Services, information officers feel that their main task is to serve the press, and these officers have frequent daily contacts with reporters. For the policy officer, however, public affairs is only one, and seldom the most important, demand upon his time. Some lower-echelon officers have no more than 2 or 3 contacts a year with the press, including telephone calls; some higher-ranking officials normally spend several hours weekly with the press. Generally speaking, higher level officials also perceive a greater stake than their lower level colleagues in dealing with the press because they are so closely identified with Administration policy.

The Department of State also relies upon the press for information. As Cohen correctly notes, information in official channels is quite specialized.[5] Formal government channels are used chiefly to communicate information on problems upon which the Department is working. Frequently, the need for verification and special handling means that the nongovernment sources will provide the first news of an impending crisis. For these reasons, Department officials keep a close watch on foreign news on the tickers of the wire services, including UPI, AP, Reuters, and Agence France Presse. As one desk officer comments, the press "often gives news, in advance of our Embassy, of crisis or other newsworthy items in the foreign press." While most officers obtain this information from the media, reporters also offer this kind of information in their personal encounters with officers.

Of course, the value of the press as a source of information for officials lies primarily outside their narrow field of specialty. The official information is usually restricted to those who have a need to know. Thus, Department officers depend on the informal channels of information in the Department and the

---

[5] Bernard C. Cohen, *The Press and Foreign Policy* (Princeton: Princeton University Press, 1963), p. 209.

press to provide them with information about developments in other policy areas. Sometimes reporters also help to bridge the communications barrier between higher- and lower-level officials in the Department. As one prominent foreign affairs reporter expounds, "You carry ideas from the middle and lower levels to people at the top."

Moreover, the press is very important in providing Department officers with information about public opinion on foreign affairs. At least, the press provides the officer with information about the image of foreign events that is being portrayed to the public. Officials usually perceive the press also as the source of public reaction to these events. Department officers thus claim that they are informed about public opinion because they read a mountain of newspapers. Although many reporters deny that they represent public views, some feel that they represent the public interest simply in the way they question officials.

Press Interest Served by the Department

Just as the Department relies heavily upon the press to inform the public and to keep itself informed, the press depends upon the Department to provide it with information and interpretation of United States foreign policy. In the first place, no private media can hope to maintain its own representatives in all of the areas of the world which may vitally affect American interests, and news organizations must rely upon diplomatic sources of information. In the second place, the State Department is often the best source for the confirmation or denial of reports or rumors which private channels receive from abroad concerning American foreign policy and actions. In the third place, the Department regularly makes news by holding press conferences, conducting investigations, announcing policy decisions, and so on, which must be covered by the private media.

Indeed, 25 of the reporters in this study rely chiefly on the State Department for foreign affairs information. Since most foreign offices in the world require reporters to work exclusively through a press office, the most significant fact in the reporters' relations with the State Department is access to both information and policy officers. An experienced foreign correspondent who has served as a British press officer remarks, "It is a pleasure here to find that I can see policy people directly." Many reporters develop close personal relations with policy officers. The regular, full-time reporters have frequent, often daily, personal contacts with policy officers. Frequent contacts may produce unexpected stories for reporters. They also provide protection for a reporter's informants in the event of an investigation and help to insure that the reporter will not be just one of several hundred strange faces when he descends on a policy officer during a crisis.

Reporters utilize different sources for different purposes. When newsmen are concerned with long-range coverage, they depend upon sources who deal with fundamental policy, e.g., the Secretary, the Under-Secretary, and Presidential Advisers, because only these officials have a sense of direction beyond what has been verbalized. When reporters want facts and opinions about current policy developments, they frequently seek out the middle and lower echelon sources who have more specific information and are less tied to official policy. When reporters want fresh ideas and interpretations, they utilize sources, regardless of level, who can engage in a frank exchange of views with reporters. A few reporters speculate that the best source of new ideas in the Department are either off-beat areas, such as intelligence or legal affairs, or schedule "C" types who participate in decisions but are not so closely tied to the Department. The regular, full-time foreign affairs reporters develop sources at all levels in the Department; other reporters are usually restricted to lower level sources.

Most reporters also rely upon information officers. Access to these officers is important to newsmen for a number of reasons. First, information officers are the basic contact point for newsmen in the Department; when policy officers become inaccessible to them, reporters depend entirely upon information officers to fulfill their needs. Even during more tranquil periods information officers serve as formal channels through which to express requests and complaints. Second, information specialists provide reporters with official statements of American policy daily through the mechanism of the noon briefing. Third, information officers are a great convenience to the reporter who is interested in a routine story or wants to check out parts of his story with someone in the Department in the evenings or on weekends. Fourth, a surprising number of newsmen rely upon at least one information officer in the Department for ideas and interpretations on broad foreign policy issues.

It is the regular, full-time reporters—those representing the wire services, the radio and television networks, the news magazines, and some newspaper bureaus—who deal frequently, in a few cases hourly, with information officers in the Department. Reporters for other newspaper bureaus, newspaper chains, and news services see information specialists less frequently, perhaps weekly; syndicated columnists and reporters for the trade and ethnic press seldom deal with information officers in the Department. As might be expected, reporters with a neutral role orientation are more likely to see information officers than their more politically-minded colleagues. Some of the reporters who seldom or only occasionally deal with information officers actually rely more heavily upon them since these reporters have fewer contacts with policy officers in the Department than the regulars.

The dependence of the press upon the State Department has increased in recent years due to changes in the field of mass communications. On the one hand, although the daily newspapers still dominate the organization for the collection of foreign policy information, the five-minute newscast on the radio every hour, and longer, but less frequent, newscasts on television have largely taken over the spot news function from newspapers. On the other hand, the printed media, and particularly national newspapers and the weekly news magazines, have turned to the analysis and interpretation of foreign affairs in order to market their products. Both developments have made these news organizations more dependent upon the information services of the State Department than ever before.

Reporters who work for national newspapers, weekly news-magazines, news services, and some newspaper chains, as well as syndicated columnists, are increasingly dependent on policy makers in order to be in a position to engage in interpretive reporting. At the same time, radio and television require much more in the way of facilities from the State Department than newspapers or magazines ever require in presenting the spot news. It is much more difficult to provide radio and television the same kind of assistance that the Department can provide newspapermen simply by releasing written statements or holding informal briefings. The electronic media require special sound and visual equipment in order to realize their potential as news media.

Other Mutual Interests

Cooperation among individual officers and reporters on these essential interests is strengthened by other factors. First, officials and reporters who agree on policy are probably more likely to play complementary roles in the opinion-policy process. Although no attempt was made in this study to investigate the policy attitudes of officers and reporters, previous studies suggest that (at least prior to the Vietnam War) reporters have generally accepted the basic premises of American foreign policy.

Second, officers and reporters operate in the same milieu in Washington and share many of the same experiences. Indeed, information officers are often recruited from the ranks of reporters. The interaction between Department officers and reporters sometimes extends into the social sphere, and personal friendships naturally increase their willingness to be responsive to each other's needs.

Third, officers and reporters are often engaged in the performance of similar tasks. Information officers, policy officers, and reporters are similarly engaged in the attempt to understand current developments in foreign affairs and to anticipate future developments. As one desk officer confesses, "I'm doing the same kind of analysis as the newsmen—we can talk their language."

CONFLICT OF INTERESTS

Despite the mutual dependence of the State Department and the press, they often serve different interests in the communications process. After all, "there are moments when the interests of a government serving the people and a press informing the people do not directly coincide."[6] The reporters' job is to obtain the most current and accurate information on foreign affairs and to disclose it to the public. His approach to international news often reflects the exigencies of the newspaper or broadcasting industry. The official's job is to conduct the nation's foreign relations. His concern for policy often causes him to withhold information until it is ready for public scrutiny.

The Department uses the devices of public information to serve the primary function of conducting foreign policy. If the full disclosure of information contributes to the actions undertaken to carry out a policy, then the Department releases information. If complete secrecy best serves the actions undertaken to carry out a policy, then the Department withholds information until it is practical to release it. Since the Department is responsible for the actual conduct of foreign relations, it cannot divorce information policy from the actions undertaken to carry out policy. Since the press is not responsible for foreign relations, it can divorce information and policy.

The discretion which Department officers must exercise when dealing with information on foreign affairs is sometimes overlooked by the public and the press. For example, there was some question in the fall of 1962 as to why the State Department was so hesitant to acknowledge the probable missile build-up in Cuba. Many citizens received the erroneous impression that former Senator Keating of New York, who was one of the first public figures to call attention to the build-up, had better access to information about Cuba than the government. The problem from the Government's standpoint, however, was not a scarcity of information; on the contrary, the problem was the volume of intelligence which had to be checked and verified. The distinction between Senator Keating and the Department in this instance was not a matter of access but rather a matter of responsibility. Unlike the Senator, the State Department could not call attention to the possibility of offensive

<hr/>

6 Robert J. Manning, "Government Information Plans and Policies," Part 1, *Hearings* before the House Subcommittee on Government Information, 88th Congress, 1st Session, March 25, 1963, p. 85.

missiles in Cuba until it was prepared to take action, and it could not take action until the probability that there was a missile buildup in Cuba became a certainty.

Department officers must also distinguish the public's need for information from the demands of the private channels of communication. The exigencies of news organizations are often quite unrelated to the public need to know. The press often brings pressure upon the State Department for the release of information before Department officers have an opportunity to study and evaluate it. As a result, information emerges from the Department in bits and fragments since the press itself is not always in a position to correlate this information with relevant information that has gone before. In many such instances the public would be better served if there were "interludes of privacy" in which the Department could give some order and coherence to current information on foreign affairs.[7] In this sense, it might be argued that reporters often want the news before it is news.

On the other hand, "it is the responsibility of the reporter to get at the news while it is still news,"[8] and it is unrealistic to expect or to want the press to bide its time until the foreign-policy makers feel free to disclose all of the information desired by the public. Indeed, private news organizations would abdicate their legitimate function of keeping the public currently informed if they always waited until the Department was ready to release information of its own volition. If the press did not exert pressure upon the Department for information, the public would seldom be informed in time to participate in any meaningful sense in foreign policy decisions.

Moreover, there is a basic conflict of interests over the content of foreign affairs stories in most of the private news media. In the first place, the Department wants the press to convey to the public a balanced picture of the factors underlying its policy so that it will receive public support; news organizations often want headlines which suggest sensational and usually

7 *Ibid.,* p. 99.
8 Douglas Cater, "Government by Publicity," *The Reporter,* March 19, 1959, p. 16.

negative stories because there is a great deal of competition within the communications industry for the sale of this kind of news. What the press finds newsworthy is only occasionally what the Department feels is important. Thus, Department officers accuse reporters of trying to make events sound more newsworthy than they really are. Reporters concede this point when they argue that a good newsman is one who can make policy seem interesting and newsworthy without getting things out of proportion. Some reporters claim that this is a major point of contention between them and their editors or producers. As one television reporter complains, "I refused to give them the headlines, so they didn't carry the story." A number of Department officers accept the idea that competition among reporters and news organizations create these distortions. "If Marvin Kalb gets too balanced," one information officer explains, "he won't make the Cronkite show."

In the second place, Department officers want comprehensive coverage of foreign affairs in the private channels of communication; since reporters cannot hope to become experts in the numerous fields of foreign relations which they cover, however, they are essentially superficial. Moreover, most media of communication are a vehicle for entertainment, and they carry only a fraction of the material available on foreign affairs. The number of audience manhours devoted to international news on radio and television is only a small proportion of the total.[9] A few of the large newspaper bureaus carry some Department statements in full, but it is difficult to get smaller newspaper bureaus to carry a full explanation of policy. As one policy officer complains, "If the President makes a speech, we're lucky if three paragraphs get in the newspapers." As Cohen indicates, the coverage of foreign affairs in the press is discontinuous, spotty, and limited to a few topics of general interest.[10]

Moreover, information on foreign affairs in the private media often suffers because of the premium placed on speed in disseminating news. Reporters are sometimes obliged to write whether they have complete evidence or not, and they must go

9 Hero, *op. cit.*, pp. 111-113.
10 Cohen, *op. cit.*, pp. 97-103.

as far as they believe they are justified in going from the information at their disposal. Of course, there is a temptation in both government and journalism to wait for more of the facts before

> committing the front page to a headline or a national government to a deed. But, for journalism the temptation is arbitrarily removed by the arrival of the deadline. For government the temptation to wait is not so clearly or so easily erased.[11]

The Department must often withhold information until its impact on current international affairs can be fully assessed or until explanatory material can be prepared to accompany its release.

Since the Department and the press must often cooperate in order to pursue somewhat different interests, the relationship between them may sometimes be interpreted as one of mutual advantage.[12] Indeed, there are numerous techniques by which officials and reporters can take advantage of each other ranging from the most overt and deliberate methods to equally deliberate but more subtle means. When officials take advantage of their superior sources of information, specialized knowledge, and position to mislead reporters, they are accused of managing the news. When reporters take advantage of the sheer size of the government, the vanity of officials, and outside sources to develop exclusive stories, they are accused of manufacturing news.

Managing the News

The State Department manages the news when the information it releases to the public distorts the facts underlying its foreign policy and actions. Since there is more information generated by the State Department each day than any newspaper would find fit to print, Department officers stress—by

11 Robert J. Manning, "Foreign Policy: Building Amid Turbulence," *The Department of State Bulletin*, Vol. XLIX, No. 1265, September 23, 1963, p. 454.

12 Francis E. Rourke, *Secrecy and Publicity: Dilemmas of Democracy* (Baltimore: The Johns Hopkins Press, 1961), p. 201.

selection, emphasis, and repetition—those aspects of international affairs which they consider most important and which the press in their experience has found newsworthy. Conversely, they tend to omit those items of information which are less important or newsworthy.[13] When this natural process of selection or elimination reaches the point where the Department consciously or unconsciously releases *only* that information which tends to support its interpretation of foreign affairs and withholds all information which tends to refute that interpretation, the Department is obviously managing the news. This conscious or unconscious distortion of the news was apparent in 1963 when Department officials stressed the success of the strategic hamlet program in South Vietnam and minimized press reports concerning the daily setbacks suffered by Vietnamese forces in skirmishes with the Viet Cong. However, as one of the experienced reporters stationed at the State Department speculates, "Reports from Washington may not have been so glowing if reports from South Vietnam had not been so critical."

This temptation to manage the news as part of U.S. foreign policy is particularly strong during periods of national crisis. For example, Arthur Sylvester, who was Assistant Secretary of Defense for Public Affairs during the Cuban crisis of 1962, was widely reported to believe that "The government had an inherent right, if necessary, to lie to save itself when it's going up into a nuclear war."[14] In fact, the Executive Committee of the National Security Council did clamp such tight security on information about developments in Cuba within the administration from October 15 to 22, 1962 that at least one official spokesman did unknowingly misinform the press.

The manipulation of information was not the only way in which the Government managed the news during the Cuban crisis; it also manipulated the access of reporters to news sources. As Max Frankel indicates, "the President, the Secretaries of Defense and State, and other officials" were readily available to the news media at the height of the Cuban crisis since "they wanted

13 Cohen, *op. cit.*, Chapter VI.
14 See *Hearings* before the House Subcommittee on Government Information, *op. cit.*, pp. 146-147, 149-151, and 168-169.

to shape and color the news and were eager for public support at home and abroad." But shortly after the crisis, Mr. Frankel reports that hardly any of these officials were available for comment.[15]

Foreign affairs reporters became concerned about access to officials shortly after the Cuban crisis when the Assistant Secretary for Public Affairs asked these officials to report to the Bureau of Public Affairs: "the name of the correspondent, his organization, the general subject discussed, and the date of the interview."[16] The reporters interviewed in this study state that Department officials were very reluctant to discuss the Caribbean situation during this period, but that the Department directive did not inhibit the normal contacts between policy officials and the press. Indeed, one reporter considers the directive a personal victory for the Assistant Secretary since his policy was much milder than the policies of other departments, especially the Department of Defense.

Of course, the Department can also take advantage of the press by controlling the circumstances under which information is released to the public. Daily contact with the representatives of the press gives government information officers an acute sense of the process by which information becomes news. By manipulating the conditions under which information is released, these officers can sometimes manage the press. Information officers assume more discretionary and political roles with respect to reporters when they interpret the facts for the public and exercise discretion in timing the release of information to the public.

The danger that the government might sell its policies to the public through the communications media is heightened by the competition among news organizations and individual reporters for facts and especially interpretations of foreign affairs. This

15 Max Frankel, "Kennedy vs. The Press," *The New York Times,* November 19, 1962, p. 12.
16 See *The New York Times,* November 17, 1962, p. 3. See also the memorandum by Robert J. Manning on "Procedures Relating to Contacts with Mass Media Representatives," dated November 27, 1962, when this directive was revoked.

hunger for news makes the press especially susceptible to one of the more subtle techniques of news management, the background briefing.

Originally, the term "background" referred to material which was not newsworthy itself but which helped to place the news in perspective. More recently, however, the term background has been applied generally to information which is not formally released to the public by the Department or its spokesmen. Newsmen receive access to this kind of information only if they agree (1) not to attribute it to a specific source, (2) to accept full responsibility for it themselves, or (3) not to disclose it to the public at all.[17] Properly speaking, "background" information should be distinguished from "nonattributable" information on the one hand and "off-the-record" information on the other hand. "Nonattributable" information appears in the press under the guise of anonymous sources, e.g., "U.S. official," "a high administrative source," and "an informed official." Reporters incorporate "background" information into their stories as though it were the product of their own originial research. "Off-the-record" information is occasionally offered to responsible reporters either to persuade a disbelieving reporter to accept the Department line or to dissuade a reporter from publishing a story which the Department feels is contrary to the national interest; it is not to be printed under any circumstance or in any form.

Department officers justify the use of these methods of avoiding formal responsibility for statements which are either too sensitive or too conjectural to place officially on the record on the grounds that official pronouncements automatically become something of a state document. These techniques also enable Department officers to serve a number of domestic purposes, however. Information released by an unidentified spokesman, for example, may take the form of a trial balloon in which the Department attempts to assess public reaction to matters pend-

---

17 See Department of State, "Definitions—Ground Rules for Discussion with the Press, Interviews, Press Conferences, and Press Briefings," in Part 4, *Hearings* before the House Subcommittee on Government Information, *op. cit.*, p. 406.

ing in the Administration. Or, it may be used to promote a program before it is formally presented to the Congress.[18] On the other hand, it may serve petty bureaucratic purposes such as the report that Adlai Stevenson wanted another Munich at the time of the Cuban crisis in 1962.[19]

Reporters, who have become increasingly dependent on "background" information now that their news organizations are placing more emphasis than ever before on the analysis and interpretation of foreign affairs, usually accept this kind of information when they are faced with the choice of either receiving information on this basis or not getting it at all. Indeed, when reporters themselves initiate the request for background information, they believe the system operates to everyone's advantage. Reporters realize that Department officers will talk more candidly on background and that officials can keep reporters from going too far astray in their speculations about the meaning and significance of current foreign policies and events. The main difficulty is that the public cannot judge for itself the importance of background material because they do not know the real source.[20]

While it may be conceded that a certain amount of information on foreign affairs must be reported in this way if it is going to be reported at all, the practice of carrying background information in the press provides the government with a unique opportunity to color the ups and downs of foreign affairs. For example, Max Frankel reports that during the Cuban crisis in 1962:

> spokesmen and press officers were instructed from time to time to reflect hope or optimism or firmness about negotiations, without allowing themselves to be quoted but were given few facts to issue and often conveyed judgments without knowing the facts on which they were based.[21]

[18] Douglas Cater, "Government by Publicity," *The Reporter*, April 2, 1959, p. 29.
[19] See Steward Alsop and Charles Bartlett, "In Time of Crisis," *The Saturday Evening Post*, Vol. 235, December 8, 1962, pp. 15-16.
[20] Samuel J. Archibald, "Rules for the Game of Ghost," *Columbia Journalism Review*, Winter 1968, Vol. VI, p. 20.
[21] Frankel, *loc. cit.*

Under these conditions, the public must rely entirely upon the reporter to check and verify this information, and the reporter and his editor or producer must assume full responsibility for the contents of the story. One diplomatic reporter complains that this is an attempt by Department officials to make newsmen take responsibility for what newsmen do not want to say.

Manufacturing News

Reporters manufacture news in the eyes of Department officials when the play up the more sensational aspects of foreign affairs. In many instances the exclusive stories of reporters are based on leaks of information within the Department and the government. A leak suggests something that should not happen, but leaks often occur precisely because some official feels that it is in the national interest for the public to have certain information. For example, one reporter indicated that people in State and Defense Departments were very concerned in 1960 that valuable information was being lost about the redeployment of Soviet missiles after President Eisenhower pledged that the United States would not resume U-2 flights over Russia. These people singled out this reporter and provided him with pictures which demonstrated what the U-2's could do in order to create public support for a continuation of the flights.

Leaks are bound to occur whenever there are hundreds of journalists talking to hundreds of officials. To the extent that these leaks are a function of the size of an organization, they are a natural consequence of bureaucracy. Of course, some reporters exploit this consequence more than others. For example, one policy official with previous experience in a high information post notes that "when Reston and Krock of the *New York Times* see a story coming, they really go after it." If a reporter is on to a story, he calls as many officials as possible in order both to harden his story and to cover his tracks.

There are a number of methods whereby reporters attempt to develop these stories. First, they can play one official off against another. As one foreign affairs reporter explains, "If you pick up something on background, it may be that you can take that information elsewhere and strike a bargain. 'I have this, I'm going to print it.' " "The problem you have," explains a country officer, "is their showing you an erroneous story. Then, you must decide whether to let it go or correct it." Once a reporter has developed his story, he has to decide what are the strongest terms he can use. He avoids details except where he is absolutely certain of his facts. His story starts other reporters working.

Second, reporters are always looking for those who are dissatisfied with policy. One experienced reporter indicates that the more sensational leaks come from those who disagree with policy. Another reporter explains that sometimes there is a war among bureaus and among desks in bureaus. "If somebody's ox is being gored," relates still another reporter, "they are usually anxious to talk about it." This mode of operation usually angers top officials. As one Assistant Secretary complains, "————————— seldom deals with me personally; he spends most of his time in the back corridors of the Department."

Third, reporters sometimes are able to play on the vanity of the leaker. As one experienced reporter expounds, "I am impressive. I reach him when he is tired. I have a tip. I give him a hard fact. If he is honest, he won't lie. He can say two things —confirm or no comment. An official does not like to lie; we trap him. He knows he will give you an answer in the end; he knows he will go to bed with you, but you must court him. It is very important how you approach these people. If you go to ————————— with a clumsy question, you will be dismissed. If he thinks you are a worthy partner, . . ."

Although the State Department is not impregnable as a source, there are several factors which limit the accessibility of news sources within the Department to reporters. First, the substance of foreign policy and the Department policy-making machinery have become so complicated that it is difficult— even for the most experienced reporters—to find the man who has the information they need for a particular story. This problem is compounded by the rapid turnover of personnel in the Department. Second, there is no compelling reason for most policy officers, especially lower echelon officers, to talk to reporters, and it may sometimes be dangerous for them to do so. Third, the pressure of official business plus the sheer number of reporters covering the Department conspire to limit the accessibility of the few officials whom reporters covering the big story of the moment are most anxious to see. This is especially characteristic of Department-press relations during periods of crisis. As James Reston expounded before the Moss Subcommittee in 1963, "In 20 years my experience has been that the officials who were informed at the moment of crisis were not available, and the officials who were available at the moment of crisis were not informed."[22]

Many reporters who cover the Department find it necessary to develop personal sources of information in the White House and in other departments and agencies of the government. Moreover, many of the regular, full-time foreign affairs reporters rely heavily on Congress for information. One such reporter states that Congress is a good source for undeveloped leaks—ideas that something may be developing in this or that direction. Reporters take the leads obtained on the Hill and develop them in the executive agencies.

Virtually all reporters rely upon some nongovernmental sources of information on foreign affairs as well. The most obvious such source for reporters is other reporters and other news organizations. While it is unlikely that any really good information is traded informally between reporters of different news organizations or even between reporters of the same news organization, there is friendly cooperation on inconsequentials. This inbreeding of information may become quite important when reporters' sources dry up and they are left to talk to each other.

Moreover, the two major wire services and some of the larger newspapers and broadcasting networks each employ a number of experienced overseas correspondents to collect information from international sources, and many of these correspondents have developed considerable expertise in foreign affairs. With the aid of rapid communications, these news agencies can often provide excellent leads to reporters covering the State Department in Washington.

Some reporters also consult various nongovernmental organizations with independent access to information about foreign

[22] James Reston, Part 1, *Hearings* before the House Subcommittee on Government Information, *op. cit.*, p. 56.

affairs. Many of the younger reporters are recent graduates of universities in the Northeast and they have contacts with functional and area specialists in these institutions. Such sources are particularly valuable to reporters when government sources dry up in a developing or crisis situation, and they need some expert guidance in order to speculate meaningfully about foreign events.

Finally, many full-time foreign affairs reporters also cover the foreign embassies in Washington as part of their beat. Reporters often rely upon embassy officials to present contrary views. Since the diplomatic representatives of these countries are sometimes anxious to comment on developments which the United States government prefers to keep quiet, embassy row is an excellent source of ideas and leads which reporters can subsequently follow-up in the Department and the government.

Indeed, the Department of State has frequently been compelled to release material which it has been temporarily withholding from the public because the press has received part of the information from outside sources. This pressure to release information prematurely is especially strong within the State Department when the information being printed by the mass media is inaccurate or misleading. Moreover, the incessant demand for official confirmations or denials of such reports may lead the government itself astray. As Professor Rourke indicates:

> the fact that government officials initially issued false state-
> ments on the [U-2] affair may be traced in part to the con-
> sideration that they were under strong pressure from the
> media of communication for a speedy official explanation of
> what had occurred.[23]

There are relatively few occasions when the government can successfully control the dissemination of foreign policy information in this country. As Arthur Sylvester, Assistant Secretary of Defense for Public Affairs, told the Moss Subcommittee, "The opportunity for controlling is very small and the opportunity, in situations where a government may think it needs

[23] Rourke, *op. cit., pp.* 201-202.

to do it, is so limited as to be less than the three fingers on your hand in my time."[24]

In view of the access of reporters to a variety of sources and in view of the techniques which reporters have developed to exploit these sources, it is fair to conclude that if the State Department has manipulated the news, "the principal onus rests on the printed and electronic press itself."[25] For example, background briefings, whether they are held in Washington or elsewhere:

> are in most instances a response to the desires of news correspondents themselves. They are completely free agents— free to attend or not to attend; free to use, reject, or amend what they are told by officials. It is not possible for officials to make self-serving use of this technique unless the newsmen are inadequate to their responsibilities.[26]

As one newsman acknowledged, "Any government administration at any level will almost always seek to put its best foot forward and announce whatever news it creates in the manner most advantageous to its interests. This we expect, and have long learned to cope with."

This fact was amply demonstrated in a confrontation between the Department spokesman and the reporters at the noon briefing at the State Department on February 18, 1964.[27] On that occasion the Department spokesman, Richard Phillips, reminded reporters that with certain exceptions "No funds available under the Foreign Assistance Act of 1964 would be used to furnish assistance to any country that has not taken appropriate steps by February 14 to prevent its ships and aircraft from carrying any equipment, materials or commodities to and from Cuba." Mr. Phillips further stated that under special authority granted to the President in the Act:

> we have concluded that except for the Governments of the United Kingdom, France, Yugoslavia, Spain and Morocco,

[24] Hearings before the House Subcommittee on Government Operations, op. cit., p. 66.
[25] Arthur Krock, "Mr. Kennedy's Management of the News," Fortune, Vol. LXVII, No. 3, March 1963, p. 202.
[26] Ibid., p. 120.
[27] Transcript of Press and Radio News Briefing, February 18, 1964.

all aid recipient governments which could be affected by the statute had taken appropriate steps by February 14.[28]

"With respect to the United Kingdom, France, and Yugoslavia," Mr. Phillips continued, "the very small residual military training and sales arrangements involved are being terminated." However, with respect to Spain and Morocco he stated, "no new obligations of funds authorized under the Foreign Assistance Act are being entered into" until these two governments clarify what steps they have taken to prevent their ships and aircraft from carrying goods to and from Cuba.

Although the Department spokesman had warned reporters that once having made this statement, he was not in a position to respond to any questions, he was subjected to intensive questioning by reporters. Newsmen became suspicious when there was no parallel between the operative language of the Act and what he said was being terminated. As John Hightower of the Associated Press stated:

> we can't report this unless you tell us what 'no new obligation of funds' means, whether it means we are telling the Spanish Government we will not enter into any new aid program with you, or whether it means we are hereby halting the obligation of funds for the general programs we have had with you. If the latter inference, you are cutting off your aid; if its the former, it doesn't mean anything.[29]

When Mr. Phillips continued to evade the questions of reporters, Mr. Hightower announced that, as one member of the Correspondent's Association in the State Department, he would like to go on record as formally protesting the inadequacy of the statement and the lack of officials present at this briefing to amplify it adequately for normal news coverage. This motion was quickly seconded, and if the Department hoped to give the impression that it was getting tougher with countries trading with Cuba, this scheme was not entirely successful. Most of the initial stories in the press indicated that the amount of aid to be cut in the case of Spain and Morocco was very small.

[28] See Section 614(a) of the Foreign Assistance Act of 1964.
[29] Transcript, *op. cit.*

CORRELATES OF PERCEIVED ANTAGONISM

The fact that State Department officials and foreign affairs reporters may take advantage of one another naturally leads them to perceive some antagonism in their professional relations. To what extent do officials and reporters perceive antagonism in their relations with each other? What variables are most closely associated with perceived antagonism among them?

The data in Tables 7.1 and 7.2 support the existence of perceived antagonism in the professional relations of State Department officers and foreign affairs reporters. Moreover, the data show differences within each group in the degree of antagonism which they perceive in their relations with counter position

Table 7.1 Department Officers' Perceptions of Relations with Reporters

	ALWAYS COOPER- ATIVE	USUALLY COOPER- ATIVE	MORE COOPER- ATIVE	BOTH COOPER- ATIVE AND ANTAG- ONISTIC	MORE ANTAG- ONISTIC	USUALLY ANTAG- ONISTIC	ALWAYS ANTAG- ONISTIC	NO RE- SPONSE	N
Information officers' relations with reporters are —	0	20	10	8	0	0	0	2	40
Policy officers' relations with reporters are —	0	9	8	12	1	5	0	5	40

Table 7.2 Reporters' Perceptions of Relations with Department Officers

	ALWAYS COOPER- ATIVE	USUALLY COOPER- ATIVE	MORE COOPER- ATIVE	BOTH COOPER- ATIVE AND ANTAG- ONISTIC	MORE ANTAG- ONISTIC	USUALLY ANTAG- ONISTIC	ALWAYS ANTAG- ONISTIC	NO RE- SPONSE	N
Reporters' relations with information officers are —	0	13	10	9	2	3	0	3	40
Reporters' relations with policy officers are —	0	8	7	9	7	7	0	2	40

holders. It is plausible that perceived antagonism between officials and reporters arises out of the different interests which each serves in the opinion-policy process, but then how does one explain the fact that perceived antagonism is not equally shared by all officials and reporters?

Students of the government and the press offer ambivalent and sometimes conflicting explanations for the fact that some officials and reporters are much more likely than their colleagues to perceive antagonism in their relations with counter position holders. On the one hand, Cohen argues that personality factors rather than positional variables explain the differences among information and policy officials in favorable and unfavorable attitudes toward foreign affairs reporters.[30] On the other hand, Nimmo contends that role orientations reflecting some positional variables explain differences among reporters and information officials in the perception of their relations with each other as cooperative or competitive.[31] Both Cohen and Nimmo want reporters to become more heavily engaged in the analysis and interpretation of foreign affairs, but Cohen feels that this might "increase the area of compatibility" between reporters and officials while Nimmo argues that "interpretive material . . . produces problems."[32]

This uncertainty over which variables are related to perceived antagonism among officials and reporters raises basic questions about the conflict between them. If perceived antagonism among members of each group is related to variables which reflect individual characteristics and perceptions, then the conflict between the government and the press may be quite malleable because these factors may be controlled. If perceived antagonism among members of each group is related to positional variables which reflect the competing demands of policy and opinion, then the conflict is probably inherent in the democratic management of foreign affairs. What variables are

30 Cohen, *op. cit.*, pp. 146-166. Cohen does not speculate about possible differences among reporters in their attitudes toward officials.

31 Don D. Nimmo, *Newsgathering in Washington* (New York: Atherton Press, 1964) pp. 53-59, 212-219. Nimmo does not deal with the relations between policy officials and reporters.

32 *Ibid.*, pp. 44-59, 213-214; Cohen, *op. cit.*, pp. 269-274.

related to perceived antagonism between officials and reporters and what theory of conflict between the government and the press is supported by these findings?

Biographical Data

There are variations among members of each group in age, amount of professional experience, and amount and type of education; and these variables may be related to perceived antagonism among officers and reporters. If conflicts between Department officers and reporters are cumulative, age and professional experience should be positively related to perceived antagonism among officers and reporters. If experience as a counter position holder is salutary, it should be negatively related to perceived antagonism. If competence has a mellowing influence, it should be negatively related to perceived antagonism. If education has a moderating influence, it should be negatively related to perceived antagonism among officers and reporters.

The above assumptions suggest the following hypotheses:

1. Older individuals are more likely than their younger colleagues to perceive antagonism in their relations with counter position holders.[33]

2. Individuals with more professional experience are more likely than their less experienced colleagues to perceive antagonism in their relations with counter position holders.[34]

3. Information officers with prior experience as reporters are less likely than their colleagues to perceive antagonism in their relations with reporters.

4. Individuals who have earned advanced academic degrees

[33] James Reston, *The Artillery of the Press: The Influence on American Foreign Policy* (New York: Harper & Row, 1967), p. 93. Similarly Nimmo argues that the younger reporters will find information officers more helpful. See Nimmo, *op. cit.,* pp. 81-82.

[34] Cohen suggests that the length of experience is not associated with unfavorable attitudes toward reporters although he speculates that in some instances experienced officers may be more likely than their colleagues to get along with reporters because they may have more self-confidence. See Cohen, *loc. cit.*

are less likely than their colleagues to perceive antagonism in their relations with counter position holders.[35]

5. Individuals who majored in one of the social sciences as undergraduates in college are less likely than their colleagues to perceive antagonism in their relations with counter position holders.

6. Among Foreign Service Officers in policy positions, those who are less competent as measured by their rate of promotion are more likely than their colleagues to perceive antagonism in their relations with reporters.[36]

The results indicate that there is no relationship between perceived antagonism and individual characteristics among policy officers and reporters. Moreover, there is no association between the individual characteristics of reporters and perceived antagonism for information officers. Among information officers, however, there are some unexpected relationships between some of these individual variables and perceived antagonism for reporters. Age is not related to perceived antagonism for reporters. Information officers with more professional experience than their colleagues are *less,* not more, likely than their colleagues to perceive antagonism in their relations with reporters. Information officers with prior experience as reporters themselves are *more,* not less, likely than their colleagues to perceive antagonism in their relations with reporters. Although amount of education is not related to perceived antagonism for reporters, information officers with social science majors in college are less likely than their colleagues to perceive antagonism in their relations with reporters. There is no relation between the competence of policy officers and perceived antagonism for reporters.

Data on Stereotyped Images

The individuals in these groups have varying images of the personal qualities and performance characteristics of counter position holders. If officers and reporters are mutually dependent upon one another, individuals who rate counter position

35 Reston, *op. cit.,* pp. 90-93.
36 Cohen, *op. cit.,* pp. 154-55. See Chapter IV.

holders lower on the qualities of intelligent, informed, skillful, responsible and helpful should be more likely than their colleagues to perceive antagonism in their relations with counter position holders.

The above assumptions suggest the following hypothesis:

7. Individuals who rate counter position holders lower on the qualities of intelligent, informed, skillful, responsible and helpful are more likely than their colleagues to perceive antagonism in their relations with these counter position holders.[37]

With a single exception, the results show that there are no relationships between officials' and reporters' ratings of each other on these five qualities and perceived antagonism for counter position holders. The exception is that reporters who rate policy officers lower on the quality of helpful are more likely than their colleagues to perceive antagonism in their relations with policy officers.

Positional Data

The reporters in this study occupy similar positions in a variety of news organizations; information and policy officers in this study occupy varying positions in the State Department. These variables may be relevant, although students of the Department and the press have been reluctant to predict the existence much less the direction of these relationships.[38] If the conflict between the government and the press arises out of the different functions which these institutions perform in the opinion-policy process, individuals who occupy positions which are more sensitive to these pressures should be more likely than individuals in other positions to perceive antagonism in their relations with counter position holders.

The above assumptions suggest the following hypotheses:

8. Department officers who occupy policy positions are more likely than those who hold information posts to perceive antagonism in their relations with reporters and vice versa.[39]

37 Ibid., pp. 149-166.
38 Ibid., pp. 108, 156-157.
39 Ibid., pp. 156-157. Cohen is doubtful whether there is less antagonism

9. Individuals who have less frequent contacts with counter position holders are more likely than their colleagues to perceive antagonism in their relations with them.[40]

10. Reporters who work for news organizations which are believed to have an edge over other media in interpretive reporting (weekly newsmagazines, national newspapers, news services, trade press, and some newspaper chains as well as syndicated columnists) are more likely than reporters who work for news organizations which are believed to be at a disadvantage in interpretive reporting (wire services, radio and television networks, local and regional newspapers, some newspaper chains, and the ethnic press) to perceive antagonism in their relations with Department officers.[41]

11. Reporters who devote full time to foreign affairs (the reporters for the wire services, the television and radio networks, newsmagazines, and national newspapers) are more likely than reporters who do not devote full time (the reporters for the trade and ethnic press, most newspaper chains, news services, and local and regional newspapers as well as syndicated columnists) to perceive antagonism in their relations with Department officers.

12. Reporters who have spent less time than their colleagues on their present assignment because of the personnel policies of their news organizations are more likely than their colleagues to perceive antagonism in their relations with Department officers.[42]

13. Department officers who hold political appointments are more likely than their colleagues to perceive antagonism in their relations with reporters.[43]

between information officers and reporters than there is between policy officers and reporters.

[40] Nimmo, *op. cit.*, p. 133.
[41] Students of the press are quite ambivalent about the impact of interpretive reporting on government-press relations. Nimmo argues that interpretation causes problems. See Nimmo, *op. cit.*, p. 57. Both Cohen and Reston seem to take the opposite position. See Cohen, *op. cit.*, pp. 269-273. Also see Reston, *loc. cit.*
[42] Kopkind, Andrew, "Times' Square," *The New York Review of Books*, Vol. VIII, November 3, May 4, 1967, p. 13.
[43] Nimmo, *op. cit.*, p. 66. Nimmo suggests that information officers who hold

14. Department officers who hold positions of Country Director, Office Director, Public Affairs Advisor, and higher-level positions are more likely than their lower-level colleagues to perceive antagonism in their relations with reporters.

15. Policy officers in regional bureaus are more likely than those located in functional bureaus of the Department to perceive antagonism in their relations with reporters.[44]

16. Among country officers and directors, those who are more likely than their colleagues to deal with countries which are hostile to the United States are more likely than their colleagues to perceive antagonism in their relations with reporters.

17. Public affairs advisors and other information specialists are more likely than information officers in the P-area to perceive antagonism in their relations with reporters.

The results suggest that there is more perceived antagonism between Department policy officers and reporters than there is between Department information officers and reporters. However, there is no relationship among any of these groups between frequency of contact with counter position holders and perceived antagonism for them.

Among part-time reporters, those who work for news organizations which stress interpretive reporting are more likely than their colleagues to perceive antagonism in their relations with information officers. Among full time reporters, those who work for news organizations which stress interpretive reporting appear to be more likely than their colleagues to perceive antagonism in their relations with policy officers. Perceived antagonism among reporters for Department officers is not related to the time which a reporter has held his present post.

political appointments may be more likely than information specialists who belong to the civil service to have competitive relations with the press.

[44] Officers in the regional bureaus are thought to be engaged in more "substantive" work than officers in functional bureaus by Foreign Service personnel. See John E. Harr, *The Anatomy of the Foreign Service—A Statistical Profile* (New York: Carnegie Endowment for International Peace, 1965), pp. 18-19. Since Foreign Service Officers are more likely than other career types to hold positions in regional bureaus, and since these officers are less likely than other career types to hold positions in functional bureaus, this variable also reflects different career services.

There is no relationship between any of these positional variables and perceived antagonism among information officers for reporters. Although none of the relationships between the positions held by policy officers and perceived antagonism for reporters are statistically significant, all of them run in the expected direction. Four out of five policy officers with political appointments perceive antagonism in their relations with reporters. Those policy officers who hold higher level positions, who work in the regional bureaus, and who deal with countries with whom the United States has generally hostile relations, all tend to be more likely than their colleagues to perceive antagonism in their relations with reporters.

Data on Role Expectations and Attitudes

The individuals in each of these groups hold varying role expectations and attitudes. If the more discretionary and political role expectations of officers and reporters are conflicting, individual factor scores representing these role expectations should be associated with perceived antagonism. Moreover, if the conflict between officers and reporters is exacerbated by varying attitudes toward the informational requirements of policy on the one hand and the public on the other, individual factor scores reflecting these attitudes should also be associated with perceived antagonism.

The above assumptions suggest the following hypotheses:

18. Individuals who are more likely than their colleagues to hold discretionary and political role expectations for themselves are more likely than their colleagues to perceive antagonism in their relations with counter position holders.[45]

19. Individuals who are less likely than their colleagues to hold discretionary and political role expectations for counter

45 Nimmo, op. cit., Chapter III. Nimmo argues that information officers and newsmen who play down the "discretionary and political nature of their service" share role orientations which promote cooperative relations between them, while those officers and reporters who assert the political segments of their job hold divergent role orientations and have competitive relations. Cohen suggests that Department officers who accept the need for public information on policy may be more favorably disposed toward the press. See Cohen, op. cit., pp. 153-154.

position holders are more likely than their colleagues to perceive antagonism in their relations with counter position
holders.[46]

20. Reporters who are more likely than their colleagues to
stress the informational requirements of the public or to deny
the informational requirements of policy are more likely than
their colleagues to perceive antagonism in their relations with
Department officers.[47]

21. Department officers who are more likely than their colleagues to stress the informational requirements of policy or to
deny the informational requirements of the public are more
likely than their colleagues to perceive antagonism in their relations with reporters.[48]

The results indicate that reporters who hold discretionary
role expectations for themselves and reject such role expectations for policy officers are more likely than their colleagues to
perceive antagonism in their relations with policy officers. There
is no relationship between perceived antagonism either among
reporters and information officers for each other or among policy
officers for reporters on the one hand and these role expectations
on the other hand.

Among part-time reporters those who are more likely than
their colleagues to reject the informational requirements of policy are more likely than their colleagues to perceive antagonism
in their relations with information officers. This relationship is
not statistically significant in the case of reporters' attitudes
toward policy officers. Moreover, there is no relationship between the attitudes of reporters toward the informational
requirements of the public and perceived antagonism for Department officers.

Policy officers who are more likely than their colleagues to
stress the informational requirements of policy are more likely
than others to perceive antagonism in their relations with re-

[46] *Ibid.*
[47] Nimmo finds "that secrecy is not a big problem" for information officers
and reporters. See Nimmo, *op. cit.*, p. 177.
[48] Andrew H. Berding, *Foreign Affairs and You* (New York: Doubleday and
Company, 1962), pp. 157-158.

porters. However, there is no relationship either between information officers' attitudes toward the informational requirements of policy and perceived antagonism for reporters or between Department officers' attitudes toward the informational requirements of the public and perceived antagonism for reporters.

OPINION VERSUS POLICY NEEDS

This study indicates that perceived antagonism among State Department officers and foreign affairs reporters is not cumulative. Indeed, more experienced information officers are *less,* not more, likely than their colleagues to perceive antagonism in their relations with reporters. Education may also help to moderate the conflict between officers and reporters, at least insofar as information officers are concerned. Among information officers, however, prior experience as a reporter is not salutary, since it is positively related to perceived antagonism for reporters. Finally, competence does not mellow the conflict among Foreign Service Officers in policy positions since there is no relationship between their competence and perceived antagonism for reporters.

This study further suggests that neither role expectations nor stereotyped images are consistently related to perceived antagonism among officers and reporters. There are several reasons for this. First, it is difficult to determine which role expectations are more discretionary and political than others. Second, a relationship between role expectations and perceived antagonism may not exist because these expectations may not reflect role behavior. Third, the relationship between either role expectations or stereotyped images on the one hand and perceived antagonism on the other hand may not hold if one group is not really dependent upon the other. Since reporters are dependent upon policy officers, their stereotyped image of policy officers and their role expectations for policy officers tend to be associated with perceived antagonism for policy officers. Since Department officers are not so dependent upon reporters, their stereotyped image of reporters and their role expectations for reporters are not associated with perceived antagonism for reporters.

This study does indicate, however, that perceived antagonism among officers and reporters is associated with attributes of the office or position which these individuals hold in their respective organizations. Reporters who, because of the character of their position, are heavily engaged in interpretive reporting consistently tend to be more likely than their colleagues to perceive antagonism in their relations with policy officers; Department officers who, because of the character of their position, are more sensitive to pressures on policy consistently tend to be more likely than their colleagues to perceive antagonism in their relations with reporters. The most striking variable among Department officers in this regard is the distinction between information and policy positions.

Moreover, the study shows that the attitudes of officials and reporters towards the Department's manipulation of information as an instrument of policy are related to perceived antagonism among them. Policy officers who, because of the character of their responsibilities, are more likely than their colleagues to accept the informational requirements of policy are more likely than the others to perceive antagonism in their relations with reporters. Reporters who, because of the character of their responsibilities, are more likely than their colleagues to reject the informational requirements of policy are more likely than other reporters to perceive antagonism in their relations with information officers. Since positional and attitudinal variables reflect the substantive interests and responsibilities of foreign affairs reporters and officials in the opinion-policy process, they provide support for the theory that the conflict between officials and reporters is inherent in the democratic management of foreign affairs.

Perceived Antagonism Among Department Officers for Reporters

In his discussion of the "policy-makers' views of the press" Cohen stresses personality factors rather than positional variables. He argues that "The line of distinction that seems most valid here as elsewhere is not between P-area people [information officers] and desk people [policy officers], or even between political appointees and career officials, but between those people in all classifications and every level in the Department who are confident in their dealings with the press and those who are not."[49] The data in this study indicate that positional variables are very important in explaining perceived antagonism among Department officers for reporters.

In the first place, information officers are less likely than policy officers to perceive antagonism in their relations with reporters. After all, most information officers, unlike policy officers, regard it as their main job to serve the press. Few information officers, moreover, are as close as policy officers to the substantive problems of foreign policy; consequently, they are less likely than policy officers to perceive antagonism for reporters because of their fear of press disclosures.

In the second place, policy officers who hold political appointments and occupy higher level positions, and who work in one of the regional bureaus tend to be more likely than their colleagues to perceive antagonism in their relations with reporters. Moreover, if the selection of the population of policy officers had been somewhat different, it may have been possible to demonstrate an even stronger relationship between the positions occupied by officers and perceived antagonism for reporters. For example, some of the countries with whom officers in the regional bureaus deal are basically friendly to the United States; others are hostile. As might be expected, virtually all of the policy officers who deal with Communist countries or Middle East countries accept the informational requirements of policy and perceive antagonism in their relations with reporters; virtually all of the officers who deal with countries which are formally allied with the United States and which are not located in the Middle East reject the informational requirements of policy and perceive less antagonism in their relations with reporters.

The extent to which an officer's position affects his relations with the press does not escape the notice of foreign affairs reporters. As one reporter comments, "It is always very difficult

49 Cohen, op. cit., p. 157.

to get information out of the Middle East Bureau because of the hostility between Israel and the Arab states, and because of the fact that the United States has a large Jewish population. Generally, it is possible to get information on troop strength in NATO," this reporter continues, "but it is quite difficult in the case of Italy and Turkey. Italy has a large Communist party, and the government doesn't want to give them any cause for opposition moves."

Generally, Department officers whose positions make them particularly sensitive to press publicity are more likely than their colleagues to perceive antagonism in their relations with reporters. Unfortunately, it is difficult, if not impossible, to test the other hypothesis that Cohen suggests: that officials who are self-confident in their dealings with the press are less likely than other officials to perceive antagonism in their relations with reporters.[50] If experience, education, and level—the intervening variables in this portion of the study—reflect self-confidence among policy officials in their dealings with reporters, however, the association between these variables and perceived antagonism disappear when positional variables are individually controlled.

Perceived Antagonism Among Reporters
for Department Officers

Positional variables are also related to perceived antagonism among reporters for Department officers. Competition among various channels of communication in the field of spot news has created a growing demand for the interpretation of current events, especially among reporters who work for national newspapers, weekly newsmagazines, news services, and some newspaper chains, as well as syndicated columnists. As one experienced press officer in the State Department explains, "There has been a growing demand for backgrounding because of the competition that radio and TV pose for newspapers. People usually already know the traditional 'Who', 'What', 'When', and 'Where' by the time the newspapers hit the street. Thus, reporters for these news organizations have to work much harder

50 *Ibid.*

on their stories. They have to provide analysis, and this means that they need to discuss the meaning and implications of current events with policy officials."

Moreover, some news organizations provide their reporters with a better opportunity than other news agencies to engage in interpretive reporting. As one experienced reporter for a small bureau expounds, "Larger bureaus staff the State Department as a 'beat', meaning that one man devotes exclusive attention to foreign affairs. He thus has the opportunity, not to say duty, to do more than routine handout reporting. He can develop stories, policy trends, backgrounders, situationers; spot changes in emphasis; do considerably more interpretive reporting. The small bureaus often do little more than move in on big stories, make cursory checks of the noon briefing, attend mass background luncheons, make occasional telephone checks of public affairs officers. Their interest is not sustained but transitory; they are impelled more by crisis than thoughtful continuous coverage."

Reporters who work for news organizations which stress interpretive reporting or which hire full-time foreign affairs reporters tend to be more likely than their colleagues to perceive antagonism in their relations with Department officers because they are more dependent upon these officers for the meaning and implications of current events. Moreover, despite James Reston's statement to the contrary, the new generation of well-educated reporters are also more likely than their colleagues to perceive antagonism in their relations with Department officers because they welcome the opportunity to do more conscientious and careful work on major problems.[51]

Why are reporters who are heavily engaged in interpretive reporting more likely than their colleagues to perceive antagonism in their relations with Department officers? In the first place, interpretive reporters must probe more deeply than their colleagues into the details of a story. This does not mean, however, that they have any greater need than straight news reporters to disclose information being withheld by the Department. Indeed, the opposite is true. What bothers interpretive

51 Reston, *op. cit.*, p. 93.

reporters is not so much the predilection of Department officers to hold up the release of information—"We expect this and are prepared to cope with it"—but rather the inability or unwillingness of many policy officers to speak frankly with them even on a not-for-attribution basis.

In the second place, interpretive reporters want Department officers to speculate about the meaning of events. These reporters are at least as interested in the officials' opinions and frame of reference as they are in knowing all the facts available to officials. Perceived antagonism among these reporters for Department officers is associated with the perception that these officials, especially policy officers, are not as "helpful" as they could be. Department officers are considered unhelpful by these reporters either because they are unable to step outside their official role and question what they are doing or because they are unwilling to do so.

In the third place, interpretive reporters are more likely than their colleagues to feel that they should not only interpret the facts for the public but also that they should bring public views and needs to the attention of Department officers and attempt to influence policy officers. Many of these reporters incorporate into their stories the views of those who are especially critical of policies and actions undertaken by the State Department and the administration in power. Some of these reporters advocate policies based on their own analysis of foreign problems. Department officers, particularly those with political appointments, are very sensitive to press criticism and advocacy.

Positional variables also help to explain why reporters perceive less antagonism in their relations with information officers than they do in their relations with policy officers. First, reporters who work for news organizations that stress spot news; that is, the reporter who practically never comes to the Department and who does not want to spend much time there, and the reporter who works there all the time and is interested in a great amount of routine find that the information officer is a great convenience. Second, reporters who work for news organizations that stress interpretive reporting, especially those who are engaged in foreign affairs reporting on a part-time basis, feel that the information officer is an initial contact whose value for in-depth reporting is limited. Since interpretive reporters are not so dependent on information officers as they are on policy officers, however, they are less likely than other reporters to regard information officers as important and less likely than one might expect to give information officers low ratings on the quality of "helpful."

There is a whole new generation of well-educated reporters engaged in the interpretation of foreign affairs, but Cohen and Reston are surely engaged in wishful thinking when they suggest that the more reporters become engaged in the field of interpretive reporting, the less they are likely to perceive antagonism in their relations with officials.[52] After all, it is precisely those reporters who are more heavily engaged in the thoughtful interpretation of foreign affairs who are most likely to perceive antagonism in their relations with Department officers and who, in turn, are regarded as the most dangerous by Department officials. These findings provide additional support for the theory that the conflict between the government and the press is inherent in the democratic management of foreign affairs.

* * *

Although the data does not allow an extension of these findings about Department-press relations to government-press relations generally, it may be useful to consider the relations between American foreign affairs officers and reporters abroad, as previous studies of the press and foreign affairs fail to distinguish sufficiently between source-channel relations at home and abroad. All of the reporters and Department officers questioned on this point contend that relations between officers and reporters are more antagonistic in the State Department than they are overseas.

They offer several reasons for this. First, they contend the U.S. Foreign Service Officers and American reporters spend more time together abroad than they do in Washington since their numbers are relatively small and they co-exist in a foreign setting. Second, American correspondents and officials overseas are united by the common task of studying a foreign situation and preparing periodic reports on it for their respective organi-

<hr>

52 *Ibid.* Also see Cohen, *op. cit.*, p. 278.

zations. Third, American reporters and officials, especially when they are stationed in hostile countries, discover that the exchange of information between them is mutually beneficial because each has access to sources not readily available to the other.

The circumstances under which source-channel relations occur in the State Department are significantly different from those overseas. The sheer size of the Department in Washington makes it difficult for reporters to develop the personal contacts they need in order to cover the breadth of American foreign policy. The substance of this policy as well as the policy-making machinery in Washington are so complicated that it is difficult—even for the experienced reporters—to find the man who has the information they want for a story. Moreover, some of the regular newsmen estimate that it takes at least a year before Department officials will really talk to you. Even then, the turnover of key personnel in the Department makes the development of sources a continuing problem for the reporter.

The interests of reporters and officials are also somewhat different in Washington than they are abroad. Correspondents and officials overseas focus on the foreign situation; in Washington these same groups are primarily concerned with U.S. policy. As one policy officer who deals frequently with the press explains, "The area of cooperation is the study of foreign situations; the area of competition is U.S. policy." Of course this is oversimplified. The interpretation of developments abroad have obvious foreign policy implications, and officials often share with newsmen an interest in explaining American policy to the public. Nevertheless, Department officers and reporters have important and often different interests at stake in the interpretation and assessment of U.S. policy, and conflicts between the press and the Department usually develop in this area.

Moreover, there is less reason for policy officers to see reporters in the State Department than abroad. The mutual exchange of information which frequently occurs abroad is less characteristic of source-channel relations in Washington where the division of labor between reporters and officials is more distinct. Department officers are the primary source of policy information for reporters in Washington; reporters are the main channel between top Department officials and the American public. As one officer stated, "Except at the top level, officers have no need for the press. Nothing is pushing you here in Washington to be forthcoming." This aspect of the relationship between reporters and Department officers is also evident in the comments of newsmen: "Most of the people with whom you deal in the Department don't have to talk to you."

Chapter 8

The State Department and Pressure Groups

THE RELATIONSHIP which has grown up between the State Department and the press is a necessary, but not a sufficient, one. Neither the Department nor the American people can depend solely upon the press to keep them informed on public opinion and foreign policy. Before taking up the relationship between the State Department and pressure groups, it is important to understand the limits of the press as an intermediary between the State Department and American society.

In the first place, the press is not an authoritative channel of communications. The State Department cannot adequately inform the people of the way in which American interests are involved, and spell out what it is doing and why it is doing it simply by furnishing information to the press or to Congress for that matter; the Department must also make this information available to the general public in a form which can be traced directly to those responsible for American foreign policy. It is important for the people in a democracy to have access to an authoritative account of how the Department is conducting the nation's foreign relations. The American people also need direct, personal channels through which they can make their views known to the officials who make foreign policy decisions. These individuals and organizations cannot rely solely upon Congress and the press to bring their interests and attitudes to bear on

218

the day-to-day decisions of the State Department. After all, the right of petition is no less important than freedom of the press in a democratic country.

In the second place, the press is not always a neutral purveyor of facts. It would be unwise for the State Department to leave the job of ascertaining and interpreting American foreign policy solely to the press. Even with the guidance of press conferences and prepared releases, newsmen are still free to interpret and slant. The Department needs some capability of countering what it considers a bad tendency or bias in the press. One information officer indicates, for example, that the Department labored in the late 1950's to show that there are two sides to the Middle East problem so that the roof would not fall in if the government gave some assistance to Nasser. Similarly, it would be unfortunate if private groups and individuals had to depend entirely upon the press to carry their views to government officials. The views of some groups might not be considered newsworthy. The attitudes and activities of other groups might be reported in an unfavorable light. Organized labor, for example, has traditionally received unfavorable coverage in the press.[1]

In the third place, the press cannot meet all of the specialized needs of the Department and the public. Public opinion studies show that perhaps a third of the American people are effectively isolated from foreign affairs information in the press.[2] Moreover, the press simply cannot and does not provide the kind of detailed information required by those most directly concerned with foreign affairs. The Department regularly publishes in the *Department of State Bulletin* and the *American Foreign Policy: Current Documents* series the texts of treaties and other material which may affect various groups throughout the country. Likewise, the Department compiles volumes of historical documents, such as the *Foreign Relations* series, for serious students of American foreign policy. The press also fails to provide for the

1 Leila A. Sussmann, "Labor in Radio News: An Analysis of Content," *Journalism Quarterly*, Vol. XXII, No. 1, March 1945, pp. 207-214.

2 The foreign affairs questions asked in national opinion surveys by the American Institute of Public Opinion (Gallup), the National Opinion Research Center (Roper), and *Time* Magazine are reported in the winter issues of *The Public Opinion Quarterly* for 1962 and 1963.

private exchange of information. Individuals and organizations who desire private and detailed consultations with the State Department about the effect of its policies on their interests and attitudes cannot make use of the press. Many of these groups are in competition with similar groups in this or other countries; they cannot be expected to share information with the Department if it cannot be done privately so that it does not help their competitors.

In order to satisfy legitimate demands for communications which cannot be met by working through the press alone, the State Department has developed a number of other channels of communication with the public. Although the State Department does have some programs which bring it into direct contact with individuals in American society, it necessarily depends upon other institutions, i.e., Congress, other departments and agencies of the government, and nongovernmental organizations to help it reach various segments of the public. This chapter deals with nongovernmental organizations or pressure groups as a channel of communication between the State Department and the American people.

COMMUNITY OF INTEREST

The State Department and pressure groups share a number of interests in the opinion-policy process. On the one hand, the State Department has a stake in reaching the American public and its constituent pressure groups with information about foreign policy; it also has an interest in finding out how its policies are affecting various groups in the domestic public. These groups, on the other hand, have an interest in getting information about Department policies and passing this information on to their members. They also have a stake in bringing their interests and attitudes to the attention of the Department.

In order to provide for these mutual interests, the State Department and pressure groups consult one another at fairly frequent intervals. These consultations provide for the exchange of service, information, support, and cooperation between them. Since private organizations with an interest in foreign affairs are involved in both the dissemination of information to the public and the transmission of information to the Department, these consultations are relevant to both the opinion-forming and policy-making processes.

In the Formation of Public Opinion

Both the State Department and pressure groups depend upon public understanding and support for their policies and proposals, and both are concerned with the wide differences between the interpretations which are given to foreign events by those who follow foreign affairs fairly closely and the interpretations which are given to these same events by other citizens. Attitude research shows that there is a significant gap between what the general public, including even the college-educated segment of it, and the attentive public, consisting of individuals with a special interest and knowledge of foreign affairs, think about American foreign policy.[3]

The leaders of nongovernmental organizations are concerned with this gap for several reasons. First, many of these organizations have international interests which cannot be adequately supported because the group's membership is not sufficiently aware of international problems. Second, many of these groups acknowledge a responsibility for educating their membership on foreign problems. Department officers are concerned with this gap because public support for its policies is never very stable when the public supports a policy for one set of reasons and the Department supports it for another.

NGO leaders and Department officials realize that if they are going to increase public understanding as well as support for their policies, they must educate their respective constituencies. Although it is naive and hypocritical for NGOs and Department officials to think that a better informed public will invariably support their policies, there is some empirical evidence to support the notion that "There is greater attachment to society and susceptibility to social influences—a force that produces

3 William C. Rogers, Barbara Stuhler, and Donald Koenig, "A Comparison of Informed and General Public Opinion on U.S. Foreign Policy," *The Public Opinion Quarterly,* Vol. XXXI pp. 242-252.

support for official government policies"—among those who are better informed on foreign affairs.[4]

How NGOs Serve State Department Interests. State Department officers are fully conscious of the contribution which nongovernmental organizations can make to the education of the general public on foreign affairs. At one time the Department estimated that more than half of the some 6,500 national organizations in this country concerned themselves with foreign affairs, and about 300 had effective educational and informational programs in the field of international relations. The Department also estimated that these groups issued a total of 9,000 to 12,000 publications (depending on whether regional and local publications were included).[5]

The capacity of these groups for reaching the general public is truely impressive. Rosenau divides organization media into three categories: programmatic, assemblematic, and memorandummatic. Programmatic media involve arranging an agenda, compiling a speakers' list, developing topics or materials for discussion, and distributing plans for mobilizing community interest in an issue. Assemblematic media encompass panel discussion, lectures, and conferences. Memorandummatic media include newsletters, pamphlets, house organs, and fact sheets.[6]

From the Department's standpoint, these organization media are attractive because they reach down into the very fabric of American society. They are the woof of private governments crisscrossing the warp of public governments. As one public affairs official states, "No media of mass communications can quite compare to the communications network of organizations in its power to arouse interest or inform opinion over a long period."[7] There is a growing body of empirical data which support the

4 William A. Gamson and Andre Modigliani, "Knowledge and Foreign Policy Opinions: Some Models for Consideration," *The Public Opinion Quarterly*, Vol. XXX, No. 2, 1966, p. 197.

5 The files of the Office of Public Services of the State Department.

6 James N. Rosenau, *Public Opinion and Foreign Policy* (New York: Random House, 1961), pp. 83-96.

7 Assistant Chief, Group Relations Section, "Report and Recommendations on Group Relations Section of Division of Public Liaison," Cochrane, Friedman, and Seamans files, Department of State, n.d.

importance of these nongovernmental organizations as mediators between government and mass society.

In the first place, there is a clear correlation between organization membership and political interest. Almond and Verba show that in five countries, including the United States, a person who belongs to an organization is more likely than one who does not "to be politically active, to be informed about politics, to be involved and care about political affairs, to believe himself to be a competent citizen, and to express support for democratic norms."[8] These authors conclude that membership in voluntary organizations plays an important role in the maintenance of a "participatory political system."[9]

In the second place, studies show that these groups play an important role in mass communications. According to Lazarsfeld and Berelson, mass communications are more indirect than commonly supposed; the mass media actually reach various opinion leaders who in turn pass on what they read and hear to those with whom they are influential. Lazarsfeld and Berelson referred to this hypothesis as "the two-step flow of communications."[10] Although the original hypothesis is now considered a gross oversimplification of what actually takes place in mass communications, the importance which these authors attributed to interpersonal influences in the communications process has actually been expanded by later authors.[11] It is now acknowledged that the audience for mass media is not made up of "isolated and atomistic individuals as once supposed but rather of individuals living within and subject to a variety of group influences."[12] These interpersonal relations are not only channels of information, but sources of social pressure and support as well.[13]

8 Sidney Verba, "Organization Membership and Democratic Consensus," *The Journal of Politics*, Vol. XXVII, No. 3, August 1965, p. 475.
9 *Ibid.*
10 Paul F. Lazarsfeld, Bernard Berelson, and Hazel Gaudet, *The People's Choice: How the Voter Makes up his Mind in a Presidential Campaign* (New York: Columbia University Press, 1948).
11 Elihu Katz, "The Two-Step Flow of Communications," *The Public Opinion Quarterly*, Spring 1957.
12 V. O. Key, Jr., *Public Opinion and American Democracy* (New York: Alfred A. Knopf, 1960), pp. 366-367.
13 Katz, *loc. cit.*

In the third place, it is argued that organizations provide a valuable forum for bringing about attitudinal change. One reason given for this is that organization members are more exposed than nonmembers to a heterogeneous political environment. The data now available suggest, however, that organizations may not provide their members with more opportunity than nonmembers to confront those who disagree with them under conditions which allow for discussion and debate.[14] At the same time, the homogeneity of organization membership does enhance the value of organization media as a means of reaching new audiences. Organizations are better able to tailor their information to fit the "specific resistances and sensitivities" of organization membership, and consequently they are more likely to be effective than the mass media both in reaching new audiences with foreign policy information and in bringing about attitudinal change.[15]

How the State Department Serves NGO Interests. NGO leaders depend upon the Department for much of the information they need to carry out their information-education programs. Organization requests for information, speakers, and publications have steadily increased during the postwar period. The Department has encouraged these organizations to maintain and to improve these programs by fulfilling as many of their specific requests as possible. Although the Department is responsive to all organizations which request assistance, Department information officers try to maintain a regular working relationship with key leaders in some 300 nongovernmental organizations. These organizations:

1. Are national in scope and importance.
2. Have active local chapters in most states.
3. Have an interest in various phases of international affairs.
4. Have effective informational and educational media for the dissemination of knowledge about foreign affairs.
5. Have a major committee and at least one staff officer with international affairs responsibilities.

[14] Verba, *op. cit.*, p. 495.
[15] Joseph T. Klapper, *The Effects of Mass Communications* (Glencoe: The Free Press, 1960), pp. 103, 106.

6. Promote an international relations, educational, and information program for members and other citizens.

7. Are regarded as being in good repute by the Department and by other national organizations in the same category.

8. Make public pronouncements on international relations matters and keep the public informed about their activities.

9. Show sufficient interest to attend some of the briefings to which they are invited.[16]

In working with nongovernmental organizations generally and the above groups in particular, Department information officers provide support for all three types of organization media. In the first place, Department officers try to work as closely as possible with the organization personnel who are responsible for planning the foreign affairs programs of these groups. Department officers can often provide up-to-date information on policies or events of interest to these groups. These officials can also help organization leaders anticipate those issues which will be most salient to their members two or three years from now when the organization program will be implemented. They can also monitor some organization activities and help group leaders avoid costly errors. The leaders of a national veterans organization, for example, often have a Department representative sit in on the meetings of the executive committee which determines the final wording of the resolutions to be presented to organization members at their annual convention in order to avoid factual errors and other problems which might embarrass the organization.

In the second place, Department officers have tried to support the assemblematic media of these organizations. Since 1944-1945, the Department has made every effort to fulfill the increasing demand for the appearance of its officers at organization meetings throughout the country. In 1967 the Speaking and Conference Arrangements Division arranged for Department officers to make 829 speeches to nongovernmental organizations outside the Washington area; during the same period another 112 speeches outside the Washington area were made under the

16 The Office of Public Services, "List of Selected U.S. National Organizations," June 10, 1965.

auspices of other bureaus of the Department.[17] Department officers also meet frequently with groups visiting the State Department and the Washington area.

Closely allied with these individual speaking engagements are the various national, regional, and local foreign policy briefing conferences arranged by the State Department in cooperation with various private organizations and media. National and regional conferences for nongovernmental groups have been held regularly since 1945, except for the period 1953-1960. In 1963 the Department inaugurated a program of "community meetings on foreign policy" which is an adaptation of the conference technique to the local level. The advantage of these speaking and conference engagements is that they enable government officials and private citizens to engage in face-to-face, give-and-take discussions on foreign affairs.

Whether conferences are sponsored by the State Department or held under the auspices of one private organization or another, the individuals attending them pay their own expenses. Because the expense involved in sending out speakers for conference and other speaking engagements is quite high, the Department, at the instigation of the Appropriations Committees of Congress, now asks the organizations requesting speakers "whether they are prepared to reimburse the actual and necessary expenses incurred in connection with their invitations."[18] It is estimated that these organizations defray about 25 percent of these costs.[19]

In the third place, Department officers prepare material which can be used in the memorandummatic media of groups. Pamphlet materials are used by the Department both to answer the specific requests of groups and individuals for information, and to disseminate information to those organizations and media which have a standing request for such material. Official pamphlets and leaflets meet a number of group needs. First, they provide facts and ideas which can be utilized by organization

[17] *Hearings* before the House Appropriations Subcommittee, The Department of State, 90th Congress, 1st Session, March 2, 1967.

[18] *Hearings* of Senate Appropriation Subcommittee, Department of State, 87th Congress, 2nd Session, September 17, 1962, pp. 152-153.

[19] *Hearings* of House Appropriations Subcommittee, *op. cit.*, p. 287.

editors in their own publications. Second, they provide reference material which can serve as the basis for group study and discussion programs.

However, costs have always held the Department's publication program to a minimum. Even in the early 1950s, when the Department's publications program reached its peak, the average print-run was only 50,000 to 60,000 copies. Since 1953 both the number of separate publications and the number of prints have been sharply cut. In spite of the increase in public demand for publications, for instance, the average print-run in 1961-1962 was 10,000 to 12,000.[20] Since there are over 25,000 high schools alone in the country, this means that the Department cannot even furnish every high school library with basic printed material on American foreign policy.

Effectiveness of Organization Liaison. There is a general consensus that liaison between organization leaders and Department information officers has never been as effective in informing the public as the staunchest advocates of the organization approach on both sides have desired. On the one hand, the Conference Group of nongovernmental organizations stated in January of 1962 that "The greatest single barrier to progress in NGO effectiveness has been the almost total absence of rational, productive, satisfactory working relationships between the NGOs and the Department of State—including the U.S. Mission [to the United Nations]."[21] Within the Department itself, it is frankly admitted that the Office of Public Services has operated "at a pace and level far below its potentialities in terms of (1) the experience and ideas of its staff members, (2) public demand for their services, and (3) the much higher level of activities of this Office prior to 1953."

A number of group leaders recognize, on the other hand, that they have not been able to represent themselves in their best light and that they have not used the resources of the State Department sufficiently.[22] Few organizations have put the

20 See *Hearings* before the House Appropriations Subcommittee from 1950-1962.
21 The Conference Group of National Organizations, "Pathways to Excellence: A Progress Report on the NGO Performance Project," January 1962, p. 11.
22 *Ibid.*

amount of resources needed into education in international affairs to make a real impact on their members at the local level, and Department officials especially feel that groups have not provided them with the kind of support they need in Congress and in the Administration. Many of these groups are so anxious about their tax-exempt status as non-profit and non-lobbying groups that they have not adopted those political action programs which are consistent with such a status.[23]

In the Making of Foreign Policy

The State Department and pressure groups also share an interest in consulting one another on policy matters. After all, both nongovernmental and governmental organizations are actively engaged in foreign relations, and each is increasingly dependent upon the other to carry out its policies. Nongovernmental organizations depend upon the State Department for foreign information since few of them have the resources available to the government abroad. Of course, these groups also depend upon the government to establish national policies in relations with foreign governments.

The State Department, in turn, depends upon nongovernmental organizations for information on the effects of its actions and the actions of foreign governments on NGO interests and attitudes since these groups know their own situation much better than the State Department does. The Department needs this information both because it seeks to serve these domestic interests and because it depends upon these groups to support its policies at home and abroad.

In order to satisfy this mutual need for consultation, the Department and pressure groups have developed various channels of communication. The direct consultations between the State Department and pressure groups may be either formal or informal. Informal consultations tend to be personal, sporadic, and specific. They are usually initiated by leaders of nongovern-

---

23 "There is nothing to preclude doing helpful work for legislators—the provision of factual information which they and their staffs need in gaining knowledge of the issues with which they must deal." See Conference Group, "Notes on the Goals Seminar," p. 8.

mental organizations, although Department officials do consult NGO leaders, too. These informal consultations may be initiated over the phone if the participants know each other. In many cases, however, they begin with a formal written communication addressed to the Secretary of State. Such communications may simply contain, without comment, the resolutions passed by the organization's membership at its recent convention, or they may contain a formal letter explaining the organization's position. The communication may even contain a research paper or study which organization leaders hope will receive the careful attention of Department officials.

Organization leaders usually accompany this written communication with a request for an opportunity to discuss the relevant policy matter with policy officials. These informal consultations may be arranged through an information officer or by the participants themselves. Although informal consultations may occur at any level, NGO leaders usually try to see policy officials at top levels in the Department at least once a year and whenever anything really important comes up.

Formal consultations tend to be highly structured, periodic, and concerned with both general and specific policies. They are usually established by Department officials in recognition either of the legitimate demands of various groups for participation in the decision-making process, or of the need for special assistance from nongovernmental experts. The creation of an office to handle the Department's relations with a particular group usually means that informal consultations have been going on between the Department and the group or groups concerned for some time.

The Department provides special channels for the representation of a number of key groups in the conduct of certain aspects of policy. During the presidency of John F. Kennedy, for example, an Office for the Special Assistant to the Secretary of State for Labor Affairs and a Director of Commercial Affairs and Business Activities were established, both to symbolize the stake of labor and business in American foreign policy and to serve the interests of these groups abroad. In both instances, interested organizations were consulted about the appointment of individuals to these and related positions.

It is not possible to provide this kind of access to all of the groups which have a stake in American foreign policy. Consequently, the Department has developed a number of formal advisory committees through which the representatives of a much larger number of groups can participate. The Bureau of African Affairs, for example, has an Advisory Committee comprising some one hundred individuals who are formally consulted annually on American policies toward that continent. Leaders of key nongovernmental organizations are also asked to serve on numerous ad hoc commissions appointed by the President or the Secretary of State to look into various facets of U.S. foreign policy.

The Department also consults many individuals. As of July 1966, there were well over 300 consultants on the rolls of the Department; most of them were attached to the Bureau of Intelligence and Research.[24] Some of these consultants make infrequent visits to the Department for which they receive per diem and travel expenses. Others provide services for which they receive additional compensation. A brief account of the "Purpose for Which Hired" shows that the Department consults these persons on a wide variety of problems.

State Department officials and NGO leaders do not always need to exchange information directly; much information is channeled indirectly through Congress, the White House, other departments and agencies of the government, and the press. Indeed, many students of the State Department and pressure groups feel that the influence of officials and NGO leaders depends upon their effectiveness in these other arenas.[25]

There is no question that many nongovernmental organizations prefer the congressional setting for their lobbying activities. After all, as representatives of specific geographic constituencies, Congressmen and Senators are particularly susceptible to the demands and promises of important domestic groups. Moreover, if a Congressman or Senator carries a group's request

[24] U. S. Department of State, "Consultants on the Rolls as of July 1, 1966."
[25] Bernard C. Cohen, "The Influence of Non-Governmental Groups on Foreign Policy-Making," *Studies in Citizen Participation in International Relations* (Boston: World Peace Foundation, 1959), p. 14.

to the State Department, he gives the organization's views additional weight and urgency.

Most nongovernmental organizations with an interest in foreign affairs also emphasize the importance of the White House as a point at which they can effectively bring group influence to bear on American foreign policy. A number of the NGO respondents commented that the White House was more susceptible to domestic pressures than the State Department. In most instances NGO leaders also feel that it is at the White House that the big decisions are actually made.

Only slightly less important than the White House as a point at which indirect group pressure can be brought to bear on American foreign policy are other departments and agencies in the executive branch. Most groups bring pressures on those departments of government that are most susceptible to their influence. When leaders of business organizations want to influence American foreign policy on international trade, for example, they would never think of simply going to the State Department. They deal mainly with the Commerce Department. As one leading business executive put it, "I've never gone to see Secretary of State Rusk, but I know Jack Conner personally, and I would feel free to call on him if something came up." Similarly, organized labor relies heavily on the Labor Department, farm groups on the Department of Agriculture, and so on.

Finally, most pressure groups are actively engaged in conducting information campaigns both in their own organizations and for the general public on behalf of foreign policies which they favor. These public affairs programs are often designed to bring general public pressure on the Department, usually in the form of public correspondence.

How NGOs Serve State Department Interests. Nongovernmental organizations can provide the Department with valuable information and perspective on both the international situation and domestic conditions. On the international side, many of these groups are closer than the Department and the Foreign Service to developments which affect them most directly. The subsidiaries or affiliates of American business and other organizations overseas, for example, are usually the first to encounter the discriminatory practices of a foreign government or its people. If these groups or organizations do not report these instances to the Department (and they frequently do not), the Department may not be aware of them.

In addition, pressure groups can conduct programs abroad which the Department itself cannot easily undertake.[26] Business, educational, farm, labor, and other groups are all engaged both in training foreign personnel in their country and in providing skilled personnel to participate in government projects abroad. In some cases, these organizations undertake actions which complement official policy. A number of American groups have actively participated with government assistance in international relief programs for the Biafrans in Nigeria. In other instances, nongovernmental organizations actually conduct official American programs abroad. For example, in the 1960s the American Institute for Free Labor Development (AIFLD), a private, nonprofit corporation founded by the AFL-CIO, conducted United States-Latin American labor programs.[27]

On the domestic side these organizations have a more detailed understanding than the State Department of the domestic ramifications of various foreign policies on their particular interests. Many of these associations represent important segments of the American public, and in the process of forming their position on foreign policy questions, these organizations serve as an initial screen of interests in a given sector of American society. Their policies may in some cases represent the first approximation of the national interest.

These groups can also teach the State Department a great deal about public attitudes on foreign affairs. Most of these groups have a more spontaneous and detailed picture than the State Department of public reactions to international events and Department policies. Unlike the Department, they have strong roots in local communities and receive regular communications from local representatives throughout the nation.

26 Chadwick F. Alger, "The External Bureaucracy in United States Foreign Affairs," *Administrative Science Quarterly*, Volume VII, 1962-1963, p. 68.
27 Senate Committee on Foreign Relations, "Survey of the Alliance for Progress," Senate Document No. 91-17, 91st Congress, 1st Session, 1969 (Washington, D.C.: Government Printing Office, 1969) pp. 573-593.

The State Department sometimes credits these organizations with the passage of key measures through Congress, such as the Trade Expansion Act of 1962. Moreover, the Department often concludes that individual organizations have played a key role in building general public support for possible changes in American foreign policy. The U.S. Chamber of Commerce, for example, is thought to have made it possible for the State Department to open up trade with Communist countries by openly supporting such a policy when most observers might have felt that it would be unalterably opposed.

How the State Department Serves NGO Interests. The State Department assists nongovernmental organizations in a number of ways. First, it provides them with information on foreign situations which may affect their interests or attitudes. For example, it conducts a "Comprehensive Reporting Program" in which all of the agencies of the government who do not have their own system of collecting information abroad can participate. The information collected by the Foreign Service is disseminated to interested nongovernmental organizations in this country by the appropriate domestic departments of the government.

The Department also represents the interests of many domestic groups in negotiations with foreign governments. The Office of Commercial Affairs and Business Activities of the State Department, for example, handles many of the problems which arise in sharing international television broadcast time. The Department also assists religious organizations in this country by working with foreign governments to safeguard their missionaries operating abroad.

The Department promotes the interests of American groups and individuals overseas by providing countless services to them. The Department, for instance, has undertaken the exploration of mineral deposits in foreign nations to help determine the advisability of American private investment abroad. The Department also advises American businesses and other groups on the political risks involved in operating in various foreign countries.

Finally, the Department assumes for all these groups the

responsibility for determining what is in the national interest. Business organizations trading with Communist countries clearly do not want this responsibility.

Effectiveness of Department-NGO Consultations. There is a general consensus that consultations between NGO leaders and State Department officials have never been as effective in the policy-making process as many on both sides have desired. Many policy officers complain that they are constantly harassed by group pressures. As one such official put it, "They usually have a hobby horse which they beat to death; they use every opportunity to press their views." Another policy official states that he would solicit group views on policy matters if these groups ever allowed him to forget them.

At the same time, Department liaison officers, whose job it is to deal with nongovernmental organizations, are often discouraged by the role which these organizations are willing to play in policy making. Many of them are only interested in their immediate interest or attitude; they have no broad outlook on policy and often do not even give the policies with which they are concerned any hard thought. As one key liaison official states, "Businessmen are peculiar. If something hits their pocketbook, they are effective; but on other things they are terribly disorganized." Another liaison official complains that the business groups in his field hold trade information which would be helpful to the State Department because of the competition within the industry.

The testimony of leaders of nongovernmental organizations seems to verify the fact that they do not very frequently communicate their views directly to the State Department. Some NGO leaders in this study do not submit organization views to the Department at all. Many of the others make their views known within the Department only when they feel that their vital interests or basic attitudes are at stake in a decision. This suggests that group views are perceived by Department officials at least as frequently as they are communicated directly to these officials by leaders of nongovernmental organizations.[28]

[28] Similar findings are reported by those who have studied lobbying in Congress. See Raymond A. Bauer, Ithiel de Sola Pool, and Lewis Anthony

Moreover, NGO leaders express dissatisfaction with the consultations they do have with Department officials. The principal complaint is that there is no real exchange of views. As one NGO leader explains, "The Department is not seriously interested in group views. If it were, it would make more of an effort to find out what they are and what the reasons for them are." NGO leaders claim that State Department officials want them to help "pull their irons out of the fire," but they are not really interested in developing a constituency.

CONFLICT OF INTERESTS

Both the State Department and pressure groups have a stake in the regular exchange of information concerning foreign policy, but mutual consultations can quickly lead to conflict because each of them serves different interests in the opinion-policy process. The State Department has the responsibility under the President for the conduct of American foreign policy; it must represent the nation as a whole in dealing with foreign governments. In carrying out its foreign policy responsibilities, the State Department must sometimes sacrifice certain domestic interests in the name of the national interest. This gives rise to the charge that the State Department really represents various foreign interests. One NGO leader complained, for example, that "U.S. officials don't know anything about the _____ field. They are being taken in by foreigners. They carry out foreign people's wishes."

Pressure groups, by definition, represent minority interests and attitudes, although they may couch their proposals in terms of the national interest. In carrying out their responsibility for promoting the interests and attitudes of their organization, leaders of nongovernmental groups must sometimes advocate policies which make problems for the State Department overseas. This gives rise to the charge that group influences in the Department are really inimical to the national interest. As

Dexter, *American Business and Public Policy* (New York: Atherton Press, 1964).

former Secretary of State Dean Acheson warns, "There are so many opportunities for special groups to profit at the general expense that we cannot expect concern for the public welfare to be sufficient as the sole restraint upon them."[29]

Closely related to this conflict of interests is the conflict over how foreign policy objectives are to be determined in a democratic government. The State Department usually insists that national interests and objectives be determined by officials who are either elected by the people or appointed by elected officials to make these decisions.

Nongovernmental organizations usually feel that the national interest is something which should be arrived at through a process of bargaining among all of the affected domestic groups. Moreover, State Department officials have their antennae directed abroad. Department officers often feel that they cannot consult groups on foreign problems because this would compel them to divulge sensitive information. The antennae of nongovernmental organizations are pointed inward; they are concerned with the effect of Departmental policies upon their special interests and attitudes. NGO leaders often favor complete disclosure of information although some groups prefer secrecy once they have been informed so that competing interests will not counterbalance their influence on important policies.

Finally, the State Department and pressure groups have different priorities in the opinion-policy process. The State Department is less interested in group assistance in making decisions than it is in organization help in explaining decisions to the public and to Congress. The Department needs organizational assistance in building public support for its policies because it lacks a "well-defined, dependable, organized constituency."[30] Although there are many groups and individuals throughout the country with interests in various facets of American foreign policy, the Department lacks, "even across this wide

29 Dean Acheson, *Power and Diplomacy* (Cambridge: Harvard University Press, 1958), p. 28.
30 The International Studies Group of the Brookings Institution, *Governmental Mechanism for the Conduct of United States Foreign Relations* (Washington: The Brookings Institution, 1949), p. 55.

band of interests, primary interaction with a composite or co-
hesive social category."[31] Moreover, unlike many other government departments and agencies, the State Department simply
has no regional or local offices from which it can inconspicuously
carry on a grass roots information-education program.[32] All of
the Department's information activities must be conducted
from the national level—in full view of a suspicious Congress.
As a result, the State Department finds it extremely difficult to
educate the public on the complexity and diversity of both the
substance of foreign policy and the foreign policy-making
process.

Pressure groups are less concerned with Department assistance
in educating their membership on foreign affairs than they are
in developing some influence over Department officers making
decisions which affect their special interests. Nongovernmental
organizations are handicapped in bringing their views to the
attention of the State Department. Many groups are actually
discouraged from presenting their views because of the prestige
of an organization which claims to represent the national interest.[33] Although virtually all pressure groups feel that they
should make their views known to the Congress, a sizeable
number of these groups do not feel that they should submit
their views directly to the Department. Indeed, former Secretary of State Rusk made it clear to his subordinates early in his
administration of the Department that he did not want them to
take domestic political views into account in making decisions
at their level.[34]

Moreover, the Department is subject to such a wide range
of group pressures on any given issue that these pressures offset
each other, leaving the State Department free to determine its

[31] Joseph La Palombara, *Interest Groups in Italian Politics* (Princeton, N.J.:
Princeton University Press, 1964), p. 271.

[32] Since the 1940s, the State Department has displayed its material at some
750 public libraries across the country, and limited quantities of its material
has also been available at some 19 volunteer distribution centers, such as the
World Affairs Council of Northern California, Minnesota United Nations
Association, and the International House, New Orleans.

[33] La Palombara, *op. cit.*, p. 347.

[34] Dean Rusk, "A Fresh Look at the Formulation of Foreign Policy," *Department of State Bulletin*, Vol. 44, No. 1134, March 20, 1961, p. 398.

own policy.[35] As one Department official stated, "We always welcome opposite views because that enables us to make a decision quite apart from these pressures."

Nongovernmental organizations also have less leverage in the State Department than they do in some other government agencies because Department officials are less dependent upon them than other government officials for information upon which to make public policy. The State Department usually has more information than pressure groups on the foreign circumstances within which American policy must be pursued.

Thus, the State Department is primarily concerned with selling its policy to nongovernmental organizations and through them to the people after government policies have been quietly nurtured within the Administration, and pressure groups are chiefly interested in being consulted in policy matters while there is still an opportunity to influence policy. When officials take advantage of superior sources of information, specialized knowledge, and position to mislead the public, they are accused of propagandizing the public. When pressure group leaders take advantage of their freedom of action, lack of official responsibility, and stature to impose their views on the government, they are accused of propagandizing the State Department.

Propagandizing the Public

The Department of State is accused of propagandizing the public when it molds and directs public opinion to suit its own interests. The Department has a number of distinct advantages in directing public opinion if it chooses to use them. In the first place, the Department is sometimes the only reliable source for information on foreign events. In the second place, its pronouncements carry the full weight and prestige of the government behind them. In the third place, its ability to mask its policy behind the ambiguous symbol of national security may largely discredit other views and interpretations of foreign affairs.

Leaders of nongovernmental organizations make the following arguments to support their contention that the Department is actually engaged in propagandizing the American people on

[35] Cohen, *op. cit.*, p. 19.

foreign affairs. First, they contend that the Department is only interested in working with groups which support its policy. There is some evidence to support this contention. There are, for example, few opposition groups included in the list of 300 nongovernmental organizations selected by the Bureau of Public Affairs for special attention. Moreover, a number of top echelon officials in the Department made verbal comments which suggest the importance they may give the distinction between friendly groups and opposition groups: "Pressure groups are helpful if they don't oppose us; we use them when they are favorable."

Second, the leaders of nongovernmental organizations argue that the Department only presents one side of the story. Although it is doubtful if the Department could really be expected to present all sides of every issue, NGO leaders contend that there is never any unexpected discussion at Department briefings or conferences; Department officials simply reiterate old policy inflexibly. By creating a climate of acceptance among key leaders of nongovernmental organizations, some NGO leaders charge that the Department deprives the opposition of organized support.

Third, these leaders claim that Department policies are so frozen by the time they are discussed with nongovernmental organizations and the public that Department officials are not seriously interested in group views. As one NGO leader states, "Sometimes, but not always, policy officers talk so much that there is insufficient exchange of views or discussion." Comments by Department officials themselves tend to substantiate these complaints. One Department officer states that "The view of a pressure group is not of a lot of use to the Department; the chief value of such a group is in educating the public."

Propagandizing the State Department

Nongovernmental organizations are accused of propagandizing the State Department when they try to impose their views on the country as a whole. Pressure groups may have a number of advantages over the State Department in their efforts to obtain their objectives. In the first place, some of these groups can undercut American foreign policy by taking independent actions at home or abroad. In the second place, nongovernmental organizations may be more creditable because the public wants to believe what the group is saying.

Department officials generally accept the efforts of nongovernmental organizations to bring their interests and attitudes to bear on foreign policy in the regular decision-making process, but they resent efforts by such groups to impose their narrowly conceived views on the Department and the government. Department officials are especially distressed by the willingness of some of these groups to take policy into their own hands if the Department does not see things their way.

One of the most flagrant ways in which some nongovernmental organizations interfere in the regular processes for making foreign policy in recent years is the economic intimidation of American business enterprises which engage in peaceful trade with Eastern European countries.[36] Although the Congress and the Executive have found it in the national interest to allow certain types of trade with these Communist countries, a number of groups, including local American Legion posts and the John Birch Society, have tried to impose their own views of the national interest on the country. One Florida chiropractor organized such a protest, using the slogan, "Buy Your Communist Merchandise At 'Super Giant'."

Moreover, Department officials claim that many of the organizations which are most critical of Department policies are not really interested in finding out the truth about foreign events and issues. They are just as set in their beliefs as they accuse the State Department of being. Interestingly, relatively few opposition groups are located in Washington, D.C., or have established contacts in the State Department and the government.

Most Department officials accept the role played by opposition groups; what really rankles some of them, however, is the refusal of opposition group leaders who gain new insights into American foreign policy to pass this information along to group

[36] See letter of the Secretaries of State, Defense, and Commerce to the six major American cigarette manufacturers, Department of State press release, No. 240, October 11, 1965.

members. The American Legion, for example, was invited by the State Department to conduct a detailed investigation of their oft-made charge that Department ranks were filled with disloyal and unfit personnel.[37] In 1964 a distinguished group of Legion members received liberal access to key Department personnel in Washington and abroad in order to conduct such an investigation. In its final report the Legion Committee expressed "its satisfaction in regard to the overwhelming majority of the Department's employees,"[38] but this report was given minimal circulation among Legion members and was not even released as an official publication of the parent organization. A number of Department officials claimed that Legion leadership was afraid to give the publication any wider circulation or status because the report's findings were not in tune with the views of the membership. According to one high-ranking Department official, Legion officials confessed, "We don't know how to face the membership; they will think we have been doped."

A final reason why Department officials often dismiss the views of pressure groups as propaganda is that they do not represent the people they purport to represent. To the extent that many of these NGO leaders represent no one but themselves, these officials do not feel that their views merit any special attention. One Department official, for example, objected to the fact that leaders of the National Council of Churches exploit their positions by suggesting that they represent the people in the pews.

CORRELATES OF PERCEIVED ANTAGONISM

The State Department and pressure groups are dependent upon one another for the satisfaction of both complementary and conflicting interests. The Department wants nongovernmental organizations to serve as mediators between it and mass

37 Excerpt from Address by the Honorable Dean Rusk, Secretary of State, to the National Commander's Dinner for Distinguished Guests of The American Legion National Convention, Miami Beach, Florida, September 10, 1963.
38 The American Legion Special Liaison Committee, "Report on the U.S. Department of State," September 1964, p. 4.

society. Many groups either do not accept Department policies or refuse to participate in the Department's information programs. Pressure groups want a major voice in making those Department policies which affect their special interests. The Department does not always want to give these groups access to such decisions. Since each attempts to influence the other, the relationship between them is one of mutual influence.

Most studies of government and pressure groups seek to describe how much influence government officials and NGO leaders exercise over one another.[39] One conclusion which emerges from these studies is that influence is inversely related both to the perception on the part of the person or persons being influenced that pressure is being applied and to the hostility which the person or persons being influenced have toward the goals of those attempting to influence them.[40] It is not clear, however, whether the perception of pressure is rooted in an attitude of hostility or whether hostility is generated by pressure tactics.[41] The strategy to be employed in this section is to study the hostility or perceived antagonism among officials and NGO leaders not as a subtle measure of lack of influence but as an indicator of some of the problems of democracy and foreign policy.

The data in Tables 8.1 and 8.2 support the existence of perceived antagonism in the professional relations of State Department officers and NGO leaders. Moreover, the data show differences among Department officers and NGO leaders in the degree of cooperation or antagonism which they perceive in

---

[39] Most of the literature in this country on government and pressure groups deals with Congress and lobbying. Some of the more recent works include: Lester W. Milbrath, *The Washington Lobbyists* (Chicago: Rand McNally & Company, 1963); Abraham Holtzmann, *Interest Groups and Lobbying* (New York: The Macmillan Company, 1966); and Harmon Zeigler and Michael Baer, *Lobbying: Interaction and Influence in American State Legislatures* (Belmont, Calif.: Wadsworth Publishing Company, Inc., 1969).

[40] See Zeigler, *op. cit.*, p. 118; Donald R. Matthews, *U.S. Senators and Their World* (Chapel Hill, N.C.: The University of North Carolina Press, 1960), p. 176; and Andrew M. Scott and Margaret A. Hunt, *Congress and Lobbies: Image and Reality* (Chapel Hill, N.C.: The University of North Carolina Press, 1965), p. 51.

[41] Zeigler, *loc. cit.*

Table 8.1 Department Officers' Perceptions of Relations with Pressure Group Leaders

	ALWAYS COOPERATIVE	USUALLY COOPERATIVE	MORE COOPERATIVE	BOTH COOPERATIVE AND ANTAGONISTIC	MORE ANTAGONISTIC	USUALLY ANTAGONISTIC	ALWAYS ANTAGONISTIC	NO RESPONSE	N
Information officers' relations with pressure group leaders	1	25	3	2	1	0	0	8	40
Policy officers' relations with pressure group leaders	0	20	4	5	2	2	0	7	40

Table 8.2 Pressure Group Leaders' Perceptions of Relations with Department Officers

	ALWAYS COOPERATIVE	USUALLY COOPERATIVE	MORE COOPERATIVE	BOTH COOPERATIVE AND ANTAGONISTIC	MORE ANTAGONISTIC	USUALLY ANTAGONISTIC	ALWAYS ANTAGONISTIC	NO RESPONSE	N
Pressure group leaders' relations with information officers	4	20	0	0	0	0	1	11	36
Pressure group leaders' relations with policy officers	4	15	3	0	2	2	0	10	36

their relations with counter position holders. It is plausible that perceived antagonism between officials and NGO leaders arises out of the different functions which each of these groups perform in the opinion-policy process, but this does not explain the fact that perceived antagonism is not equally shared by all officials and lobbyists.

If differences in perceived antagonism among officials and NGO leaders are distributed randomly, then these differences have no meaning. Previous studies of government and pressure groups suggest, however, that these differences may not be random. Some authors indicate that perceived antagonism is associated with the personal qualities or performance characteristics of officials or NGO leaders.[42] Still other authors suggest that perceived antagonism is associated with positional variables, such as type of group and the kind of influences each type can bring to bear on the State Department.[43] Some of these authors also contend that perceived antagonism among officials and NGO leaders is related to differences among them over foreign policy issues.[44]

If perceived antagonism among members of each group is related to variables which reflect individual characteristics, then the conflict between the government and pressure groups may be quite malleable because these factors may be controlled. If perceived antagonism among members of each group is related to positional variables which reflect differences over policy, then the conflict is probably inherent in the democratic management of foreign affairs because these differences will always exist in a free society. What variables, if any, are related to perceived antagonism among Department officers and pressure group leaders? What theory of conflict between the government and pressure groups do these findings support?

Biographical Data

There are variations among members of each group in age, amount and type of professional experience, and amount and type of education; these variables may be related to perceived antagonism among officers and NGO leaders. If conflicts between Department officers and NGO leaders are transitory, age and length of professional experience should be negatively related to perceived antagonism among Department officers and NGO leaders. If relations between NGO leaders and other position holders are antagonistic, prior experience in one of these positions should be positively related to perceived antag-

---

42 Zeigler, *op. cit.*, p. 139; Scott and Hunt, *op. cit.*, p. 50.
43 Cohen, *op. cit.*, pp. 18-19.
44 Zeigler, *op. cit.*, p. 118; Matthews, *op. cit.*, p. 178; Scott and Hunt, *op. cit.*, p. 51.

onism. If education has a moderating influence, it should be negatively related to perceived antagonism among officers and NGO leaders.

The above assumptions suggest the following hypotheses:

1. Younger individuals are more likely than their older colleagues to perceive antagonism in their relations with counter position holders.[45]

2. Individuals with less professional experience are more likely than their colleagues to perceive antagonism in their relations with counter position holders.[46]

3. Information officers with prior experience as reporters are more likely than their colleagues to perceive antagonism in their relations with NGO leaders.

4. Information officers with prior experience in the Foreign Service of the United States are more likely than their colleagues to perceive antagonism in their relations with NGO leaders.

5. Individuals who have earned advanced academic degrees are less likely than their colleagues to perceive antagonism in their relations with counter position holders.[47]

6. Individuals who majored in one of the social sciences as undergraduates in college are less likely than their colleagues to perceive antagonism in their relations with counter position holders.[48]

The results indicate that older information officers and NGO leaders are no more or less likely than their colleagues to perceive antagonism in their relations with counter position holders; however, older policy officers are more likely than their younger colleagues to perceive antagonism in their relations

[45] Henry Ehrman, "French Bureaucracy and Organized Interests," *Administrative Science Quarterly*, March 1961, p. 552. Ehrman argues that the younger generation of French bureaucrats regard themselves as the "counter-lobby."
[46] Zeigler, *op. cit.*, pp. 121, 152. Zeigler finds that the attitudes of legislators toward lobbyists become more favorable as experience increases.
[47] Ehrman, *op. cit.*, p. 550. Ehrman contends that "general education immunizes officials against group pressures." Also Zeigler feels that better-educated officials are more willing to accept persuasive material and be more tolerant of pressures. Zeigler, *op. cit.*, p. 125.
[48] *Ibid.*

with NGO leaders. Professional experience is not related to perceived antagonism among these groups. Information officers with prior experience either as reporters or Foreign Service officers are more likely than their colleagues to perceive antagonism in their relations with NGO leaders. There is no relationship between the amount or kind of education of Department officers and NGO leaders and perceived antagonism among them.

Data on Stereotyped Images

The individuals in this study have varying images of the personal qualities and performance characteristics of counter position holders. If Department officers and NGO leaders are suspicious of one another, individuals who rate counter position holders lower on the qualities of intelligent, informed, skillful, responsible, and helpful are more likely than their colleagues to perceive antagonism in their relations with counter position holders.

This assumption suggests the following hypothesis:

7. Individuals who rate counter position holders lower on these qualities are more likely than their colleagues to perceive antagonism in their relations with these counter position holders.[49]

The results show that NGO leaders who rate Department officers lower on these qualities are no more or less likely than their colleagues to perceive antagonism in their relations with Department officers. Department officers who rate NGO leaders lower than their colleagues on the qualities of intelligent, informed, and skillful are no more or less likely than they are to perceive antagonism in their relations with NGO leaders.

---

[49] Scott, *op. cit.*, p. 32. Scott and Hunt report that congressmen who rely upon NGO leaders for information are more likely to find their relations with them cooperative. This suggests that both level of information and helpfulness would be negatively related to perceived antagonism. Also, see Zeigler, *op. cit.*, p. 35. Zeigler indicates that many officials feel that NGO leaders are irresponsible because they represent and push minority interests. This would lead us to expect that responsibility and helpfulness are negatively related to perceived antagonism.

However, Department officers who are more likely than their colleagues to rate NGO leaders lower on the quality of responsible are more likely than they are to perceive antagonism in their relations with them. Information officers who are more likely than their colleagues to rate NGO leaders lower on the quality of helpful are also more likely than their colleagues to perceive antagonism in their relations with NGO leaders; but there is no relation between policy officers' ratings of NGO leaders on the quality of helpful and perceived antagonism.

Positional Data

The NGO leaders in this study occupy similar positions in a variety of groups; officials occupy varying positions in the State Department. These variables may also be related to perceived antagonism among NGO leaders and Department officials. If the conflict between officials and NGO leaders arises out of the different functions which these groups perform in the opinion-policy process, individuals who occupy positions which are more sensitive to these pressures should be more likely than their colleagues to perceive antagonism in their relations with them. If the conflict between officials and NGO leaders arises largely out of differences over policy, individuals who are more likely than their colleagues to differ with counter position holders should be more likely than their colleagues to perceive antagonism in their relations with them.

The above assumptions suggest the following hypotheses:

8. Policy officers are more likely than information officers to perceive antagonism in their relations with NGO leaders, and NGO leaders are more likely to perceive antagonism in their relations with policy officers than with information officers.

9. Department officers who hold political appointments are more likely than their colleagues to perceive antagonism in their relations with NGO leaders.[50]

10. Department officers who hold positions of Country Director, Office Director, Public Affairs Advisor, and higher level

[50] La Palombara, op. cit., pp. 386-387. La Palombara indicates that political appointees are more sensitive than their colleagues to group pressures in a bureaucracy.

positions are more likely than their colleagues at lower levels to perceive antagonism in their relations with NGO leaders.

11. Policy officers in regional bureaus are more likely than those in functional bureaus to perceive antagonism in their relations with NGO leaders.

12. Among policy officers in regional bureaus, those who deal with countries with whom the U.S. has generally hostile relations are more likely than their colleagues to perceive antagonism in their relations with NGO leaders.

13. Individuals in more frequent contact with counter position holders are less likely than their colleagues to perceive antagonism in their relations with them.[51]

14. NGO leaders who devote full-time to foreign affairs are more likely than their colleagues to perceive antagonism in their relations with Department officers.

15. Leaders of economic groups are less likely than leaders of other groups to perceive antagonism in their relations with Department officers.[52]

16. Leaders of organizations which support the State Department are less likely than leaders of opposition groups to perceive antagonism in their relations with Department officers.[53]

17. Leaders of non-membership groups are less likely than leaders of membership groups to perceive antagonism in their relations with Department officers.[54]

As expected, the results indicate that policy officers are more likely than information officers to perceive antagonism in their relations with NGO leaders; NGO leaders are more likely to

[51] Zeigler, op. cit., pp. 95-96. Zeigler argues that "interaction increases not only positive evaluation but also congruence of perceptions."

[52] Cohen, op. cit., pp. 6, 8, 12, 18-19. Cohen repeatedly indicates that economic interests have better access and are perceived by officials as having more legitimate interests at stake than other groups.

[53] Zeigler, op. cit., pp. 134-135. Zeigler points out that organizations which are part of the establishment can just supply information; outsiders must persuade. Stewart also contrasts the process of consultation with the technique of campaigns. See J.D. Stewart, British Pressure Groups: Their Role in Relations to the House of Commons (London: Oxford University Press, 1958).

[54] Stewart, op. cit., pp. 39, 106. Stewart argues that membership organizations often prefer public forms of pressure which are disliked by officials.

perceive antagonism in their relations with policy officers than with information officers. There is no relationship between the sensitivity of positions held by Department officers and perceived antagonism for NGO leaders. Indeed, policy officers in regional bureaus appear to be *less,* not more, likely than their colleagues to perceive antagonism in their relations with NGO leaders. Perceived antagonism for NGO leaders is negatively associated with frequency of contact among Department officers. However, there is no relationship between frequency of contact with Department officers by NGO leaders and perceived antagonism for Department officers. Except for the fact that NGO leaders who represent groups who oppose Department policies are more likely than their colleagues to perceive antagonism in their relations with policy officers, there are no relationships between the character of the positions held by NGO leaders and perceived antagonism for Department officers.

Data on Role Expectations and Attitudes

The individuals in each of these groups hold varying role expectations and attitudes. If the more discretionary and political role expectations of officers and NGO leaders conflict, then these role expectations should be associated with perceived antagonism.[55] Moreover, if the conflict between officers and NGO leaders is exacerbated by varying attitudes toward the informational requirements of policy on the one hand and the public on the other hand, these attitudes should also be associated with perceived antagonism.

The above assumptions suggest the following hypotheses:

18. Individuals who accept the more discretionary and political segments of their own role are more likely than their colleagues to perceive antagonism in their relations with counter position holders.

19. Individuals who reject the more discretionary and political expectations of counter position holders are more likely

---

[55] Factors measuring role expectations are not employed in this chapter because they obscure significant relationships among individual items and perceived antagonism.

than those who accept these role expectations to perceive antagonism in their relations with counter position holders.

20. Policy officers, who are less likely than their colleagues to feel that they should interpret the national interest for domestic groups or that they should solicit the views of interest groups on policies which affect group interests, are more likely than their colleagues to perceive antagonism in their relations with NGO leaders.

21. NGO leaders, who are less likely than their colleagues to feel that policy officers should play a leading role in opinion-making in this country or that policy officers should determine what information is released to the public, are more likely than their colleagues to perceive antagonism in their relations with policy officers.

22. NGO leaders, who are more likely than their colleagues to feel that they should submit their views directly to Department officers, are more likely than their colleagues to perceive antagonism in their relations with policy officers.

23. NGO leaders, who are more likely than their colleagues to stress the informational requirements of the public or to deny the informational requirements of policy, are more likely than their colleagues to perceive antagonism in their relations with Department officers.

24. Department officers, who are more likely than their colleagues to stress the informational requirements of policy or to deny the informational requirements of the public, are more likely than their colleagues to perceive antagonism in their relations with NGO leaders.

The results suggest that information officers who reject the more discretionary and political role expectations of pressure group leaders are more likely than their colleagues to perceive antagonism in their relations with them. There are no relationships between the attitudes of these groups on role expectations and perceived antagonism toward each other.

Policy officers, who feel that they should interpret the national interest for domestic groups, are more likely than their colleagues to perceive antagonism in their relations with lobbyists; however, there is no relation between perceived antagonism for

NGO leaders and policy officers' acceptance of the need to solicit the views of interest groups which affect group interests. Leaders of nongovernmental organizations who are less likely than their colleagues to feel that policy officers should play a leading role in opinion-making or in determining what information to release to the public, are more likely than their colleagues to perceive antagonism in their relations with policy officers. Moreover, NGO leaders, who are more likely than their colleagues to feel that they should submit their views directly to Department officers, are more likely than their colleagues to perceive antagonism in their relations with policy officers.

As expected, NGO leaders, who are more likely than their colleagues to deny the informational requirements of policy, are more likely than their colleagues to perceive antagonism in their relations with policy officers. However, NGO leaders who are more likely than their colleagues to stress the informational requirements of the public are *less,* not more, likely than their colleagues to perceive antagonism in their relations with policy officers. There is no relationship between the attitudes of NGO leaders toward the informational requirements of democracy and foreign policy and perceived antagonism for information officers. Moreover, there is no relationship between Department officers' attitudes toward the requirements of information policy and perceived antagonism for NGO leaders.

OPINION VERSUS POLICY NEEDS

This study provides no support for the notion that perceived antagonism among State Department officers and NGO leaders is transitory. Older policy officers are more, not less, likely than their younger colleagues to perceive antagonism in their relations with NGO leaders. As expected, prior experience as a reporter or Foreign Service officer is related to perceived antagonism among information officers for NGO leaders. There is no evidence that education serves to moderate perceived antagonism between officials and pressure group leaders.

The data indicate that officials and lobbyists play some conflicting roles in the opinion-policy process. Distrust for lobbyists and the rejection of the officials' role segments involving NGO leaders reveal the conflict of roles underlying perceived antagonism among policy officers for them. The awareness of the NGO leaders' need to influence policy officers combined with the rejection of policy officers' role in influencing domestic opinion suggests the conflict of roles underlying perceived antagonism among NGO leaders for policy officers.

The data further suggest that perceived antagonism is not associated with all positional variables. Positional variables reflecting the sensitivity of officials to pressure are not related to perceived antagonism for NGO leaders; Department officers who are political employees or high-ranking officials are no more likely than other officials to perceive antagonism in their relations with NGO leaders. Moreover, type of group is not related to perceived antagonism among NGO leaders for Department officials; leaders of economic groups or membership groups are no more likely than the leaders of other organizations to perceive antagonism in their relations with officials.

The data indicate, however, that positional variables which reflect a concern for policy and especially differences over policy are related to perceived antagonism between Departmnt officials and NGO leaders. This finding is important because it provides additional support for the theory that the conflict between the State Department and pressure groups is inherent in any system which attempts to conduct its foreign policy on a democratic basis.

Perceived Antagonism Among NGO Leaders for Department Officials

Perceived antagonism among NGO leaders for State Department policy officers arises out of group efforts to influence Department policies. All of the NGO leaders who perceive antagonism in their relations with policy officials feel that they should submit their views directly to the State Department. There is no evidence in this study that economic groups are any more or less likely than other pressure groups either to bring their demands to bear on the State Department or to come into conflict with the Department. Rather, it is the leaders of organizations which generally oppose the Department and its policies who are more likely than their colleagues to perceive antagonism in their relations with policy officials.

These findings are not surprising, but they are significant for democratic government. After all, group leaders would probably not be as hostile toward Department officials if it were not for the fact that leaders of opposition groups feel that they have a right to be consulted on policies which affect their special interests as a part of the democratic process. Many of these groups, however, do not feel that they receive a fair hearing, even when Department officials meet with them.

As an "outsider trying to convince insiders," it is not surprising that opposition groups feel that their views are not taken seriously. In view of the difficulty which any group has in measuring its influence, a group's assessment either of its impact on the Department or the Department's responsiveness to its views is largely a function of whether the group agrees or disagrees with Department policy. If a group agrees with the Department, it either does not need to influence the Department or it can too easily convince itself that its influence is effective. If a group disagrees with the Department, it is hard for the group to convince itself that its views are taken very seriously.

Similarly, a group's attitude toward the Department's information program is at least in part a function of whether the group agrees or disagrees with Department policy. If a group agrees with the policy of the Department, it usually feels that that policy has been made perfectly clear. If a group disagrees with the policy of the Department, however, it seldom feels that the Department has presented all of the relevant information.

Distrust of the Department's information program is manifest among NGO leaders who perceive antagonism in their relations with policy officers. NGO leaders, who are less likely than their colleagues to feel either that policy officers should play a leading role in opinion-making in this country or that policy officers should determine what information is released to the public, are more likely than their colleagues to perceive antagonism in their relations with policy officials. It makes no difference whether the Department is managing its information policy in order to meet the requirements of policy or of the public; NGO leaders, who are less likely than their colleagues to accept the Department's information policy, are more likely than their colleagues to perceive antagonism in their relations with policy officials.

In view of the above relationship, it is curious that NGO leaders are less likely to perceive antagonism in their relations with information officers than they are in their relations with policy officers. The explanation for this finding is to be found in the varying expectations which NGO leaders have for information and policy officers. NGO leaders apparently feel that access to information about policy is a prerequisite for influencing policy decisions, but they feel that information officers exercise little control over information policy and provide little or no access to policy decisions.

There are essentially two reasons why most NGO leaders have fewer contacts with information than policy officers. First, NGO leaders feel that policies are made by officials at higher echelons in the State Department, but the information officers designated to serve them are located at lower echelons in the Department. Second, organization leaders feel that few information officers, regardless of the level at which they operate, can provide them with access to information or policy decisions. As one opposition leader comments on the role of a high level liaison officer, "_____'s office doesn't operate to bring views on policy. He doesn't get into substantive questions."

NGO leaders, especially those whose organizations support Department policies, do maintain minimum contact with information officers. Some of them find that information officers can provide them with useful services and information. Although most organization leaders do not depend upon information officers to arrange consultations with policy officers for them, a few NGO leaders keep information officers informed of their activities so as not to undermine the position of these liaison officers in the State Department. After all, the Office of Public Services and other liaison offices are the formal contact points for these organizations in the Department, and it is in their interest to maintain these contacts in the event that their access to other officials is blocked for one reason or another.

Thus organizations rely upon the formal information channels largely for routine services, help in arranging individual or group interviews with policy officials, and general information. Although most NGO leaders do not have an especially high regard for information officers, this lack of esteem does not manifest itself in the form of perceived antagonism, because NGO leaders do not rely primarily upon these officials either for information or access to policy officials.

Perceived Antagonism Among Department Officials for NGO Leaders

Perceived antagonism among Department officials for NGO leaders also arises out of the policy differences between them. Department officials who are engaged in direct consultations with leaders of nongovernmental organizations deal mainly with groups which support their policy. As one policy official put it, "The groups we deal with see things pretty much as we do." Department officials who are not engaged in direct consultations are only exposed to the publicized attempts of opposition groups to force the Department's hand. Consequently, officials who have less frequent contact than their colleagues with NGO leaders are both more likely than their colleagues to perceive antagonism in their relations with NGO leaders and more likely than their colleagues to regard NGO leaders as irresponsible.

Moreover, policy officers are more likely than information officers to perceive antagonism in their relations with NGO leaders. This finding indicates that there is a division of labor between information and policy officers in the State Department with respect to group liaison. Information officers backstop the information-education programs of nongovernmental organizations; NGO leaders come to these officers for information on general foreign policy questions. Policy officers conduct foreign policies in the interest of the nation and its constituent pressure groups; NGO leaders contact these officials either when they desire specific information on policy developments or when they want to influence Department policy decisions.

Since information and policy officers either encounter different NGO leaders or the same leaders on essentially different missions, it is not surprising that the steretotyped image of NGO leaders held by information and policy officers differs considerably. Information officers are less likely than policy officers to feel that NGO leaders are well informed because the NGO leaders they encounter always want information. Information officers are more likely than policy officers to feel that NGO leaders are helpful because they are an important channel of communications for information officers. Indeed, those information officers who are less likely than their colleagues to feel that NGO leaders are helpful are more likely than their colleagues to perceive antagonism in their relations with NGO leaders.

Policy officers may be more likely than information officers to perceive antagonism in their relations with NGO leaders because policy officers are less likely than information officers to emphasize the domestic conditions which affect policy; they have their antennae directed toward the rapidly changing international situation. Those policy officers who are less likely than their colleagues to feel that they should interpret the national interest and foreign interests for domestic groups are more likely than their colleagues to perceive antagonism in their relations with NGO leaders.

Moreover, information officers who have been Foreign Service officers are more likely than their colleagues to perceive antagonism in their relations with NGO leaders. Since these information officers have had more extensive oversees experience than their colleagues, this finding provides additional support for the belief that policy officers place less importance than NGO leaders on consultations with domestic groups. Interestingly, information officers with prior experience as reporters are also more likely than those with no reportorial experience to perceive antagonism in their relations with NGO leaders, but this relationship will be discussed in the next chapter.

* * *

Although this study is not concerned with the relations between U.S. officials and representatives of American pressure groups abroad, a number of respondents in this study make some interesting observations with respect to this relationship. According to a few Department officers, the conflict between

American officials and pressure group leaders is more pronounced abroad than it is in Washington because the overseas representatives of many of these groups are so concerned with America's image in the host country that they side with that government in its dealings with American officials. Since the leaders of these same organizations in the United States are more likely than their field representatives to place events overseas in the context of American foreign policy as a whole, the Department often receives disparate views from the headquarters and field officers of the same organization.

Chapter 9

The Press and Pressure Groups

BOTH THE PRESS and pressure groups serve as intermediaries
between the State Department and the American people.
The role of each of these institutions in the opinion-policy
process has been the subject of systematic study, but there has
been little effort to examine thoroughly the relations between
these two groups. To what extent do reporters and NGO leaders
coordinate their activities? To what extent do they compete
with one another? What sources of cooperation and conflict
arise among them? These are a few of the questions to be dealt
with in this chapter.

COMMUNITY OF INTEREST

The press and pressure groups often share an interest in disseminating foreign policy information to the American public;
they also have an interest in communicating public attitudes on
foreign affairs to Departmental decision-makers. When these
two institutions share a community of interest, they have a
definite incentive to work together because the capabilites of
one complement the capabilities of the other. The resulting cooperation between the press and pressure groups has largely
been institutionalized through the emergence of reporters whose
sole job is to cover the activities of certain types of pressure
groups and the press agents of these nongovernmental organizations.

258

How NGO Interests are Served by the Press

In order to influence foreign policy, NGO leaders must be well-informed. Without superior sources of information, they are at a clear disadvantage both in dealing with government officials and in conducting information-education programs before the public. Although many of these organizations have independent sources of information abroad, including their own overseas representatives, they all rely upon the press for current information and interpretation, especially in geographic and issue areas of secondary interest to them. Approximately 60 percent of the NGO leaders in this study who listed their non-Departmental sources of information on international affairs named newspapers or news magazines, such as *The New York Times,* the *Washington Post, Time,* and so on.

There is also some evidence that NGO leaders rely upon the knowledge and experience of individual foreign affairs reporters with whom they have contacts for their assessment of foreign policy events and decisions. As one NGO leader remarks, "We should cultivate newsmen much more, both for the information and tips they can give us and for the background and experience they can provide. Richard Dudman of the *St. Louis Post Dispatch,* for example, has been very helpful to us in understanding what is going on in Vietnam." Indeed, the knowledge, skills, and contacts of a reporter are so relevant to the work of many pressure groups that one study of NGO influence at the state level finds that NGO leaders with prior experience as reporters are more effective than their colleagues in lobbying on behalf of organization interests and attitudes.[1]

One reason that the skills of a reporter may be relevant to success as an NGO leader is the fact that pressure groups, particularly at the national level, have turned more and more to indirect rather than to direct strategies of influence.[2] Reporters have many of the skills needed to influence officials indirectly

[1] Walter Dale de Varies, "The Michigan Lobbyist: A Study in the Bases and Perceptions of Effectiveness," Ph.D. Dissertation, Michigan State University, 1960, p. 80.
[2] Lester W. Milbrath, *The Washington Lobbyists* (Chicago: Rand McNally and Company, 1963), p. 215.

through the public, and they possess a knowledge of the press which is probably indispensable to any group which wants to reach segments of the general public. In short, NGO leaders depend upon the press as a channel of mass communications. Part of their job is to furnish editors and reporters with as much usuable material as possible.

NGO leaders also use the press to communicate with organization members. The ability of the leadership to receive general publicity is believed to have a bearing on its status within the organization. For this reason, many NGO leaders reprint and circulate among the membership press stories concerning their personal lives and group programs. Information carried in the general news media is probably more effective than information carried in organization media in building support for the leadership because the membership feels that it constitutes an independent evaluation of the quality of the leadership and its performance.

How Press Interests Are Served by NGO Leaders

In order to provide comprehensive coverage of foreign affairs, the press must cover the activities of pressure groups both at home and abroad. Although the activities of these groups are not as important as those of the government, they constitute a significant part of international relations; occasionally they become the focus of government actions. Because of the varied and dispersed character of these organization activities, it is particularly difficult for the press to cover them. When general publicity is in the interest of these pressure groups, the press can often depend upon the leaders of these organizations to furnish the information to reporters.

In addition, many of these groups contain individuals with special knowledge and skills in various aspects of international relations and foreign policy. These individuals may be an important source of information to reporters even when the organization they represent does not figure prominently in the news. Over half of the reporters who listed their non-Departmental sources of information on foreign affairs explicitly mentioned NGO leaders. A large portion of these reporters specifically referred to academic experts in educational or research organizations as a valuable source of opinion and interpretation on contemporary international events.

The press benefits from the efforts of NGO leaders to sell organization policies in other ways too. In the first place, the press is a business organization. It supports itself by selling advertisements and subscriptions. Nongovernmental organizations support the press by buying advertising space in the mass media. Moreover, members of nongovernmental organizations are more likely than nonmembers to be subscribers. These individual subscriptions are also important to the press.

The foreign affairs reporter must compete with other reporters for time and space in the mass media. The use and placement of his material in the media are supposedly related to the amount and intensity of audience interest in it. Since the international action and education programs of various pressure groups stimulate interest both within their own membership and among the public at large, these groups help to enlarge the interest in and demand for the output of foreign affairs reporters. As a prominent wire service reporter states, "The organization media creates and sustains interest in current news. This helps the news business."

CONFLICT OF INTERESTS

Although the press and pressure groups are both intermediaries between the public and the State Department, they perform disparate functions in the opinion-policy process. The press, which is primarily concerned with informing, evaluating, and entertaining the general public, emphasizes the public opinion-forming process. Its influence in the foreign policy-making process is derived chiefly from the part it plays in the formation of public opinion. Pressure groups, which are mainly concerned with the making of public policy, stress the foreign policy-making process. The efforts of NGO leaders to inform the public stem largely from their desire to influence the political environment which officials may take into account in making foreign policy.

The interests of reporters in informing the public as a whole and the interests of NGO leaders in influencing policy on behalf of a part of the public do not always coincide. On the one hand, reporters feel that the principal responsibility of the press is to provide objective information to an undifferentiated mass public. They believe that special attitude and interest groups have an ax to grind and that any information provided by them is slanted. Reporters are convinced that if they do not exercise independent news judgment, the press will simply become a battleground for the expression of special interest viewpoints.

On the other hand, NGO leaders represent a highly differentiated public organized into various interest and attitude groups. They depend often upon the press to bring their views to the attention of officials as well as the general public. NGO leaders feel that they contribute much of the information which officials and the public must have in order to make decisions. When reporters disregard group views, NGO leaders feel that information on American foreign policy is being distorted by reporters.

This conflict of interests between the press and pressure groups is exacerbated by the fact that reporters and NGO leaders question the very legitimacy of the role which each other plays in the opinion-policy process. Reporters not only perceive that the promotional activities of NGO leaders conflict with the ideal of an objective press, but they also feel that these activities are undemocratic. Similarly, NGO leaders not only perceive that the press's definition of news conflicts with group interests, but also that these standards are inappropriate in a democracy.

The notion that pressure groups, irrespective of their goals, are evil is not peculiar to reporters. They simply share a view of democracy which has been prevalent from the beginning of the American republic.[3] According to this view, democracy assumes that a majority of individuals within a society are capable of making rational choices. Reporters naturally perceive themselves as playing a critical role in democratic government for they have the primary responsibility for communicating information directly to the individuals who make these choices.

There are several reasons why reporters feel that pressure

[3] Harmon Zeigler, *Interest Groups in American Society* (Englewood Cliffs, N.J.: Prentice-Hall, 1964), p. 33.

groups are undemocratic. First, reporters contend that pressure groups are inimical to democratic majority rule because they invariably represent minorities. The whole idea that foreign policy might represent the minority group's interest or attitude or even a coalescence of such minority interests and attitudes is antithetic to reporters. Most reporters reject the group basis for making foreign policy because they are convinced that these groups are so tied to their selfish interests that their foreign policies would at best represent "a mere extension of domestic interests into the foreign sphere."[4]

Second, reporters argue that pressure groups violate the assumption of individualism in a democracy. Reporters themselves are engaged in a highly individualistic, competitive trade; they feel that NGO leaders subordinate the needs of individuals in their organization to the needs of the group. Moreover, reporters suspect that NGO leaders do not really speak for the groups they supposedly represent. As one prominent newspaper reporter states, "Group attitudes are usually formed by a few select and specialized position holders within an organization." Thus, pressure groups are also undemocratic because they are unrepresentative of their membership.

Third, reporters feel that pressure groups have an emotional commitment which prevents rational consideration of foreign policy problems. Reporters feel that most pressure groups take the same old positions year after year: "They are largely concerned with spreading the gospel." Reporters also feel that most groups represent lost causes: "They are a place to let off steam." With reference to groups promoting Atlantic unity, for example, one reporter remarks, "The Atlantic Community is fine, but all evidence points to the fact that we are not going to have it." In this sense, some reporters look upon attitude groups and their leaders as honorary pallbearers.

NGO leaders have a different view of the democratic process. They accept a pluralist view of democracy in which a multiplicity of groups plays a key role in forming and representing public opinion. In their view democratic majorities often

---

4 Gabriel A. Almond, *The American People and Foreign Policy* (New York: Frederick A. Praeger, 1950), p. 150.

develop out of compromises among contending interests; individuals express themselves through organizations, and organizations help to make foreign affairs intelligible to the public.

However, the leaders of nongovernmental organizations do not feel that they should be an exclusive channel of communications between the State Department and the public. They depend upon the press both as a source of foreign policy information and as a channel for organization material on foreign affairs. Pressure group criticism of the press rests on the notion that the press does not provide an objective account of what is going on in foreign affairs. What is the basis for these criticisms?

NGO Criticism of the Press

Nongovernmental organizations with an interest in foreign affairs want to influence Department policy. NGO leaders are critical of any actions by reporters which tend to diminish the influence they can exert on Department officials. There are two ways in which the press may limit NGO effectiveness. First, it can hamper group efforts indirectly by restricting the flow of information to them. Second, it can limit group efforts directly by refusing to carry group messages to the general public.

Indirect Influence. NGO leaders engage in consultations with Department officials. Even though reporters are not a direct participant in these consultations, they can hamper NGO effectiveness indirectly by influencing the flow of information among the participants and between the participants and the attentive public.

First, since these consultations are usually initiated by NGO leaders, the press hampers effective consultations simply by failing to report the fact that officials are making decisions in which various pressure groups have an important interest. NGO leaders are critical of the press for not ferreting out more information on the formation of policy.

Second, NGO leaders depend upon the press both as a source of and channel for information which may affect their relations with Department officials. NGO leaders must be well-informed on the parameters of a decision if they hope to use their influence effectively. They are very much concerned with the spotty and inaccurate coverage of foreign affairs in the press. As one NGO leader explains, "Information in the press must be checked. We do not take press information as gospel." The exasperation of NGO leaders for the press only increases when the press fails to carry the stories they offer to reporters in the hope of reaching officials indirectly.

Third, reporters sometimes compete with NGO leaders by lobbying for policies which they support. Although there is little evidence that NGO leaders are very concerned with this kind of competition in their relations with executive officials, studies of legislative lobbying indicate that there is a basis for NGO concern for press influence on legislators. Milbrath indicates that reporters are in as strong a position as most lobbyists to influence government decisions.[5] De Varies reports that "Some of the most effective lobbyists in the [Michigan] capitol are the reporters. They not only have unlimited access to the floor, but direct access to the Members during and after the sessions. I think reporters have more to do with legislation that passes than do the lobbyists."[6]

Fourth, the press may upset effective consultations between NGO leaders and officials by giving them too much publicity since it is generally agreed that a group is most effective when it is consulting officials on subjects which are not perceived as major public issues.[7] "On well-publicized matters" according to Milbrath, "the official's concern with the maintenance of his public image and support from constituents outweighs in-dividual *quid pro quo* relationships."[8]

Direct Influence. The efforts of nongovernmental organiza-tions to mobilize public support for their policies may also be thwarted by the press. Reporters play a key role in the public relations campaigns of organizations because NGO leaders are dependent upon the press to reach the general public. NGO dissatisfaction with the press may be summarized under the charges that the press is sensational, biased, and inaccurate.

5 Milbrath, *op. cit.,* p. 191.
6 de Varies, *op. cit.,* p. 261.
7 Bernard C. Cohen, *The Influence of Non-Governmental Groups on Foreign Policy-Making* (Boston: World Peace Foundation, 1959), p. 12.
8 Milbrath, *op. cit.,* p. 194.

Much of the distortion of foreign policy information which NGO leaders see in the press results from the peculiar standards which the press applies to news. As one organization leader complains, "Reporters are constantly aware of the requirement of a good story; news must be exciting and interesting. This sometimes takes precedence over issues they should describe. They are more interested in gimmicks than content." For this reason, NGO leaders feel that there is sketchy or no reporting of many happenings in Washington that ought to be news.

Although the press claims that it is neutral in the sense that it does not represent one part of society, many NGO leaders feel that press coverage of foreign affairs is biased. One source of bias is the identification of the press with business elements in the community. The press itself is a business enterprise and depends extensively upon the paid advertisements of other businesses for financial support. Labor unions are very much concerned with this pro-business bias.[9] At least one reason for this bias in reporting labor affairs is the fact that the press itself has been hampered by strikes.[10]

Press bias may also stem from the stereotyped images which reporters and their editors have of certain groups. For example, the press may ignore many of the activities of religious groups simply because reporters and editors have rigid notions about the role of religious leaders. Women's groups are also very critical of their treatment in the press. As the leader of one such group states, "Everything we do is put on the women's page. The most profound announcements are put on the women's page!"

Finally, NGO leaders complain that there are numerous inaccuracies in the press. NGO leaders are concerned about inaccurate reports on their activities in the press not only because such reports may cost them support among the general public but also because such reports cause problems for them within their own organization. As one NGO leader indicates, "Re-

[9] George M. Harrison, speech before Associated Press Managing Editors, *Editors and Publishers,* Volume 90, No. 10, November 30, 1957, p. 10.
[10] Every April *Editor and Publisher* carries the annual report of the Labor Relations Committee of the American Society of Newspaper Editors on strikes against newspapers.

porters sometimes release statements which tend to set the membership against you." Another NGO leader chastizes the press for failing "to make clear who or what body is making a policy statement and whom they represent or do not represent." This problem arises from the fact that the reporter is writing for the general public, but the NGO leader is concerned not only with the general public but also with various audiences within his own organization.

In order to offset the distortion of organization information in the press, pressure groups hire their own press agents or public relations staff. These individuals attempt to cope with the distortion of organization news in two ways. First, they help the organization prepare news releases which the press will accept as general news. Second, they establish organization media which provide alternative means of getting information to their members and sometimes to the general public as well.

Press Criticisms of NGO Leaders

The press serves as an intermediary between the State Department and the public, and individual reporters covering diplomatic news sometimes assume the role of representatives of the public as well as disseminators of public information. As representatives of the general public, they may be contemptuous of the efforts of special interest and attitude groups to influence public policy. This concern may be reflected itself in the number of books by reporters written on the evils of lobbying.[11]

As pressure groups in Washington turn more and more to indirect means of influencing public officials, however, the publicity campaigns organized by these group leaders compete directly with the values which reporters attempt to achieve in disseminating information to the general public. The conflict stems primarily from the efforts of press agents to disguise the identity and objectives of the organizations preparing and disseminating biased and false information by getting the press

11 Several recent examples are James Deakin's *The Lobbyists* (Washington, D.C.: Public Affairs Press, 1966) and Drew Pearson's and Jack Anderson's *The Case Against Congress: A Compelling Indictment of Corruption on Capitol Hill* (New York: Simon and Schuster, 1968).

to carry their stories as a part of its regular news coverage. "Naturally he [the press agent] does not want to use advertising. The advertisement is obvious special pleading, and obvious special pleading . . . is relatively ineffectual. Consequently, the public relations counsel attempts to slip his propaganda into the press as news, features, or editorials; into the newsreels under the same guise; into the magazines as unbiased articles written by disinterested authorities . . . ."[12] There are several ways in which press agents attempt to use the news as a vehicle for their special purposes.

Direct Influence. First, NGO leaders try to influence individual editors and reporters to carry information which is favorable to their organization in the mass media. Although only a few of the reporters in this study have frequent contacts with NGO leaders, those who do feel that press agents are always on their backs. For this reason reporters regard NGO leaders as supplicants of the press, and they are highly suspicious of any information which a press agent offers them. As one reporter explains, "Ninety percent of them have a selfish motive. Nothing they furnish to you is worthwhile."

Although there is no evidence in this study of unethical pressure upon individual reporters to carry pressure group messages, the Senate Foreign Relations Committee found some questionable practices in its 1963 hearings on "Activities of Non-diplomatic Representatives of Foreign Principles in the United States."[13] An American public relations firm, Selvege and Lee, which has represented overseas companies of Portugal in Angola and Mozambique, for example, had offered free trips to Africa for black editors and writers in order to counter the bad image among Americans in general and among black Americans in particular of race relations in the Portuguese overseas territories. Although there was no explicit requirement that those who made the trips had to write favorable

---

12 Institute for Propaganda Analysis, "The Public Relations Counsel and Propaganda," *Propaganda Analysis*, Vol. I, August 1938, pp. 62-64.
13 Senate Committee on Foreign Relations, *Activities of Nondiplomatic Representatives of Foreign Principals in the United States*, Hearings, 88th Congress, 1st Session, 1963 (Washington, D.C.: Government Printing Office, 1963).

stories, this was admittedly the justification for the expenditures.[14]

The efforts by various groups to censor unfavorable material is probably less apparent to reporters than their efforts to disseminate favorable information. One reason for this is that such pressures are more likely to be felt by editors than reporters because editors are more conscious than reporters of the economic requirements of the news organization.

Indirect Influence. Second, even if reporters have no direct contacts with organization press agents, they are still quite conscious of the success of these agents in placing their material in the press. Apparently, a significant amount of the information in the press is provided by press associations, feature syndicates, and the distributors of pictures, films, and other items to the mass media. Pressure groups can successfully mask both their sponsorship and goals by paying these third parties to disseminate this material to their clients rather than having the organization's own press agents push the material with individual editors or reporters.

This technique was also covered in the hearings by the Senate Committee in 1963. According to that body of testimony, it is common practice for these distributors to peddle NGO material. For example, Hamilton Wright, who heads an American public relations firm which has represented Nationalist China and other foreign principals, testifies that his organization has prepared stories for the old New York Herald Tribune News Service, the North American Newspaper Alliance, and King Features Syndicate, and furnished films and newsreels to 20th Century Fox, Radiant Films, Metro-Goldwyn-Mayer newsreel, and Universal International newsreel.[15]

The fact that information can be fed into the mass media without direct sponsorship is of great value to pressure groups because it makes their information much more credible. In the 1958-1959 publicity contract with the Republic of Free China, for example, the Hamilton Wright Organization, Inc., played up this fact by assuring the sponsor that "Many of these editors

14 *Ibid.*, pp. 1152-1155.
15 *Ibid.*, part 7.

[leading U.S.A. newspaper syndicates, such as Associated Press, United Press International, Newspaper Enterprise Association, King Features Syndicate, Central Press Association, and North American Newspaper Alliance] give us direct assignments. In 75 percent of the releases, neither the editor of the newspaper nor the newspaper reader *has any knowledge of where the material originated*. Only the editor of the syndicate knows."[16]

Although the Senate Committee was primarily interested in the propaganda activities of foreign principals in these hearings, it was apparent from the testimony that domestic pressure groups actively engaged in the same practice. The overall result is that a significant portion of the information to which the domestic public is exposed on foreign affairs is prepared, not by reporters, but by pressure groups with a special interest or attitude to present to the public.

In addition to these efforts to place organization material in the regular news stories of the mass media, nongovernmental organizations have developed their own channels of communication. Although organization media are primarily designed for the purpose of reaching organization members, they also provide an outlet for dissemination of information to a wider public. Reporters may feel that the press is placed in a financial disadvantage because it must compete with these organization media. From this standpoint, "The press agent is commercially a competitor rather than professionally a collaborator of the press."[17]

Reporters accept NGO leaders' right to petition the Department and to use the free press to get their views before the public. What they object to is the effort of NGO leaders to obtain exclusive access to a particular decision and to disguise their sponsorship of material in the press. Reporters feel that the best way for them to cope with these problems is to remain free agents—free to publish or not to publish promotional material as their conscience dictates. "The reporter wants to know what he's doing and not to be taken in by press agents." One

16 *Ibid.*, p. 736.
17 Lee Trenholm, "Press Agents Irritate the Press," *The Public Opinion Quarterly*, Vol II, October 1938, pp. 671-677.

way the reporters attempt to insure that they are not used by NGO leaders for organization purposes is to avoid them. Since half of the reporters indicate that they have little or no contact with organization leaders, this avoidance behavior is quite prevalent.

CORRELATES OF PERCEIVED ANTAGONISM

The press and pressure groups are dependent upon one another for the resources needed to reach the general public. Pressure groups depend upon the press to reach wider audiences. The press depends upon these groups for information and financial support. Because of the different objectives of these two institutions, however, mutual dependence often leads to mutual advantage. Pressure groups may take advantage of their public relations resources to propagandize the public through the press. The press may take advantage of its communication network to distort the news about these groups. To what extent does this conflict between the press and pressure groups manifest itself in the form of perceived antagonism among individual reporters and NGO leaders?

There has been little effort to study this particular question. In a survey of the attitudes of 213 newspaper editors and 171 opinion leaders selected from *Who's Who in America*, Edward L. Bernays found in 1952 that opinion leaders were more critical than newspaper proprietors of the media.[18] The press is usually critical of NGOs, however, Walter de Varies suggests that there is a disparity between what is written in the press about the activities of pressure groups in the state legislature and what is said privately by reporters covering these activities. According to de Varies, "Reporters privately perceive lobbying as an essential and desirable ingredient in the legislative process."[19]

The data in Table 9.1 support the existence of perceived antagonism in the professional relations of reporters and NGO

18 J. Edward Gerald, *Social Responsibility of the Press* (Minneapolis, Minn.: The University of Minnesota Press, 1963), pp. 105-107.
19 de Varies, *op. cit.*, p. 254.

Table 9.1   Perceived Antagonism Among Reporters and NGO Leaders

	ALWAYS COOPER-ATIVE	USUALLY COOPER-ATIVE	MORE COOPER-ATIVE	BOTH COOPER-ATIVE AND ANTAG-ONISTIC	MORE ANTAG-ONISTIC	USUALLY ANTAG-ONISTIC	ALWAYS ANTAG-ONISTIC	NO RE-SPONSE	N
Perceived antagonism among reporters for NGO leaders	0	16	3	3	2	0	1	15	40
Perceived antagonism among NGO leaders for reporters	0	15	7	0	1	1	0	12	36

leaders. Moreover, the data indicate that there are differences among both reporters and NGO leaders in the extent to which they perceive antagonism in their relations with each other. Most of the literature which has a bearing on the relations between reporters and NGO leaders attribute the conflict between them to the different roles they play in the opinion-policy process; there has been no effort to explain why some reporters and NGO leaders are more likely than others to perceive antagonism in their relations. Of course it is possible that these differences among group members are random and have no importance. But it is also possible that these differences among group members may be associated with independent variables, such as education and type of organization, which might indicate sources of perceived antagonism among them.

Although few authors have addressed themselves to the question of which variables may account for these differences of perception among reporters and NGO leaders, it is possible that many of the variables which have been employed to explain the relations between the members of these two groups and third parties may be relevant. Perceived antagonism among each of these groups for counterposition holders may therefore be related to individual characteristics, stereotyped images, and positional variables as well as role expectation and attitudes.

By carrying out these tests, it may be possible to answer a number of interesting questions. First, is perceived antagonism between holders of these two positions related to the type of pressure groups or news organization they represent, or is it related to individual variables? If perceived antagonism is related to individual characteristics, this antagonism may be quite malleable. If, on the other hand, perceived antagonism is related to positional variables, the conflict which generates it may be institutionalized to the extent that the conflict beween these two groups is inherent in a democratic political system. Second, is perceived antagonism between these two sets of position holders associated with variables which reflect real or imaginary conflict? If perceived antagonism is related to variables which reflect direct confrontation between the two groups, this suggests that conflict has a substantial basis. If, however, perceived antagonism is related to variables with role expectations which are apparently unrelated to direct interaction, the conflict may be less important than the participants themselves suggest.

Biographical Data

There are variations among members of each group in age, amount of professional experience, and amount and type of education; and these variables may be related to perceived antagonism among reporters and NGO leaders. If conflicts between reporters and NGO leaders are cumulative, age and length of professional experience should be positively related to perceived antagonism among reporters and NGO leaders. If education has a moderating influence, it should be negatively related to perceived antagonism among reporters and NGO leaders.

The above assumptions suggest the following hypotheses:

1. Older individuals are more likely than their younger colleagues to perceive antagonism in their relations with counter position holders.

2. Individuals with more professional experience are more likely than their less experienced colleagues to perceive antagonism in their relations with counter position holders.

3. Individuals who have earned advanced academic degrees are less likely than their colleagues to perceive antagonism in their relations with counter position holders.[20]

20 Bauer et al. find that it is role more than background which determined

4. Individuals who majored in one of the social sciences as undergraduates in college are less likely than their colleagues to perceive antagonism in their relations with counter position holders.

The results indicate that older, more experienced individuals are no more likely than their colleagues to perceive antagonism in their relations with counter position holders. Neither the amount nor type of education received by reporters and NGO leaders is related to perceived antagonism toward each other.

Data on Stereotyped Images

Reporters and NGO leaders have varying images of the personal qualities and performance characteristics of counter position holders. If reporters and NGO leaders are mutually dependent upon one another, individuals who rate counter position holders lower on the qualities of intelligent, informed, skillful, responsible, and helpful are more likely than their colleagues to perceive antagonism in their relations with counter position holders.

The above assumptions suggest the following hypothesis:

5. Individuals who rate counter position holders lower on characterizations of intelligent, informed, skillful, responsible, and helpful are more likely than their colleagues to perceive antagonism in their relations with them.

The results of these tests indicate that perceived antagonism among reporters for NGO leaders is not related to these perceived characterizations of NGO leaders. Moreover, these tests suggest that perceived antagonism among NGO leaders for reporters is unrelated to the characterizations of reporters as intelligent, informed, and skillful. However, NGO leaders who are more likely than their colleagues to perceive reporters as lacking the characteristics of responsible and helpful are more likely than their colleagues to perceive antagonism in their relations with reporters.

the behavior of respondents because exceptional men have long since made up the deficiencies. See Raymond A. Bauer, Ithiel de Lola Pool, and Lewis Anthony Dexter, *American Business and Public Policy: The Politics of Foreign Trade* (New York: Atherton Press, 1964), p. 155.

Positional Data

The reporters in this study occupy similar positions in a variety of news organizations; the NGO leaders in this study occupy similar positions in a variety of pressure groups. These variables may be related to perceived antagonism among reporters and NGO leaders. If these two institutions perform conflicting roles in the opinion-policy process, individuals who occupy positions which are more sensitive to these pressures should be more likely than individuals in other positions to perceive antagonism in their relations with counter position holders.

The above assumptions suggest the following hypotheses:

6. Reporters who devote full time to foreign affairs are more likely than part-time reporters to perceive antagonism in their relations with NGO leaders.

7. Reporters who work for news organizations which stress interpretive reporting are less likely than those who work for news organizations which stress straight news reporting to perceive antagonism in their relations with NGO leaders.

8. Individuals who hold positions in which they have more frequent contacts with counter position holders than their colleagues are more likely than their colleagues to perceive antagonism in their relations with them.

9. Leaders of economic groups are more likely than leaders of other groups to perceive antagonism in their relations with reporters.[21]

10. Leaders of organizations which generally support Department policies are less likely than leaders of opposition groups to perceive antagonism in their relations with reporters.

11. Leaders of membership organizations are more likely than leaders of nonmembership groups to perceive antagonism in their relations with reporters.

12. Leaders of organizations which rely primarily upon the State Department for information are less likely than the leaders of other groups to perceive antagonism in their relations with reporters.

21 Bernard C. Cohen, *The Political Process and Foreign Policy* (Princeton, N.J.: Princeton University Press, 1957), p. 101.

Contrary to expectations, the results show that part-time diplomatic reporters are *more,* not less, likely than full-time reporters to perceive antagonism in their relations with NGO leaders. However, there is no evidence that reporters who work for news organizations which stress interpretive reporting are any more or less likely than those who work for news organizations which stress straight news reporting to perceive antagonism in their relations with NGO leaders. Moreover, there is no evidence that reporters who have more frequent contacts with NGO leaders perceive any more antagonism than their colleagues in their relations with them.

There is no apparent relationship between the frequency with which NGO leaders have contacts with reporters and perceived antagonism. NGO leaders who represent economic organizations are more likely than those representing other organizations to perceive antagonism in their relations with reporters, but neither the character of the organization's membership, nor its foreign policies, nor the extent to which it is dependent upon the State Department, seem to make any difference with respect to the perception of antagonism among them in relation to reporters.

Data on Role Expectations and Attitudes

The individuals in each of these groups hold varying role expectations and attitudes. If the more discretionary and political role expectations of reporters and NGO leaders conflict, then factors representing these role expectations should be associated with perceived antagonism. Moreover, if the conflict between reporters and NGO leaders is exacerbated by varying attitudes toward the informational requirements of policy on the one hand and the public on the other hand, these attitudes should also be associated with perceived antagonism.

The above assumptions suggest the following hypotheses:

13. Individuals who are more likely than their colleagues to hold discretionary and political role expectations for themselves are more likely than their colleagues to perceive antagonism in their relations with counter position holders.

14. Individuals who are less likely than their colleagues to

hold discretionary and political role expectations for counter position holders are more likely than their colleagues to perceive antagonism in their relations with counter position holders.

15. NGO leaders who are more likely than their colleagues to stress the informational requirements of policy and who are less likely than their colleagues to stress the informational requirements of the public are more likely than their colleagues to perceive antagonism in their relations with reporters.

16. Reporters who are less likely than their colleagues to stress the informational requirements of policy and who are more likely than their colleagues to stress the informational requirements of the public are more likely than their colleagues to perceive antagonism in their relations with NGO leaders.

The results of these tests suggest no relationship between perceived antagonism and the acceptance of one's own discretionary and political role expectations. However, reporters who reject the discretionary and political expectations of NGO leaders are more likely than their colleagues to perceive antagonism in their relations with these leaders, while NGO leaders who do not expect reporters to play objective and impartial roles are more likely than their colleagues to perceive antagonism in their relations with reporters.

The results also indicate that perceived antagonism among reporters for NGO leaders is unrelated to their attitudes toward the informational requirements of policy and the public. As expected, NGO leaders who are less likely than their colleagues to stress the informational requirements of the public are more likely than their colleagues to perceive antagonism in their relations with reporters. However, NGO leaders who are more likely to stress the informational requirements of State Department policy are less, not more, likely to perceive antagonism in their relations with reporters.

OPINION VERSUS POLICY PROCESS

This study suggests that perceived antagonism among foreign affairs reporters and NGO leaders is not cumulative. Older, more experienced individuals are no more or less likely than their colleagues to perceive antagonism in their relations with counter position holders. Moreover, there is no evidence that amount or type of education moderates perceived antagonism among these individuals.

The study does indicate, however, that perceived antagonism among reporters and NGO leaders is associated with attributes of the position or organizational affiliation of the individual. Reporters who devote only part of their time to foreign affairs coverage are more likely than reporters who devote full time to foreign affairs to perceive antagonism in their relations with NGO leaders. Leaders of economic groups are more likely than leaders of other nongovernmental organizations to perceive antagonism in their relations with foreign affairs reporters.

The study further shows that the functions of foreign affairs reporters and NGO leaders are often perceived as competitive. Although there is no apparent relationship between perceived antagonism and an individual's acceptance of his own discretionary and political role expectations, individuals who are less likely than their colleagues to accept the role expectations of counter position holders are more likely than their colleagues to perceive antagonism in their relations with them.

Finally, the study shows that while NGO leaders are dependent upon foreign affairs reporters, these reporters are not really dependent upon NGO leaders. Thus, NGO leaders who are more likely than their colleagues to rate reporters low on characterizations of responsible and helpful are more likely than their colleagues to perceive antagonism in their relations with reporters, but the same relationship does not hold for reporters' ratings and perceptions of NGO leaders. Also NGO leaders who are more suspicious of the discretion exercised in the name of informational requirements of policy and the public are more likely than their colleagues to perceive antagonism in their relations with reporters, but the same relationship does not hold for reporters' attitudes toward the information requirements of policy and the public and perceived antagonism for NGO leaders.

Perceived Antagonism Among NGO Leaders for Reporters

NGO leaders perceive antagonism in their relations with foreign affairs reporters for one of two reasons. In the first place, perceived antagonism among NGO leaders for reporters is associated with the suspicion that organization leaders do not receive full and complete information about foreign affairs in the press. In part this suspicion results from the conviction that the Department manipulates the press. For example, these NGO leaders generally reject the explanations given by the Department both for releasing and withholding information. Moreover, these NGO leaders feel that the press is either not as aggressive as it should be in ferreting out information which the State Department is withholding, or too anxious to report information which the Department has a stake in releasing.

Since the leaders of nongovernmental organizations are largely dependent upon the press for current information, they want an aggressive and inquiring press. The qualities which NGO leaders most prize in a reporter are his abilities to get behind official handouts and cover-up stories and to get the facts straight and in perspective. In their view, reporters "ought to be independent of existing policy. They ought to be willing to write what they learn on almost any subject. They ought to be abrasive to the extent that they can retain sources."

In the second place, perceived antagonism among NGO leaders for reporters is related to the way in which the press treats the activities of nongovernmental organizations in general news stories. NGO leaders contend that reporters are unhelpful or irresponsible either when they refuse to cover organization activities in foreign affairs or when they put organization activities in a bad light. The major indictment of the press by NGO leaders is that it is not objective. As one NGO leader put it, "We have the worst interpretive press in the free world." Another stated that "When newsmen try to interpret, they miss the boat altogether."

Of course some nongovernmental organizations rely more than others upon the press. Cohen argues that, although all groups communicate with their constituents, economic groups are more likely than other organizations to utilize the press because they find it more necessary to justify their interests to the general public.[22] If this is true, it helps to explain why the leaders of economic organizations are more likely than other groups to perceive antagonism in their relations with reporters.

Of the two grounds for perceived antagonism among NGO leaders for reporters, the second is probably the more important one. Most NGO leaders have little or no personal contact with the reporters upon whom they ultimately depend as a source of information on foreign affairs. NGO leaders pick up their information from the media itself. However, most NGO leaders do become personally involved with reporters when they use the press to disseminate information to the general public.

Perceived Antagonism Among Reporters for NGO Leaders

Foreign affairs reporters perceive antagonism in their relations with pressure groups because reporters feel that there is a conflict between their role and the role of NGO leaders in the opinion-policy process. Reporters who are more likely than their colleagues to reject the role expectations of NGO leaders are more likely than their colleagues to perceive antagonism in their relations with them. Why do reporters feel that their role and the role of NGO leaders conflict? What role expectations for NGO leaders do they find most objectionable?

The basic reason why reporters perceive a conflict between their role and the role of NGO leaders is manifest. Reporters regard the press as an essential part of democratic government; they regard pressure groups as a threat to that system. The next question is not so easy to answer: What role or activities by pressure groups do foreign affairs reporters find most objectionable?

Cohen argues that "Reporters seem to see themselves in competition with interest groups and other expressions of public opinion." According to Cohen, this competition manifests itself in the participant roles which reporters attribute to the press (such as representative of the public, critic of government, advocate of policy, and policy-maker) and "which parallel the roles that are commonly ascribed to interest groups." This sug-

22 *Ibid.*

gests that reporters perceive the competition between the press and pressure groups arising out of their efforts to influence policy makers rather than out of their efforts to educate the public. The data in this study suggest a different interpretation.

There are at least two reasons why Cohen's reasoning cannot be accepted for the individuals in this study. First, most of these foreign affairs reporters do not accept the "participant roles" as part of their job; at most they regard these roles as natural but incidental consequences of their work, and those reporters who are more likely than their colleagues to accept participant roles are no more or less likely than their colleagues to perceive antagonism in their relations with NGO leaders. Second, these foreign affairs reporters object most to role expectations for NGO leaders in the opinion-forming (not the policy-making) process. For example, reporters who are less likely than their colleagues to feel that NGO leaders should educate the general public are more likely than their colleagues to perceive antagonism in their relations with NGO leaders.

This evidence suggests that although reporters may be concerned with pressure group efforts to influence policy directly, perceived antagonism for NGO leaders is chiefly related to the suspicion which NGO leaders arouse in reporters when they seek to influence policy indirectly by propagandizing the general public through the press. As Cohen indicates, most foreign affairs reporters feel that they have a responsibility for providing the public with an objective account of foreign policies and events. In the minds of most of these reporters, pressure groups hinder, rather than help, them because these groups are always trying to sell something.

Since NGO leaders are generally regarded as biased sources of information, some reporters do not use NGO material at all, and many others report information received from pressure groups only when it is generated by them for their own purposes. The press as an institution may be dependent upon pressure groups for financial support, but many foreign affairs reporters regard pressure groups and their leaders as irrelevant to newsgathering in Washington. They cope with the bias of pressure groups simply by "sloughing off" or "playing down" their views. This helps to explain both why foreign affairs reporters encounter NGO leaders so infrequently and why NGO leaders in turn feel that the press is so biased.

The fact that foreign affairs reporters are so independent of pressure groups may raise yet another question: Why do they perceive antagonism in their relations with NGO leaders at all? Part of the answer to this question must be that many of them do not perceive antagonism in their relations with NGO leaders because such relations are virtually nonexistent. Part-time foreign affairs reporters are more likely than full-time diplomatic reporters to perceive antagonism in their relations with NGO leaders because these part-time reporters have more contact with NGO leaders and because NGO leaders are apparently more effective in domestic than foreign affairs.

* * *

The above discussion of relations between reporters and NGO leaders underscores differences between the press and pressure groups in the opinion-policy process. In this addendum several comparisons between the press and pressure groups on the one hand and foreign affairs officials on the other hand will be considered.

In the first place, the literature suggests that the relationship between the press and foreign policy is more viable than the relationship between pressure groups and foreign policy. For example, Cohen refers to "the continuous and intimate interaction that takes place between the press and the other institutions of government as distinguished from the intermittent and politically limited or segmented contact that characterizes interest group or individual participation in policy-making."[23] How accurate is this description of relations between the State Department, the press, and pressure groups?

The data in this study indicate that although foreign affairs reporters generally spend more time than NGO leaders do in the State Department, and although they contact information and policy officers in the Department more frequently than NGO leaders do, reporters do not necessarily have any more intimate or continuous contacts than NGO leaders with in-

[23] Cohen, *The Press, op. cit.*, p. 31.

dividual officials. In this connection it is important to remember that there are more NGO leaders than reporters. Moreover, these reporters are essentially generalists; they see many different officials on many different problems. NGO leaders specialize on problems which concern the interests or attitudes of their particular organization. The contacts of NGO leaders with individual officials who conduct policies in which these organizations have a special interest are probably no less frequent and intimate than the interaction which foreign affairs reporters have with individual officials.

In the second place, a number of reporters and press officers in this study argue that reporters are better informed than NGO leaders on foreign affairs. However, the evidence suggests that this comparison is difficult if not impossible to make because the press and pressure groups seek essentially different kinds of information. The press emphasizes current news; it has an intense interest in the day-to-day changes in foreign affairs which constitute headline news for broad segments of the American public. NGO leaders are primarily concerned with basic foreign policy developments which may affect organization interests. The public requires both kinds of information in order to insure that foreign policy is being made on a democratic basis.

Chapter 10

Conclusion

THIS BOOK HAS BEEN concerned with the interactions among four key groups in the opinion-policy process: State Department policy officers; State Department information officers; foreign affairs reporters; and the leaders of nongovernmental organizations. Although cooperation among these groups has been described in some detail, the main focus of this study has been on the conflicts between them. The objectives of the study have been: (1) to describe the pattern of perceived antagonism among these counter position holders, (2) to identify sources of perceived antagonism among these groups, and (3) to discuss the significance of these correlates of perceived antagonism for theories of conflict between democracy and foreign policy.

PATTERNS OF PERCEIVED ANTAGONISM

The study shows that all groups perceive antagonism as well as cooperation in their relations with counter position holders. The overall pattern of perceived antagonism among these groups is shown in Figure 10.1. The average amount of perceived antagonism among members of a dyad is represented in Figure 10.1 by the length of the arrows between the two groups. These averages are based on a seven point scale running from a low of 0 (always cooperative) to a high of 6 (always antagonistic). The average scores are generally low both because many

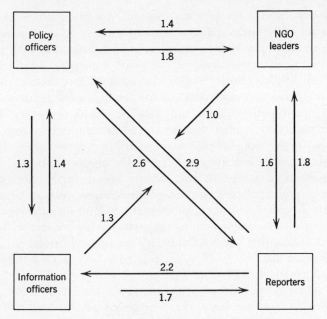

Figure 10.1   Average amount of perceived antagonism between counter position holders. Scale: one unit of perceived antagonism equals two centimeters. 0 = always cooperative; 1 = usually cooperative; 2 = more cooperative; 3 = both cooperative and antagonistic; 4 = more antagonistic; 5 = usually antagonistic; 6 = always antagonistic.

individuals are reluctant to admit that their relations with others are antagonistic and because whenever possible these individuals deal with those with whom they get along best.

Figure 10.1 illustrates the general finding that some groups are much more likely than others to perceive antagonism in their relations with counter position holders. The diagram shows that State Department information and policy officers are more likely to perceive antagonism in their relations with foreign affairs reporters than they are with NGO leaders. At the same time, reporters are more likely than NGO leaders to perceive antagonism in their relations with Department information and policy officers. Perceived antagonism is more prevelant among policy officers and reporters than it is among information officers and reporters. Policy officers perceive less antagonism in their relations with information officers than reporters; but information officers perceive no more or less antagonism in their relations with policy officers than reporters. NGO leaders are more likely to perceive antagonism in their relations with policy officers and reporters than they are with information officers.

These findings indicate that the most salient conflict in the opinion-policy process arises out of the relations between State Department policy officers and foreign affairs reporters. These findings further suggest that perceived antagonism among other groups in the opinion-policy relationship are somehow linked to this conflict. This notion is partially supported by the inter-correlations of perceived antagonism among these four groups. Among policy officers, perceived antagonism for information officers is correlated with perceived antagonism for reporters, and perceived antagonism for reporters is associated with perceived antagonism for NGO leaders. Among reporters, perceived antagonism for policy officers is related to perceived antagonism for information officers, and perceived antagonism for information officers is correlated with perceived antagonism for NGO leaders. As intermediaries between policy officers and reporters, information officers are apparently more discriminating than either of these two groups in their perceived antagonism for counter position holders since none of the perceptions of information officers are intercorrelated. By the same token, NGO leaders are less discriminating than other groups since NGO leaders, who are more likely than their colleagues to perceive antagonism in their relations with any one of the other three groups, are more likely than their colleagues to perceive antagonism in their relations with the other two counter position holders.

Figure 10.1 also points up the symmetry between each dyad in amount of perceived antagonism shared by groups. This gives the impression that the conflict between them is well-understood on both sides of the relationship. Despite this symmetry, some interesting patterns emerge in the comparison of perceived antagonism among paired groups. Information officers appear to be more likely than policy officers to perceive antagonism in their relations. Reporters seem to be more likely than State Department officers to perceive antagonism in their relations. Policy officers, information officers, and reporters appear to be more likely than NGO leaders to perceive antagonism in their relations. How is the pattern of perceived antagonism among these groups to be explained?

CORRELATES OF PERCEIVED ANTAGONISM

The study shows that perceived antagonism among these four groups stems from varying role expectations and attitudes. State Department officers, for example, are more conscious than reporters and NGO leaders of the informational requirements of policy. This does not mean, however, that this study supports Nimmo's contention that the competition between individuals in some of these groups can be predicted on the basis of their acceptance or rejection of certain discretionary and political segments of their own role or the role of others. One reason for this is that it is difficult to determine which role segments are more discretionary and political than others. Another reason is that role expectations may not reflect role behavior.

This study also indicates that some individuals in these groups perceive more antagonism than others in their relations with counter position holders. Positional variables are especially important in explaining these variations among the individuals of each group in their relations with counter position holders. One of the most striking findings in this study is that the relations between information and policy officers in the State Department on the one hand and foreign affairs reporters and NGO leaders on the other hand are quite different.

Some authors have tried to account for variations in perceived antagonism among one set of position holders by arguing that the conflicting roles of groups in the opinion-policy process are more manageable by some individuals than others. Cohen, for example, argues that officials who feel more confident in their relations with reporters are less likely than their colleagues to perceive antagonism in their relations with reporters. Although it was not possible to test this hypothesis directly, there was no relationship in this study between the variations in individuals' age, competence, education, and experience on the one hand and perceived antagonism on the other except in the case of information officers.

Indeed this study suggests that perceived characteristics are more important than the actual characteristics of individuals in explaining perceived antagonism among counter position holders. Perceived characteristics are associated with perceived antagonism under two conditions. First, this relationship occurs if one group questions the legitimacy of the role played by the other group in the opinion-policy process. Second, this relationship occurs whenever one group is clearly dependent on another. Thus, although policy officers characterize reporters as unhelpful and even irresponsible, this stereotype of reporters is not associated with perceived antagonism for reporters because policy officers accept the role of reporters in the opinion-policy process and do not feel very dependent upon them.

The correlation between inter- and intra-group variations in role expectations, attitudes, positions, individual characteristics, and perceived characteristics on the one hand, and perceived antagonism among these groups on the other hand provides some empirical evidence for suggesting some of the sources of conflict among these groups. These findings have been described in detail in the last four chapters. It is only necessary here to bring these findings together for the purpose of explaining the overall pattern of perceived antagonism among these four groups.

Perceived Antagonism Among State Department Officers and Reporters

Perceived antagonism is more prevalent in the relations of State Department policy officers and foreign affairs reporters than it is in the relations of any other dyad. Sources of perceived antagonism between these two groups are not difficult to discover. On the one hand, policy officers are responsible for the conduct of foreign relations. They are primarily concerned with the policy-making process. Their participation in the opinion-forming process is largely passive and instrumental. On the other hand, diplomatic reporters are responsible for informing the general public on foreign affairs. They are mainly interested in the opinion-forming process. Their participation in the policy-making process is incidental to their main task.

In view of the divergent roles of policy officers and reporters, it is not surprising that they have varying attitudes toward the requirements of State Department information policy. Policy officers naturally place foreign policy requirements ahead of domestic opinion needs; reporters give priority to the needs of the domestic public. These varying perceptions are the principal source of perceived antagonism among policy officers and reporters.

The conflict between policy officers and reporters is most salient for those policy officers who deal with issues which are most sensitive to publicity because they fear that reporters will disclose information which will make the conduct of foreign relations even more difficult for them. This conflict is most noticeable for those reporters who feel compelled to analyze and interpret as well as report foreign affairs because they find that policy officers are not very helpful in providing the kind of critical information and opinions they need.

Information officers in the State Department serve as brokers between policy officers and reporters. Although they owe their primary allegiance to the Department, they feel an obligation to keep the public informed on foreign affairs and to keep the Department informed on public views. Since information officers serve Department interests and are more likely than reporters to accept the need to manipulate information to serve policy ends, they run into conflict with reporters. Since information officers have the responsibility for making the case within the Department for the release of information to reporters and others, they come into conflict with policy officers.

This helps to explain why information officers perceive as much antagonism in their relations with policy officers as reporters, although both policy officers and reporters perceive less antagonism in their relations with information officers than they do with each other. This also helps to explain why perceived antagonism among information officers for policy officers is unrelated to perceived antagonism for reporters, while perceived antagonism among policy officers for information officers is associated with perceived antagonism for reporters and perceived antagonism among reporters for information officers is correlated with perceived antagonism for policy officers.

The conflict between reporters and State Department officers is more salient for the former than the latter because reporters are more dependent upon Department officers than *vice versa*. Moreover, reporters perceive less antagonism in their relations with information officers than policy officers because they have quite different expectations for and generally depend less upon information officers than policy officers. This may also explain why information officers generally get along better than policy officers with reporters. Interestingly, it is those information officers with prior experience as reporters who are most likely to perceive antagonism in their relations with reporters.

Perceived antagonism among information and policy officers occurs at higher echelons in the Department because that is where the most difficult issues of information policy must be resolved. Policy officers readily admit this conflict but information officers are reluctant to do so because they depend to a large extent upon their personal relationships with policy officials for whatever influence they have on the information policies of the State Department. Indeed, the lack of status for information officers in the Department is a distinct source of perceived antagonism among them for policy officers.

Perceived Antagonism Among State Department Officers, Reporters, and NGO Leaders.

NGO leaders represent highly differentiated segments of the American public. They are primarily concerned with translating their particular group's interests and attitudes into public policy. While they engage in direct consultations with Department officers on foreign policy issues, they have tried increasingly to influence policy decisions indirectly by building general public support for organization policies. By lobbying on behalf of their views in both the policy-making and opinion-forming processes, they come into conflict with both State Department officers and foreign affairs reporters.

The fact that NGO leaders simultaneously use both policy-making and opinion-forming channels to further their special interests and attitudes may explain why they, more than any other group, view the opinion-policy process as a composite whole. NGO leaders tend to evaluate the whole system, depending on how responsive it is to their influence. This helps to explain why perceived antagonism among NGO leaders for any one group is correlated with perceived antagonism among them for all other groups.

For example, NGO leaders who support Department policies expect policy officers both to be forthcoming and to take public views into account and expect reporters to be objective in reporting events. However, leaders of opposition groups feel that neither the press nor the Department informs the public adequately. Although NGO leaders perceive the greatest conflict between their role and that of information officers, there is less perceived antagonism among NGO leaders for information officers than for either policy officers or reporters because NGO leaders do not rely extensively upon them for anything.

Perceived antagonism among other groups for NGO leaders is based partially on the notion that pressure groups are inherently evil and undemocratic, and partially on the fact that some of these groups bring unwanted pressure to bear on the State Department and the press. Perceived antagonism among policy officers and reporters is associated with the notion that pressure groups are unhelpful in a democracy. Since policy officers have more frequent contacts with NGO leaders who support Department policies, it is those with infrequent contacts with NGO leaders who are more likely than their colleagues to perceive antagonism in their relations with them. Since pressure groups are more effective in domestic than foreign affairs, it is those reporters who cover domestic as well as foreign affairs who are likely to perceive antagonism in their relations with NGO leaders. Perceived antagonism among reporters for NGO leaders and information officers is linked because they view them both as press agents.

The study suggests that information officers are less likely than policy officers to perceive antagonism in their relations with NGO leaders because they see NGO leaders as allies of the Department in building support for Department policies. Apparently, it is the information officers with prior experience as reporters who perceive antagonism in their relations with NGO leaders.

Department officers are sensitive to the criticism of outside groups; this probably explains why perceived antagonism among them for reporters and NGO leaders is associated. Nevertheless, there is more antagonism between Department officers and reporters than there is between Department officers and NGO leaders. Department officers are especially concerned with reporters because they have learned that public opposition to their policies follows the headlines. Reporters are more concerned than NGO leaders with their relations with Department officers because they are more dependent than pressure group leaders upon access to these particular officials in order to perform their job.

DEMOCRACY VERSUS FOREIGN POLICY

In the introduction to this book, it was suggested that the requirements of foreign policy-making and public opinion formation in a democracy might be incompatible because of conflicting demands for: (1) secrecy and publicity, (2) speed and deliberation, and (3) unity and dissent. To what extent does perceived antagonism among these key groups in the opinion-policy process arise from these varying requirements?

The study supports the notion that democracy and foreign policy require conflicting information policies. Department officers, who have a primary responsibility for the nation's foreign policies, perceive antagonism in their relations with reporters because the press seeks the full disclosure of information. Reporters, who have a primary responsibility for informing the public, perceive antagonism in their relations with Department officers because these officials manipulate information for policy reasons.

Moreover, this study provides some evidence that the element of time is a source of conflict between democracy and foreign policy. Department policy officers feel that there is no time for consultations with reporters and NGO leaders because foreign events will not wait for public advice and consent. Reporters feel that Department officers should release information immediately so that the public will have an opportunity to be heard before the policy is fully formed. Department officers may perceive less antagonism for NGO leaders than reporters because the former are less likely than the latter to expect the immediate disclosure of information.

Above all, this study supports the notion that the conflict between foreign policy and democracy arises out of the varying requirements for unity and dissent. Department officers perceive antagonism in their relations with interpretive reporters and leaders of opposition groups because these individuals bring the assumption of mass support for Department policies into question. These reporters and NGO leaders perceive antagonism in their relations with Department officers because the latter want public support, not a public dialogue. The evidence suggests, for example, that reporters are less concerned with formal efforts of the Department to withhold information than they are with the failure of officials to talk frankly with reporters, even on a background basis.

Thus, sources of perceived antagonism among discrete individuals, playing key roles in the opinion-policy process, support the idea that the conflict between these groups is inherent in the democratic management of foreign affairs. However, this does not mean the democratic form of government is any more or less suitable than other forms of government for the conduct of foreign affairs.

After all, much of the apparent conflict between democracy and foreign policy is actually derived from the juxtaposition of the domestic and foreign requirements of policy. The fact is that the requirements for the internal functioning of the state and the requirements placed upon the state by its external environment are often conflicting. Under these circumstances any form of government would appear to clash with the external demands placed upon it. The object of foreign policy is not to insure that external requirements will be given a priority, but rather to achieve the right balance between domestic and foreign considerations.

Democracy may place more emphasis than autocracy on genuine communications between government and the public, but international communications makes it increasingly dubious that any modern government can expect to hide the essential facts about its foreign policy from its domestic public. Likewise, democracy may open the way for more dissent than other forms of government, but it is not at all clear whether open self-criticism of foreign policy has a more or less destabilizing effect on the conduct of foreign relations in the long run. The state which allows internal dissatisfaction to build over a long period may find its discretion even more impaired than the state which allows dissent on a continuing basis.[1]

In short, the conflict between democracy and foreign policy reflects in part the larger clash between the internal and external demands on foreign policy makers. Democratic government fosters expectations which bring this conflict into the open, but that may be *more*, not less, conducive to an effective foreign policy.

[1] Kenneth N. Waltz, *Foreign Policy and Democratic Politics: The American and British Experience* (Boston: Little, Brown and Company, 1967), pp. 306-311. Comparative studies of national adaptation in democratic and autocratic societies seem to offer the best prospects for resolving this question. See Stephen A. Salmore and Charles F. Hermann, "Foreign Policy as a Dependent Variable in the U.S. and the U.S.S.R.," an unpublished paper prepared for an American Political Science Association Round Table in The Comparative Study of Foreign Policy, September 1969, pp. 18-19.

Appendix A

Research Design

The research on this book began with a survey of the literature on the opinion-policy process, especially the literature on relations between the State Department, the press, and pressure groups. This review of literature was followed by field research, including an examination of unpublished documentary materials in the State Department and two sets of interviews with policy and opinion elites. The first set of approximately 100 interviews consisted of exploratory talks between July 1962 and March 1964 with about 80 officials in the State Department and approximately 20 reporters and leaders of nongovernmental organizations. The second set of 156 interviews consisted of a highly structured questionnaire administered between June and September of 1966 to 40 State Department policy officers, 40 Department information officers, 40 foreign affairs reporters, and 36 leaders of nongovernmental organizations.

The forty policy officers represented a stratified random sample of officials holding positions as country officers, division chiefs, country directors, office directors or higher level positions in the State Department.[1] The forty policy officers included 15 officers representing a 7 percent sample of desk officers and division chiefs; 15 officers representing a 20 percent sample of country and office directors, and 10 officers

[1] The policy positions in the State Department are defined as those listed in the May 1966 Telephone Directory of the State Department, as amended by the list of new "Country Director" positions on p. 7 of the May 1966 issue of the Department of State Newsletter. For the purpose of this study the State Department was defined so as to exclude positions in autonomous agencies, such as the United States Information Agency (USIA), the Arms Control and Disarmament Agency (ACDA), and the Agency for International Development (AID).

at the bureau and department level, including all but one of the five regional assistant secretaries. At the division and office level, officers were selected from regional and functional bureaus so that they were roughly proportional to the number of policy positions in regional and functional bureaus on the overall list.

The forty information officers in this study included virtually all of the officials in the Department who hold positions as office directors, public affairs advisors, or higher level positions and whose primary responsibility is to handle public relations for the State Department.[2] Twenty of these position holders were located in the Bureau of Public Affairs or "P" area. The other twenty positions were scattered throughout the State Department since most top level officials in the regional and functional bureaus as well as the Department Secretariat had their own information officer.

Of the 40 foreign affairs reporters, 25 constitute virtually all of the "regulars" who covered diplomatic news for the wire services, weekly news magazines, radio and television networks, and newspapers; the remaining 15 reporters represented a stratified random sample of syndicated columnists as well as reporters for the trade and ethnic press, the newspaper chains, and the news services on the "Correspondents List" of the State Department.[3] In the case of reporters who were not Department regulars or columnists, the reporter who was most likely to cover foreign affairs stories for the selected news organization was interviewed.

Of the 36 NGO leaders, 32 were chosen from "The List of Selected National Organizations" compiled by the Office of Public Services in the State Department.[4] Organizations were selected from this list so as to insure that each type of pressure group (business, labor, religious, etc.) was represented, roughly proportional to its numbers on the overall list and to make certain that those groups which frequently represent other organizations in the same category (U.S. Chamber of Commerce, AFL-CIO, National Council of Churches, etc.) were included. The representatives of four groups not well represented on the Department's

[2] The information positions in the State Department are also based on the May 1966 Telephone Directory of the State Department. Officers in the Historical Office were not included, and some information specialists of lower rank, such as organization liaison officers, were included because of the importance of their work for this study.

[3] Office of News, Department of State, "Correspondents List," November 1965.

[4] Office of Public Services, Department of State, "List of Selected U.S. National Organizations," June 10, 1965. The criteria for placing organizations on this list are found on p. 9 of Chapter 7.

list were also interviewed. As in the case of reporters, the individual who was most likely to handle the organization's dealings with the State Department was interviewed.

Separate questionnaires were prepared in advance for each of these groups. These questionnaires were designed both to obtain a balanced view of the relations among the groups and to elicit information required to test hypotheses concerning perceived antagonism among them. These generalizations were either drawn from the literature on policy and opinion elites or generated by the author on the basis of the first set of exploratory interviews.

Four types of data were required in order to test these propositions. First, respondents were asked for biographical information, such as age, education, and experience. This type of information was solicited mainly from reporters and NGO leaders during the interviews because it was already available on State Department officers in *The Biographic Register* of the State Department and related agencies.

Second, an instrument was included in each questionnaire which taped the stereotyped images of these groups for one another. Respondents were asked to rate the individuals in the other three positions on the qualities of intelligent, informed, skillful, responsible, and helpful.

Third, a number of questions were asked about the character of the offices held by these individuals in their respective organizations. Information and policy officers occupy a variety of positions or offices in the State Department; NGO leaders and reporters occupy similar positions in a variety of nongovernmental organizations.

Fourth, all respondents were asked a number of open-ended questions concerning their role expectations for each of the four groups. In addition, all respondents were asked (1) the same four sets of eight different questions about their role expectations for each group and (2) the same set of ten questions concerning their attitudes toward the withholding and releasing of information by the State Department.

A brief pretest indicated that respondents in each population were familiar with the language used and prepared to answer the questions asked in their questionnaire. It was assumed that these respondents also shared a common understanding of such key terms as "facts" and "interpretation," since some of the hypotheses to be tested were based on distinctions between these terms. However, the assumption of intersubjectivity was not warranted in the case of the illustrative terms above. The four questionnaires are found in Appendices B through E.

The interviews were all conducted by the author. They usually lasted at least one hour. Most of the questions were given orally in order to encourage respondents to elaborate on their answers, and considerable care was taken to record at the time what the respondents actually said. Respondents were asked to mark a number of scaled items in the questionnaire, but these items were set up so that they could be left with the respondent in the event that the interview schedule could not be completed in the time available. In a few cases respondents filled out the entire questionnaire themselves.

A number of internal checks were run to determine the reliability of the interview data. These checks indicated that no discernible bias had been introduced either by the sequence in which individuals were interviewed or by the manner in which the questionnaire was administered. For example, it did not seem to matter whether the author filled out the scaled items for the respondent during the interview or whether the respondent later filled out these items for himself.

Since variations in individual characteristics, stereotyped images, positional factors, and role expectations and attitudes may help to explain the relations among policy and opinion elites, they are the independent variables in this study. There are two types of independent variables: continuous and discontinuous. The data on role expectations and attitudes are continuous and these variables are treated as such. The data on stereotyped images are continuous, but these variables are dichotomized. Biographical and positional data may be either continuous or discontinuous, and these variables are all dichotomized. When variables based on continuous data are dichotomized, they are divided as close to the median value as possible. When variables based on discontinuous data are dichotomized, the basis for the classification is explained in the text.

Perceived antagonism among policy and opinion elites is what this research is designed to explain; consequently, measures of perceived antagonism among these position holders are the dependent variables in this study. In order to measure perceived antagonism among these position holders, each respondent was asked to characterize his relations with counter position holders as always cooperative, usually cooperative, compatible, usually antagonistic, or always antagonistic. If the respondent answered compatible, he was then asked whether he thought that his relations with these counter position holders were more cooperative or more antagonistic. Some respondents insisted that their relations with counter position holders were both cooperative and antagonistic. Viewed as a whole, these responses fall along a continuum: always cooperative; usually cooperative; compatible—more cooperative; compatible—both cooperative and antagonistic; compatible—more antagonistic; usually antagonistic; always antagonistic.

The tests employed in this research for determining whether two variables are related require that both variables be either continuous or discontinuous. Thus, in tests involving independent variables which are continuous, the dependent variable remains continuous. However, in tests involving independent variables which are dichotomized, the dependent variables must be dichotomized. In these cases, the distinction between those in each group who perceive antagonism in their relations with counter position holders and those who do not is drawn as close to the median value as possible.

The primary aim of this research is to establish whether there is a significant relationship between the independent variables and perceived antagonism. A significant relationship is said to exist if the probability of its occurring by chance is less than one in twenty (.05). When continuous variables are used, the probabilities are calculated from Pearson's correlation coefficient (r). When dichotomized variables are used, the probabilities are based on chi-square values (χ^2) or Fisher's exact test, whichever is appropriate.[5]

The secondary aim of this research is to state the degree of relationship between variables. When continuous data are used, Pearson's r is the measure of degree of association. Pearson's r is .00 when there is no relationship between variables, and attains the limits of ± 1.00 when the relationship is perfect. When dichotomous data are used, the contingency coefficient (C) is the measure of degree of association. The C is .00 when there is no relationship between variables; if the C based on dichotomous variables is divided by .707, it attains the limits of ± 1.00 when the relationship is perfect.[6]

In view of the large number of variables in this study, these calculations are not reported in the text. However, selected findings in each chapter are reported in Appendix F. In each instance, the number of cases (N), the chi-square value if calculated (χ^2), the probability (P), and the direction and degree of relationship (r or C) will be reported. From time to time, respondents are quoted to illustrate a finding; however, no citations accompany these quotations because all respondents were assured at the beginning of the interview that the information and opinions expressed by them during the interview would be attributed neither to them personally nor, in the case of NGO leaders and reporters, to their respective organizations.

---

5 If the requirements for the chi-square test are not met, Fisher's exact test is performed. See S. Siegel, *Nonparametric Statistics for the Behavioral Sciences* (New York: McGraw-Hill Book Company, 1956).

6 Herbert M. Blalock, *Social Statistics* (New York: McGraw-Hill Book Company, 1960), p. 230.

Appendix B

Interview Schedule–Information Officers

Name _____   Position _____

In the first set of questions, I wish to explore the functions performed in this country by information officers in the State Department.

1. How would you describe your job? What are the most important things you do? What part, if any, do you play in the formation of public opinion on foreign affairs in this country? What part, if any, do you play in the formation of foreign policies in this country?

2. To what extent do you feel that *information officers* should or should not do the following things:

	Check One				
	ABSO-LUTELY MUST	PREFER-ABLY SHOULD	MAY OR MAY NOT*	PREFER-ABLY SHOULD NOT	ABSO-LUTELY MUST NOT
	1	2	3	4	5	6

a. Interpret the facts underlying policy for the public?   _____

b. Advise policy-makers on information policies?   _____

300

c. Apply pressure within the Department for a more liberal information policy?

_____

d. Handle routine information activities for the State Department?

_____

e. Exercise discretion in timing the release of information to the public.

_____

f. Keep the public informed on policy deliberations prior to the time that formal policy statements are released?

_____

g. Participate actively in policy-making?

h. Systematically analyze general public opinion on foreign affairs?

_____

* If you answer "May or May Not," please indicate whether you feel that information officers (3) "should unless the situation precludes it" or (4) "should not unless the situation requires it."

3. What do you believe to be the extent of the State Department's obligation to inform the public? What are the sources of this obligation? What limits would you set on this obligation?

In this next set of questions, I wish to determine how compelling you find various reasons for releasing or withholding information.

4. To what extent do you feel that the Department should or should not do the following things:

Check One

	ABSO-LUTELY MUST	PREFER-ABLY SHOULD	MAY OR MAY NOT*	PREFER-ABLY SHOULD NOT	ABSO-LUTELY MUST NOT
	1	2	3	4	5	6

a. Release information because it may strengthen this government's negotiating position?

b. Release information because it may promote domestic political support for Department policies?

c. Release information because it may reduce the number of misleading speculations which are being made in public?

d. Release information because it may improve public understanding of existing programs and policies?

e. Release information because the public has a "right-to-know"?

f. Withhold information because it may embarrass friendly governments and their leaders?

g. Withhold information be-
cause it may discredit the
State Department and the
Administration in power?

_____

h. Withhold information because it may expose differences of opinion within the
Department and the government?

_____

i. Withhold information because it may endanger na-
tional security?

_____

j. Temporarily withhold information because it may require explanatory material
not yet available?

_____

* If you answer "May or May Not," please indicate whether you feel that the
Department (3) "should unless the situation precludes it" or (4) "should not
unless the situation requires it."

5. What do you feel are the most effective ways for the Department
to get its message to the public? What special difficulties, if any, do you
feel that the Department has in getting its message to the public?

6. Much of the information which is available to newsmen and the
leaders of nongovernmental organizations in the Department is provided on a "not-for-attribution" basis. What are the advantages and
disadvantages of making information available on this basis—both for
the Department and the public?

7. To what extent do you feel that public opinion is a factor in
foreign policy-making in this country? With respect to what types of
foreign policy do you feel that public opinion is most important? Least
important? Whose opinions are most important with respect to these
policies? Whose opinions are least important? How are these opinions
made known to the Department? To you? What would you regard as the
most reliable sources for information on the state of general public
opinion on foreign policy issues?

The next set of questions deals with the relations between information officers and policy officers.

8. What part, if any, do policy officers play in the formation of public opinion on foreign affairs in this country? How frequently do you encounter policy officers? What problems do policy officers create for you?

9. To what extent do you feel that policy officers should or should not do the following things:

Check One

	ABSO-LUTELY MUST	PREFER-ABLY SHOULD	MAY OR MAY NOT*	PREFER-ABLY SHOULD NOT	ABSO-LUTELY MUST NOT
	1	2	3	4	5	6

a. Determine what information is released to the public?

b. Inform information officers of policy deliberations prior to decisions?

c. Play a leading role in opinion-making in this country?

d. Take time off to meet with reporters and pressure group leaders?

e. Interpret United States national interests and the interests of foreign countries to domestic groups?

f. Take public opinion into account in the formation of foreign policy?

g. Solicit the views of pressure groups on policies affecting their special interests?

h. Solicit the views of nongovernmental experts on policies in their field of specialization?

---

* If you answer "May or May Not," please indicate whether you feel that
policy officers (3) "should unless the situation precludes it" or (4) "should
not unless the situation requires it."

10. What special qualities would you ascribe to a "good" policy
officer?

11. How would you rate the policy officers you deal with on the following qualities:

Intelligent	5	4	3	2	1	Unintelligent
Informed	5	4	3	2	1	Uninformed
Skillful	5	4	3	2	1	Unskillful
Helpful	5	4	3	2	1	Unhelpful
Responsible	5	4	3	2	1	Irresponsible

12. Would you describe the relations between information officers and
policy officers as

a. Always cooperative?
b. Usually cooperative?
c. Compatible?*
d. Usually antagonistic?
e. Always antagonistic?

* If you respond "compatible," please indicate whether you feel that relations
are "more cooperative" or "more antagonistic."

The next set of questions deals with the relations between information officers and reporters.

13. What part, if any, do reporters play in the formation of public opinions on foreign affairs in this country? How frequently do you encounter reporters? What problems do reporters create for you?

14. To what extent do you feel that reporters should or should not do the following things:

Check One

	ABSO-LUTELY MUST	PREFER-ABLY SHOULD	MAY OR MAY NOT*	PREFER-ABLY SHOULD NOT	ABSO-LUTELY MUST NOT
	1	2	3	4	5	6

a. Report the facts avoiding any interpretation whatever?

b. Interpret the facts for the public?

c.. Incorporate statements of Department policy in their material whether they agree or disagree with it?

d. Verify information obtained from unauthorized sources in the Department before publication in any form?

e. Write without regard for the editorial views of their news organization?

f. Work through Department information officers?

g. Attempt to influence policy officers?

h. Bring public views and
needs to the attention of
Department officers?

---

* If you answer "May or May Not," please indicate whether you feel that reporters (3) "should unless the situation precludes it" or (4) "should not unless the situation requires it."

15. What qualities do you ascribe to a "good" reporter?

16. How would you rate reporters you deal with on the following qualities:

a.	Intelligent	5	4	3	2	1	Unintelligent
b.	Informed	5	4	3	2	1	Uninformed
c.	Skillful	5	4	3	2	1	Unskillful
d.	Helpful	5	4	3	2	1	Unhelpful
e.	Responsible	5	4	3	2	1	Irresponsible

17. Would you describe the relations between information officers and reporters as

a. Always cooperative?
b. Usually cooperative?
c. Compatible?*
d. Usually antagonistic?
e. Always antagonistic?

* If you respond "compatible," please indicate whether you feel that relations are "more cooperative" or "more antagonistic."

The next set of questions deals with the relations between information officers and the leaders of nongovernmental organizations.

18. What part, if any, do the leaders of nongovernmental organizations play in the formation of public opinion on foreign affairs in this country? How frequently do you encounter the leaders of nongovernmental organizations? What problems do these leaders create for you?

19. To what extent do you feel that the leaders of nongovernment organizations should or should not do the following things:

Check One

	ABSO-LUTELY MUST	PREFER-ABLY SHOULD	MAY OR MAY NOT*	PREFER-ABLY SHOULD NOT	ABSO-LUTELY MUST NOT
	1	2	3	4	5	6

a. Exercise their own discretion in applying organization policies to current situations?

b. Consult the membership prior to the adoption of basic organization policies?

c. Prepare material of special interest for release in the organization media?

d. Help to educate the general public on foreign affairs?

e. Mobilize support within the organization for policies adopted by the leadership?

f. Propose adjustments of the organization's special interests in favor of national and possibly foreign interests?

g. Bring pressure to bear on members of Congress to support organization policies?

h. Submit organization views directly to policy officers in the State Department?

* If you answer "May or May Not," please indicate whether you feel that pressure group leaders (3) "should unless the situation precludes it" or (4) "should not unless the situation requires it."

20. What qualities would you ascribe to a "good" leader of a nongovernment organization?

21. How would you rate the leaders of nongovernment organizations you deal with on the following qualities:

a. Intelligent	5	4	3	2	1	Unintelligent
b. Informed	5	4	3	2	1	Uninformed
c. Skillful	5	4	3	2	1	Unskillful
d. Helpful	5	4	3	2	1	Unhelpful
e. Responsible	5	4	3	2	1	Irresponsible

22. Would you describe the relations between information officers and the leaders of nongovernmental organizations as

a. Always cooperative?
b. Usually cooperative?
c. Compatible?*
d. Usually antagonistic?
e. Always antagonistic?

* If you respond "compatible," please indicate whether you feel that relations are "more cooperative" or "more antagonistic."

23. What is your official title? How many years have you held the same general position? What rank do you presently hold?

24. How many years have you been with present organization? In this type of work? What has been your specialty?

25. Have you ever served as a policy officer? reporter? NGO leader? If so, in what capacity?

26. What is the highest academic degree which you have earned? Where did you receive it? What was your undergraduate major? How many years of formal schooling do you have beyond the Bachelor's degree?

Appendix **C**

Interview Schedule–Policy Officers

Name _____ Position _____

In the first set of questions, I wish to explore the functions performed by policy officers in the State Department.

1. How would you describe your job? What are the most important things you do? What part, if any, do you play in the formation of public opinion in this country? What part, if any, do *you* play in the formation of foreign policy?

2. To what extent do you feel that policy officers should or should not do the following things:

Check One

	ABSO-LUTELY MUST	PREFER-ABLY SHOULD	MAY OR MAY NOT*	PREFER-ABLY SHOULD NOT	ABSO-LUTELY MUST NOT
	1	2	3	4	5	6

a. Determine what information is released to the public?

b. Inform information officers of policy deliberations prior to decisions?

c. Play a leading role in opinion-making in this country?

_____

d. Take time off to meet with
reporters and pressure
group leaders?

_____

e. Interpret United States national interests and the interests of foreign countries
to domestic groups?

_____

f. Take public opinion into account in the formation of
foreign policy?

_____

g. Solicit the views of interest
groups on policies affecting
their special interests?

_____

h. Solicit the views of nongovernmental experts on policies in their field of specialization?

_____

* If you answer "May or May Not," please indicate whether you feel that
policy officers (3) "should unless the situation precludes it" or (4) "should not
unless the situation requires it."

3. What do you believe to be the extent of the State Department's
obligation to inform the public? What are the sources of this obligation?
What limits would you set on this obligation?

In the next set of questions, I wish to determine how compelling you find various reasons for releasing or withholding information.

4. To what extent do you feel that the Department should or should not do the following things:

Check One

	ABSO-LUTELY MUST	PREFER-ABLY SHOULD	MAY OR MAY NOT*	PREFER-ABLY SHOULD NOT	ABSO-LUTELY MUST NOT
	1	2	3	4	5	6

a. Release information because it may strengthen this government's negotiating position?

b. Release information because it may promote domestic political support for Department policies?

c. Release information because it may reduce the number of misleading speculations which are being made in public?

d. Release information because it may improve public understanding of existing programs and policies?

e. Release information because the public has a "right-to-know"?

f. Withhold information because it may embarrass friendly governments and their leaders?

g. Withhold information be-
cause it may discredit the
State Department and the
Administration in power?

_____

h. Withhold information because it may expose differences of opinion within the
Department and the government?

_____

i. Withhold information because it may endanger na-
tional security?

_____

j. Temporarily withhold information because it may require explanatory material
not yet available?

---

* If you answer "May or May Not," please indicate whether you feel that the
Department (3) "should unless the situation precludes it" or (4) "should not
unless the situation requires it."

5. What do you feel are the most effective ways for the Department
to get its message to the public? What special difficulties, if any, do you
feel that the Department has in getting its message to the public?

6. Much of the information which is available to newsmen and the
leaders on the nongovernmental organizations in the Department is provided on a "not-for-attribution" basis. What are the advantages and disadvantages of making information available on this basis—both for the
Department and the public?

7. To what extent do you feel that public opinion is a factor in foreign-
policy-making in this country? With respect to what types of foreign
policy do you feel that public opinion is most important? Least important? Whose opinions are most important with respect to these policies?
How are these opinions made known to the Department? To you? What
would you regard as the most reliable sources for information on the state
of general public opinion on foreign policy issues?

The next set of questions deals with the relations between policy officers and information officers.

8. What part, if any, do information officers play in the formation of public opinions on foreign affairs in this country? How frequently do you encounter information officers? What problems do information officers create for you?

9. To what extent do you feel that information officers should or should not do the following things:

Check One

	ABSO- LUTELY MUST	PREFER- ABLY SHOULD	MAY OR MAY NOT*	PREFER- ABLY SHOULD NOT	ABSO- LUTELY MUST NOT
	1	2	3	4	5	6

a. Interpret the facts underlying policy for the public?

b. Advise policy-makers on information policies?

c. Apply pressure within the Department for a more liberal information policy?

d. Handle routine information activities for the State Department?

e. Exercise discretion in timing the release of information to the public?

f. Keep the public informed of policy deliberations prior to the time that formal policy statements are released?

g. Participate actively in policy-making?

h. Systematically analyze general public opinion on foreign affairs?

---

* If you answer "May or May Not," please indicate whether you feel that information officers (3) "should unless the situation precludes it" or (4) "should not unless the situation requires it."

10. What special qualities would you ascribe to a "good" information officer?

11. How would you rate the information officers you deal with on the following qualities:

a. Intelligent	5	4	3	2	1	Unintelligent
b. Informed	5	4	3	2	1	Uninformed
c. Skillful	5	4	3	2	1	Unskillful
d. Helpful	5	4	3	2	1	Unhelpful
e. Responsible	5	4	3	2	1	Irresponsible

12. Would you describe the relations between policy officers and information officers as

a. Always cooperative?
b. Usually cooperative?
c. Compatible?*
d. Usually antagonistic?
e. Always antagonistic?

* If you respond "compatible," please indicate whether you feel that relations are "more cooperative" or "more antagonistic."

The next set of questions deals with the relations between policy officers and reporters.

13. What part, if any, do reporters play in the formation of public opinions of foreign affairs in this country? Under what circumstances do you encounter reporters? To what extent do you feel that you should or should not develop personal friendships with reporters? What problems do reporters create for you?

14. To what extent do you feel that reporters should or should not do the following things:

Check One

	ABSO-LUTELY MUST	PREFER-ABLY SHOULD	MAY OR MAY NOT*	PREFER-ABLY SHOULD NOT	ABSO-LUTELY MUST NOT
	1	2	3	4	5	6

a. Report the facts avoiding any interpretation whatever?

b. Interpret the facts for the public?

c. Incorporate statements of Department policy in their material whether they agree or disagree with it?

d. Verify information obtained from unauthorized sources in the Department before publication in any form?

e. Write without regard for the editorial views of their news organization?

f. Work through Department information officers?

g. Attempt to influence policy
officers?

_____

h. Bring public views and
needs to the attention of Department officers?

_____

* If you answer "May or May Not," please indicate whether you feel that
reporters (3) "should unless the situation precludes it" or (4) "should not
unless the situation requires it."

15. What qualities do you ascribe to a "good" reporter?

16. How would you rate reporters you deal with on the following
qualities:

a.	Intelligent	5	4	3	2	1	Unintelligent
b.	Informed	5	4	3	2	1	Uninformed
c.	Skillful	5	4	3	2	1	Unskillful
d.	Helpful	5	4	3	2	1	Unhelpful
e.	Responsible	5	4	3	2	1	Irresponsible

17. Would you describe the relations between policy officers and
reporters as

a. Always cooperative?
b. Usually cooperative?
c. Compatible?*
d. Usually antagonistic?
e. Always antagonistic?

* If you respond "compatible," please indicate whether you feel that relations are "more cooperative" or "more antagonistic."

The next set of questions deals with the relations between policy officers and the leaders of nongovernmental organizations.

18. What part, if any, do the leaders of nongovernmental organizations play in the formation of public opinion on foreign affairs in this country? How frequently do you encounter the leaders of nongovernmental organizations? What problems do these leaders create for you?

19. To what extent do you feel that the leaders of nongovernment organizations should or should not do the following things:

Check One

	ABSO-LUTELY MUST	PREFER-ABLY SHOULD	MAY OR MAY NOT*	PREFER-ABLY SHOULD NOT	ABSO-LUTELY MUST NOT
	1	2	3	4	5	6

a. Exercise their own discretion in applying organization policies to current situations?

b. Consult the membership prior to the adoption of basic organization policies?

c. Prepare material of special interest for release in the organization media?

d. Help to educate the general public on foreign affairs?

e. Mobilize support within the organization for policies adopted by the leadership?

f. Propose adjustments of the organization's special interests in favor of national and possibly foreign interests?

g. Bring pressure to bear on members of Congress to support organization policies?

h. Submit organization views directly to policy officers in the State Department?

---

* If you answer "May or May Not," please indicate whether you feel that pressure group leaders (3) "should unless the situation precludes it" or (4) "should not unless the situation requires it."

20. What qualities would you ascribe to a "good" leader of a nongovernment organization?

21. How would you rate the leaders of nongovernmental organizations you deal with on the following qualities:

a. Intelligent	5	4	3	2	1	Unintelligent
b. Informed	5	4	3	2	1	Uninformed
c. Skillful	5	4	3	2	1	Unskillful
d. Helpful	5	4	3	2	1	Unhelpful
e. Responsible	5	4	3	2	1	Irresponsible

22. Would you describe the relations between policy officers and the leaders of nongovernmental organizations as

a. Always cooperative?
b. Usually cooperative?
c. Compatible?*
d. Usually antagonistic?
e. Always antagonistic?

* If you respond "compatible," please indicate whether you feel that relations are "more cooperative" or "more antagonistic."

23. What is your official title? How many years have you held this position? What rank do you presently hold?

24. How many years have you been with your present organization? In this type of work? What has been your specialty?

25. Have you ever served as an information officer? reporter? NGO leader? If so, in what capacity?

26. What is the highest academic degree which you have earned? Where did you receive it? What was your undergraduate major? How many years of formal schooling do you have beyond the Bachelor's degree?

Appendix D

Interview Schedule–Reporters

Name _____ Organization _____

In the first set of questions, I wish to explore the extent to which you and your news organization cover foreign affairs.

1. What importance does your news organization place on the coverage of foreign affairs? How is your organization's staff here in Washington organized to cover foreign affairs?

2. How would you describe your job? What are the most important things you do? How do you decide what story you will cover on foreign affairs? What is your concept of news? To what extent are you allowed to report and interpret the news as you see it? For what kind of audience do you prepare material on foreign affairs? What restrictions, if any, do you encounter in your work?

In this next set of questions, I wish to explore the functions performed by reporters in the governing process in this country.

3. What part, if any, do you feel that reporters play in the formation of public opinion on foreign affairs in this country? What part, if any, do you feel that reporters play in the formation of foreign policies?

4. To what extent do you feel that reporters should or should not do the following things:

	Check One				
	ABSO-LUTELY MUST	PREFER-ABLY SHOULD	MAY OR MAY NOT*	PREFER-ABLY SHOULD NOT	ABSO-LUTELY MUST NOT
	1	2	3	4	5	6

a. Report the facts avoiding any interpretation whatever?

320

b. Interpret the facts for the public?

c. Incorporate statements of Department policy into their material whether they agree or disagree with it?

d. Verify information obtained from unauthorized sources within the Department before publication in any form?

e. Write without regard for the editorial views of your news organization?

f. Work through Department information officers?

g. Attempt to influence policy officers?

h. Bring public views and needs to the attention of Department officers?

---

* If you answer "May or May Not," please indicate whether you feel that reporters (3) "should unless the situation precludes it" or (4) "should not unless the situation requires it."

5. What do you believe to be the extent of the State Department's obligation to inform the public? What are the sources of this obligation? What limits would you set on this obligation?

In the next set of questions, I wish to determine how compelling you find various reasons for releasing or withholding information.

6. To what extent do you feel that the Department should or should not do the following things:

Check One

	ABSO-LUTELY MUST	PREFER-ABLY SHOULD	MAY OR MAY NOT*	PREFER-ABLY SHOULD NOT	ABSO-LUTELY MUST NOT
	1	2	3	4	5	6

a. Release information because it may strengthen this government's negotiating position?

b. Release information because it may promote domestic political support for Department policies?

c. Release information because it may reduce the number of misleading speculations which are being made in public?

d. Release information because it may improve public understanding of existing programs and policies?

e. Release information because the public has a "right-to-know"?

f. Withhold information because it may embarrass friendly governments and their leaders?

g. Withhold information because it may discredit the State Department and the Administration in power?

_____

h. Withhold information because it may expose differences of opinion within the Department and the government?

_____

i. Withhold information because it may endanger national security?

_____

j. Temporarily withhold information because it may require explanatory material not yet available?

_____

* If you answer "May or May Not," please indicate whether you feel that the Department (3) "should unless the situation precludes it" or (4) "should not unless the situation requires it."

The next set of questions deals with your sources of information on foreign affairs.

7. What kind of information on foreign affairs do you require in your work? To what extent do you depend upon the State Department for this information? What sources or outlets of information do you tap in the Department? Which of these are most valuable to you? What other sources of information on foreign affairs are available to you? Your organization? White House?

8. To what extent do you receive information on a "not-for-attribution" basis from the Department? What are the advantages and disadvantages of receiving information on this basis—both for the Department and the public?

The next set of questions deals with the relations between reporters and information officers.

9. What part, if any, do information officers play in the formation of public opinions on foreign affairs in this country? How frequently do you encounter information officers? What problems do information officers create for you?

10. To what extent do you feel that information officers should or should not do the following things:

Check One

	ABSO-LUTELY MUST	PREFER-ABLY SHOULD	MAY OR MAY NOT*	PREFER-ABLY SHOULD NOT	ABSO-LUTELY MUST NOT
	1	2	3	4	5	6

a. Interpret the facts underlying policy for the publi ?

b. Advise policy-makers on information policies?

c. Apply pressure within the Department for a more liberal information policy?

d. Handle routine information activities for the State Department?

e. Exercise discretion in timing the release of information to the public?

f. Keep the public informed of policy deliberations prior to the time that formal policy statements are released?

g. Participate actively in policy-making?

h. Systematically analyze general public opinion on foreign affairs?

---

* If you answer "May or May Not," please indicate whether you feel that information officers (3) "should unless the situation precludes it" or (4) "should not unless the situation requires it."

11. What special qualities would you ascribe to a "good" information officer?

12. How would you rate the information officers you deal with on the following qualities:

a.	Intelligent	5	4	3	2	1	Unintelligent
b.	Informed	5	4	3	2	1	Uninformed
c.	Skillful	5	4	3	2	1	Unskillful
d.	Helpful	5	4	3	2	1	Unhelpful
e.	Responsible	5	4	3	2	1	Irresponsible

13. Would you describe the relations between reporters and information officers as

a. Always cooperative?
b. Usually cooperative?
c. Compatible?*
d. Usually antagonistic?
e. Always antagonistic?

* If you respond "compatible," please indicate whether you feel that relations are "more cooperative" or "more antagonistic."

The next set of questions deals with the relations between reporters and policy officers.

14. What part, if any, do policy officers play in the formation of public opinions on foreign affairs in this country? How frequently do you encounter policy officers? What problems do policy officers create for you?

15. To what extent do you feel that policy officers should or should not do the following things:

Check One

	ABSOLUTELY MUST	PREFERABLY SHOULD	MAY OR MAY NOT*	PREFERABLY SHOULD NOT	ABSOLUTELY MUST NOT
	1	2	3	4	5	6

a. Determine what information is released to the public?

b. Inform information officers of policy deliberations prior to decisions?

c. Play a leading role in opinion-making in this country?

d. Take time off to meet with reporters and pressure group leaders?

e. Interpret United States national interests and the interests of foreign countries to domestic groups?

f. Take public opinion into account in the formation of foreign policy?

g. Solicit the views of interest groups on policies affecting their special interests?

h. Solicit the views of nongovernmental experts on policies in their field of specialization?

---

* If you answer "May or May Not," please indicate whether you feel that policy officers (3) "should unless the situation precludes it" or (4) "should not unless the situation requires it."

16. What special qualities would you ascribe to a "good" policy officer?

17. How would you rate the policy officers you deal with on the following qualities:

a. Intelligent	5	4	3	2	1	Unintelligent
b. Informed	5	4	3	2	1	Uninformed
c. Skillful	5	4	3	2	1	Unskillful
d. Helpful	5	4	3	2	1	Unhelpful
e. Responsible	5	4	3	2	1	Irresponsible

18. Would you describe the relations between reporters and policy officers as

a. Always cooperative?
b. Usually cooperative?
c. Compatible?*
d. Usually antagonistic?
e. Always antagonistic?

* If you respond "compatible," please indicate whether you feel that relations are "more cooperative" or "more antagonistic."

The next set of questions deals with the relations between policy officers and the leaders of nongovernmental organizations.

19. What part, if any, do the leaders of nongovernmental organizations play in the formation of public opinion on foreign affairs in this country? How frequently do you encounter the leaders of nongovernmental organizations? What problems do these leaders create for you?

20. To what extent do you feel that the leaders of nongovernment organizations should or should not do the following things:

Check One

	ABSO-LUTELY MUST	PREFER-ABLY SHOULD	MAY OR MAY NOT*	PREFER-ABLY SHOULD NOT	ABSO-LUTELY MUST NOT
	1	2	3	4	5	6

a. Exercise their own discretion in applying organization policies to current situations?

b. Consult the membership prior to the adoption of basic organization policies?

c. Prepare material of special interest for release in the organization media?

d. Help to educate the general public on foreign affairs?

e. Mobilize support within the organization for policies adopted by the leadership?

f. Propose adjustments of the organization's special interests in favor of national and possibly foreign interests?

g. Bring pressure to bear on members of Congress to support organization policies?

h. Submit organization views directly to policy officers in the State Department?

* If you answer "May or May Not," please indicate whether you feel that pressure group leaders (3) "should unless the situation precludes it" or (4) "should not unless the situation requires it."

21. What qualities would you ascribe to a "good" leader of a nongovernment organization?

22. How would you rate the leaders of nongovernment organizations you deal with on the following qualities:

a.	Intelligent	5	4	3	2	1	Unintelligent
b.	Informed	5	4	3	2	1	Uninformed
c.	Skillful	5	4	3	2	1	Unskillful
d.	Helpful	5	4	3	2	1	Unhelpful
e.	Responsible	5	4	3	2	1	Irresponsible

23. Would you describe the relations between policy officers and the leaders of nongovernmental organizations as

a. Always cooperative?
b. Usually cooperative?
c. Compatible?*
d. Usually antagonistic?
e. Always antagonistic?

* If you respond "compatible," please indicate whether you feel that relations are "more cooperative" or "more antagonistic."

24. What is your official title? How many years have you held this position? What rank do you presently hold?

25. How many years have you been with your present oganization? In this type of work? What has been your specialty?

26. Have you ever served as a policy officer? informational officer? NGO leader? If so, in what capacity?

27. What is the highest academic degree which you have earned? Where did you receive it? What was your undergraduate major? How many years of formal schooling do you have beyond the Bachelor's degree?

Interview Schedule–NGO Leaders

Name ·_____   Organization _____

In the first set of questions, I wish to identify the nature and extent of your organization's interest in foreign affairs.

1. To what extent is it important for your organization to deal with foreign affairs? What aspects of foreign affairs are of most concern to your organization? What international affairs programs does your organization sponsor abroad? In this country? How many persons on the organization's professional staff, if any, devote full time to foreign affairs? What percentage of your time would you estimate is devoted to activities related to foreign affairs?

In the next set of questions, I wish to explore the functions you perform in your organization and in the governing process generally.

2. First, how would you describe your job? What are the most important things you do? To what extent do you participate in shaping the policies of your organization on foreign affairs? What part, if any, do you play in the formation of public opinions on foreign affairs in this country? What part, if any, do you play in the formation of foreign policies in this country?

3. To what extent do you feel that you should or should not do the following things:

Check One

	ABSO-LUTELY MUST	PREFER-ABLY SHOULD	MAY OR MAY NOT*	PREFER-ABLY SHOULD NOT	ABSO-LUTELY MUST NOT
	1	2	3	4	5	6

a. Exercise your own discretion in applying organization policies to current situations?

b. Consult the membership prior to the adoption of basic organization policies?

c. Prepare material of special interest to the membership for release in organization media?

d. Help to educate the general public on foreign affairs?

e. Mobilize support within the organization for policies adopted by the leadership?

f. Propose adjustments of the organization's special interests in favor of national and possibly foreign interests?

g. Bring pressure to bear on members of Congress to support organization policies?

h. Submit organization views directly to policy officers in the State Department?

* If you answer "May or May Not," please indicate whether you feel that NGO leaders (3) "should unless the situation precludes it" or (4) "should not unless the situation requires it."

The next set of questions deals with your sources of information on foreign affairs.

4. What kind of information on foreign affairs do you require in your work? To what extent do you depend upon the State Department for this information? What sources or outlets of information do you tap in the Department? Which of these are most valuable to you? What other sources of information on foreign affairs are available to you? Your organization? White House?

The next set of questions deals with the circulation of opinions within your organization and among the general public.

5. What techniques do you utilize to circulate information on foreign affairs? What media? How frequently? What audience? What information?

6. To what extent is international affairs dealt with at the conventions and other assemblages of your organization? To what extent do you participate in planning the programs for the international affairs activities of your organization? To what extent do you utilize the general news media to furnish information on foreign affairs to the public?

The next set of questions deals with opinion submission within your organization.

7. To what extent do you consult the membership prior to the adoption of organization policies on foreign affairs? What techniques, if any, do you use to assess the opinions of the membership on foreign affairs?

The next set of questions deals with the submission of organization opinions to the State Department and the Government.

8. Under what circumstances do you submit organization views directly to policy-makers in the State Department? With respect to what issues do you feel you will receive the most consideration? The least consideration? What techniques do you feel are most effective in bringing your views to the attention of policy officers? Of what value are the Department's conferences and speaking engagements as a means of transmitting your views to the Department?

9. Under what circumstances do you submit your views on foreign affairs to Congress? The White House? Other agencies? To what extent do you work with other organizations with common interests in foreign affairs? What value do you attribute to placing your views in the general news media?

10. What do you believe to be the extent of the State Department's obligation to inform the public? What are the sources of this obligation? What limits would you set on this obligation?

In this next set of questions, I wish to determine how compelling you find various reasons for releasing or withholding information.

11. To what extent do you feel that the Department should or should not do the following things:

Check One

	ABSO-LUTELY MUST	PREFER-ABLY SHOULD	MAY OR MAY NOT*	PREFER-ABLY SHOULD NOT	ABSO-LUTELY MUST NOT
	1	2	3	4	5	6

a. Release information because it may strengthen this government's negotiating position?

b. Release information because it may promote domestic political support for Department policies?

c. Release information because it may reduce the number of misleading speculations which are being made in public?

d. Release information because it may improve public understanding of existing programs and policies?

e. Release information because the public has a "right-to-know"?

f. Withhold information because it may embarrass
friendly governments and
their leaders?

_____

g. Withhold information be-
cause it may discredit the
State Department and the
Administration in power?

_____

h. Withhold information because it may expose differences of opinion within the
Department and the government?

_____

i. Withhold information because it may endanger na-
tional security?

_____

j. Temporarily withhold information because it may require explanatory material
not yet available?

_____

* If you answer "May or May Not," please indicate whether you feel that the
Department (3) "should unless the situation precludes it" or (4) "should not
unless the situation requires it."

12. What do you feel are the most effective ways for the Department
to get its message to the public? What special difficulties, if any, do you
feel that the Department has in getting its message to the public.

The next set of questions deals with the relations between NGO leaders
and information officers.

13. What part, if any, do information officers play in the formation
of public opinions on foreign affairs in this country? How frequently do
you encounter information officers? What problems do information
officers create for you?

14. To what extent do you feel that information officers should or should not do the following things:

Check One

	ABSO-LUTELY MUST	PREFER-ABLY SHOULD	MAY OR MAY NOT*	PREFER-ABLY SHOULD NOT	ABSO-LUTELY MUST NOT
	1	2	3	4	5	6

a. Interpret the facts underlying policy for the public?

b. Advise policy-makers on information policies?

c. Apply pressure within the Department for a more liberal information policy?

d. Handle routine information activities for the State Department?

e. Exercise discretion in timing the release of information to the public?

f. Keep the public informed of policy deliberations prior to the time that formal policy statements are released?

g. Participate actively in policy-making?

h. Systematically analyze general public opinion on foreign affairs?

* If you answer "May or May Not," please indicate whether you feel that information officers (3) "should unless the situation precludes it" or (4) "should not unless the situation requires it."

15. What special qualities would you ascribe to a "good" information officer?

16. How would you rate the information officers you deal with on the following qualities:

a. Intelligent	5	4	3	2	1	Unintelligent
b. Informed	5	4	3	2	1	Uninformed
c. Skillful	5	4	3	2	1	Unskillful
d. Helpful	5	4	3	2	1	Unhelpful
e. Responsible	5	4	3	2	1	Irresponsible

17. Would you describe the relations between NGO leaders and information officers as

a. Always cooperative?
b. Usually cooperative?
c. Compatible?*
d. Usually antagonistic?
e. Always antagonistic?

* If you respond "compatible," please indicate whether you feel that relations are "more cooperative" or "more antagonistic."

The next set of questions deals with the relations between NGO leaders and policy officers.

18. What part, if any, do policy officers play in the formation of public opinions on foreign affairs in this country? How frequently do you encounter policy officers? What problems do policy officers create for you?

19. To what extent do you feel that policy officers should or should not do the following things:

Check One

	ABSO-LUTELY MUST	PREFER-ABLY SHOULD	MAY OR MAY NOT*	PREFER-ABLY SHOULD NOT	ABSO-LUTELY MUST NOT
	1	2	3	4	5	6
a. Determine what information is released to the public?					
b. Inform information officers of policy deliberations prior to decisions?					

c. Play a leading role in opinion-making in this country?

_____

d. Take time off to meet with
reporters and pressure
group leaders?

_____

e. Interpret United States national interests and the interests of foreign countries
to domestic groups?

_____

f. Take public opinion into account in the formation of
foreign policy?

_____

g. Solicit the views of interest
groups on policies affecting
their special interests?

_____

h. Solicit the views of nongovernmental experts on policies in their field of specialization?

---

* If you answer "May or May Not," please indicate whether you feel that
policy officers (3) "should unless the situation precludes it" or (4) "should
not unless the situation requires it."

20. What special qualities would you ascribe to a "good" policy
officer?

21. How would you rate the policy officers you deal with on the following qualities:

a.	Intelligent	5	4	3	2	1	Unintelligent
b.	Informed	5	4	3	2	1	Uninformed
c.	Skillful	5	4	3	2	1	Unskillful
d.	Helpful	5	4	3	2	1	Unhelpful
e.	Responsible	5	4	3	2	1	Irresponsible

22. Would you describe the relations between NGO leaders and policy officers as

    a. Always cooperative?
    b. Usually cooperative?
    c. Compatible?*
    d. Usually antagonistic?
    e. Always antagonistic?

* If you respond "compatible," please indicate whether you feel that relations are "more cooperative" or "more antagonistic."

The next set of questions deals with the relations between NGO leaders and reporters.

23. What part, if any, do reporters play in the formation of public opinions on foreign affairs in this country? How frequently do you encounter reporters? What problems do reporters create for you?

24. To what extent do you feel that reporters should or should not do the following things:

Check One

	ABSO-LUTELY MUST	PREFER-ABLY SHOULD	MAY OR MAY NOT*	PREFER-ABLY SHOULD NOT	ABSO-LUTELY MUST NOT
	1	2	3	4	5	6

a. Report the facts avoiding any interpretation whatever?

b. Interpret the facts for the public?

c. Incorporate statements of Department policy in their material whether they agree or disagree with it?

d. Verify information obtained from unauthorized sources in the Department before publication in any form?

e. Write without regard for the
editorial views of their news
organization?

_____

f. Work through Department
information officers?

_____

g. Attempt to influence policy
officers?

_____

h. Bring public views and
needs to the attention of Department officers?

_____

* If you answer "May or May Not," please indicate whether you feel that
reporters (3) "should unless the situation precludes it" or (4) "should not
unless the situation requires it."

25. What qualities do you ascribe to a "good" reporter?

26. How would you rate reporters you deal with on the following
qualities:

a. Intelligent   5   4   3   2   1   Unintelligent
b. Informed   5   4   3   2   1   Uninformed
c. Skillful   5   4   3   2   1   Unskillful
d. Helpful   5   4   3   2   1   Unhelpful
e. Responsible   5   4   3   2   1   Irresponsible

27. Would you describe the relations between NGO leaders and reporters as

a. Always cooperative?
b. Usually cooperative?
c. Compatible?*
d. Usually antagonistic?
e. Always antagonistic?

* If you respond "compatible," please indicate whether you feel that relations
are "more cooperative" or "more antagonistic."

28. What is your official title? How many years have you held the same
general position? What rank do you presently hold?

29. How many years have you been with your present organization?
In this type of work? What has been your specialty?

30. Have you ever served as information officer? policy officer? reporter? If so, in what capacity?

31. What is the highest academic degree which you have earned? Where did you receive it? What was your major? How many years of formal schooling do you have beyond the Bachelor's degree?

Appendix **F**

Selected Findings

I. Relations Among Perceived Characteristics (Chapter 4)

    A. Characterizations of policy officers

        1. On the quality of informed.

	High	Low
Reporters	23	9
Information officers	13	16

$(N = 61; \chi^2 = 3.551; P = .10; C = .33)$

        2. On the quality of helpful.

	High	Low
Reporters	6	23
Information officers	17	15

$(N = 61; \chi^2 = 5.503; P = .02; C = -.41)$

        3. On the quality of helpful.

	High	Low
Reporters	10	19
NGO leaders	16	9

$(N = 54; \chi^2 = 3.578; P = .10; C = -.35)$

B. Characterizations involving reporters

1. Reporters' characterizations of others on the quality of helpful.

	High	Low
Policy officers	10	19
Information officers	22	12

$(N = 63; \chi^2 = 4.575; P = .05; C = -.37)$

2. Characterizations of reporters on quality of helpful.

	High	Low
Information officers	19	12
Policy officers	9	20

$(N = 60; \chi^2 = 4.362; P = .05; C = .37)$

3. Characterizations of reporters on the quality of responsible.

	High	Low
Information officers	17	6
Reporters	7	17

$(N = 47; \chi^2 = 7.705; P = .01; C = .53)$

4. Characterizations of reporters on the quality of responsible.

	High	Low
Reporters	7	17
Policy officers	20	11

$(N = 55; \chi^2 = 5.423; P = .02; C = -.42)$

C. Characterizations of NGO leaders

1. On the quality of helpful.

	High	Low
Information officers	15	8
Reporters	8	15

$(N = 46; \chi^2 = 3.130; P = .10; C = .36)$

2. On the quality of helpful.

	High	Low
Information officers	15	8
Policy officers	11	20

$(N = 54; \chi^2 = 3.561; P = .10; C = .35)$

D. Characterizations involving information officers

1. Information officers' characterizations of others on the quality of informed.

	High	Low
Policy officers	27	5
NGO leaders	6	19

$(N = 57; \chi^2 = 18.583; P = .001; C = .70)$

2. Information officers' characterizations of others on the quality of informed.

	High	Low
Reporters	17	15
NGO leaders	6	19

$(N = 57; \chi^2 = 3.810; P = .10; C = .35)$

3. Information officers' characterizations of others on the quality of skillful.

	High	Low
Policy officers	17	14
NGO leaders	6	17

$(N = 54; \chi^2 = 3.366; P = .10; C = .34)$

4. Information officers' characterizations of others on the quality of skillful.

	High	Low
Reporters	18	14
NGO leaders	6	17

$(N = 55; \chi^2 = 3.800; P = .10; C = .36)$

II. Factor Scores (Chapter 5)

   A. Differences between groups in mean factor scores

      1. Factor I.

	Information officers	Reporters	NGO leaders
Policy officers	NS	NS	.05
Information officers		NS	.05
Reporters			.05

      2. Factor II.

	NGO leaders	Information officers	Policy officers
Reporters	NS	.05	.05
NGO leaders		.05	.05
Information officers			NS

      3. No significant differences among mean factor scores for Factor III.

      4. No significant differences among mean factor scores for Factor IV.

      5. Factor V.

	Information officers	Policy officers	NGO leaders
Reporters	NS	.05	.05
Information officers		NS	.05
Policy officers			.05

      6. Factor VI.

	NGO leaders	Information officers	Reporters
Policy officers	NS	NS	.05
NGO leaders		NS	.05
Information officers			NS

   B. Intercorrelations among individual factor scores by Group

      1. Among policy officers, Factors II and V are negatively correlated $(N = 40; P = .05; r = -.41)$.

2. Among reporters, Factors I and V are negatively correlated $(N = 35; P = .05; r = -.36)$.

3. Among NGO leaders:
   Factors I and VI are correlated $(N = 30; P = .05; r = .40)$.
   Factors I and II are correlated $(N = 30; P = .05; r = .41)$.
   Factors II and VI are correlated $(N = 32; P = .05; r = .46)$.
   Factors V and VI are correlated $(N = 28; P = .05; r = .37)$.
   Factors III and IV are correlated $(N = 29; P = .05; r = -.60)$.

4. Among information officers, Factors III and V are positively correlated $(N = 34; P = .05; r = .35)$.

III. Relations Between Information and Policy Officers (Chapter 6)

A. Perceived antagonism among information officers for policy officers

1. Skillfulness of policy officers.

	Relations with policy officers	
	Cooperative	Antagonistic
Higher	9	0
Lower	13	8

$N = 30; \chi^2 = 2.930; P = .03; C = .42$

2. Information officers who are more hesitant than their colleagues to accept the informational requirements of the public (Factor VI) are more likely than others to perceive antagonism in their relation with policy officers $(N = 34; C = .05; r = -.33)$.

B. Perceived antagonism among policy officers for information officers

1. Age.

	Relations with information officers	
	Cooperative	Antagonistic
Younger	17	1
Older	12	6

$N = 36; \chi^2 = 2.837; P = .04; C = .38$

2. Level of position.

	Relations with information officers	
	Cooper-ative	Antag-onistic
Lower	14	0
Higher	15	7

$N = 36; \chi^2 = 3.685; P = .02; C = .43$

3. Policy officers who are more likely to accept the informational requirements of policy (Factor II) are more likely than their colleagues to perceive antagonism in their relations with information officers $(N = 36; C = .05; r = .32)$.

IV. Relations Between Department Officers and Reporters (Chapter 7)

A. Perceived antagonism among information officers for reporters

1. Professional experience of information officer.

	Relations with reporters	
	Cooper-ative	Antag-onistic
Less	6	12
More	14	5

$N = 37; \chi^2 = 4.544; P = .05; C = -.47$

2. Prior Experience as a reporter.

	Relations with reporters	
	Cooper-ative	Antag-onistic
No	15	5
Yes	5	12

$N = 37; \chi^2 = 5.964; P = .02; C = .53$

3. Social science major
in college.

	Relations with reporters	
	Cooperative	Antagonistic
Yes	5	10
No	7	2

$N = 24; \chi^2 = 2.844; P = .04; C = -.46$

B. Perceived antagonism among reporters for information officers

1. Among part-time reporters, those who work for news organizations which stress interpretation.

	Relations with information officers	
	Cooperative	Antagonistic
No	7	1
Yes	3	6

$N = 17; \chi^2 = 3.138; P = .04; C = .56$

2. Reporters who are more likely than others to reject the informational requirements of policy (Factor II) are more likely than their colleagues to perceive antagonism in their relations with information officers $(N = 37; P = .05; r = -.40)$.

C. Perceived antagonism among policy officers for reporters

1. Among policy officers at higher level, those with a political appointment.

	Relations with reporters	
	Cooperative	Antagonistic
No	9	7
Yes	1	4

$N = 21; \chi^2 = .817; P = .18; C = .27$

2. Among policy officers at lower level, those in ———— bureaus.

	Relations with reporters	
	Cooperative	Antagonistic
Functional	4	1
Regional	3	6

$N = 14; \chi^2 = 1.244; P = .13; C = .40$

3. Type of department officer.

	Relations with reporters	
	Cooperative	Antagonistic
Information	25	13
Policy	13	23

$N = 74; \chi^2 = 5.384; P = .05; C = .37$

4. Policy officers who are more likely than their colleagues to stress the informational requirements of policy (Factor II) are more likely than others to perceive antagonism in their relations with reporters $(N = 35; P = .05; r = .36)$.

D. Perceived antagonism among reporters for policy officers

1. Type of Department officer.

	Relations with Department officers	
	Cooperative	Antagonistic
Information	23	14
Policy	15	23

$N = 75; \chi^2 = 3.006; P = .10; C = .28$

2. Helpfulness of policy officers.

	Relations with policy officers	
	Cooperative	Antagonistic
Higher	7	2
Lower	6	13

$N = 28; \chi^2 = 3.548; P = .03; C = .47$

3. Among full-time reporters, those with news organizations which encourage interpretation.

	Relations with policy officers	
	Cooperative	Antagonistic
No	4	5
Yes	2	10

$N = 21; \chi^2 = .822; P = .18; C = .27$

4. Reporters who are more likely than others to reject the role expectations of policy officers (Factor I) are more likely than they are to perceive antagonism in their relations with policy officers $(N = 38; P = .05; r = -.34)$.

5. Reporters who are more likely than their colleagues to accept their own role expectations (Factor V) are more likely than they are to perceive antagonism in their relations with policy officers $(N = 38; P = .05; r = .34)$.

V. Relations Between Department Officers and NGO Leaders
    (Chapter 8)

A. Perceived antagonisms among information officers for NGO
    leaders

    1. Prior experience as a
    reporter.

	Relations with NGO leaders	
	Cooper- ative	Antag- onistic
No	18	1
Yes	8	5

$N = 32$; $\chi^2 = 3.618$; $P = .03$; $C = .45$

    2. Foreign Service officer.

	Relations with NGO leaders	
	Cooper- ative	Antag- onistic
No	23	3
Yes	3	3

$N = 32$; $\chi^2 = 2.546$; $P = .06$; $C = .38$

    3. Frequency of contact
    with NGO leaders.

	Relations with NGO leaders	
	Cooper- ative	Antag- onistic
Less	16	6
More	10	0

$N = 32$; $\chi^2 = 1.805$; $P = .08$; $C = -.33$

4. Responsibility of NGO
leaders.

Relations with
NGO leaders

	Cooper- ative	Antag- onistic
Higher	15	1
Lower	2	4

$N = 22$; $\chi^2 = 5.956$; $P = .01$; $C = .65$

5. Helpfulness of NGO
leader.

Relations with
NGO leaders

	Cooper- ative	Antag- onistic
Higher	13	1
Lower	4	4

$N = 22$; $\chi^2 = 3.164$; $P = .04$; $C = .50$

6. Information officers who are more likely than their colleagues to reject the role expectations for NGO leaders (Factor III) are more likely than their colleagues to perceive antagonism in their relations with them ($N = 32$; $P = .05$; $r = -.57$).

B. Perceived antagonism among NGO leaders for information officers

No significant findings.

C. Perceived antagonism among policy officers for NGO leaders

1. Age of policy officer.

Relations with
NGO leaders

	Cooper- ative	Antag- onistic
Younger	12	3
Older	7	11

$N = 33$; $\chi^2 = 4.103$; $P = .05$; $C = .47$

2. Type of policy specialty.

	Relations with NGO leaders	
	Cooperative	Antagonistic
Regional	15	7
Functional	3	6

$N = 31; \chi^2 = 1.915; P = .08; C = .34$

3. Type of Department officer.

	Relations with NGO leaders	
	Cooperative	Antagonistic
Information	26	6
Policy	20	13

$N = 65; \chi^2 = 2.423; P = .15; C = .27$

4. Frequency of contacts with NGO leaders.

	Relations with NGO leaders	
	Cooperative	Antagonistic
Less	4	7
More	15	6

$N = 32; \chi^2 = 2.370; P = .06; C = -.37$

5. Responsibility of NGO leaders.

	Relations with NGO leaders	
	Cooperative	Antagonistic
Higher	13	6
Lower	4	7

$N = 30; \chi^2 = 1.756; P = .09; C = .33$

6. Policy officers who interpret United States national interest and the interests of foreign countries to domestic groups.

	Relations with NGO leaders	
	Cooperative	Antagonistic
Yes	18	8
No	1	4

$N = 31; \chi^2 = 2.460; P = .06; C = .38$

Perceived antagonism among NGO leaders for policy officers

1. Type of Department officer.

	Relations with policy officers	
	Cooperative	Antagonistic
Information	24	1
Policy	19	7

$N = 51; \chi^2 = 3.479; P = .05; C = .54$

2. NGO's position on Department policies.

	Relations with policy officers	
	Cooperative	Antagonistic
Support	17	3
Oppose	3	4

$N = 27; \chi^2 = 2.852; P = .05; C = .44$

3. NGO leaders who are more likely than their colleagues to stress the informational requirements of policy (Factor II) are less likely than they are to perceive antagonism in their relations with policy officers ($N = 26; P = .05; r = -.46$).

4. NGO leaders who are more likely than their colleagues to stress the informational requirements of the public (Factor VI) are less likely than their colleagues to perceive antagonism in their relations with policy officers $(N = 26; P = .05; r = -.45)$.

5. Policy officers should play a leading role in opinion-making.

| | Relations with policy officers | |
	Cooperative	Antagonistic
Yes	14	1
No	4	4

$N = 23; \chi^2 = 3.493; P = .03; C = .51$

6. Policy officers should determine what information is released?

| | Relations with policy officers | |
	Cooperative	Antagonistic
Yes	14	2
No	4	4

$N = 24; \chi^2 = 2.250; P = .07; C = .41$

7. NGO leaders should submit their views directly to policy officers?

| | Relations with policy officers | |
	Cooperative	Antagonistic
Yes	10	7
No	9	0

$N = 26; \chi^2 = 3.194; P = .03; C = -.47$

VI.   Relations Between Reporters and NGO Leaders (Chapter 9)

A.   Perceived antagonism among reporters for NGO leaders

1. Amount of time spent
by reporters on foreign
affairs.

	Relations with NGO leaders	
	Cooper-ative	Antag-onistic
Part	4	5
Full	12	2

$N = 23; \chi^2 = 2.673; P = .05; C = -.46$

2. Reporters who are more likely than their colleagues to re-ject the role expectations of NGO leaders (Factor III) are more likely than their colleagues to perceive antagonism in their relations with them $(N = 24; P = .05\ r = -.45)$.

B.   Perceived antagonism among NGO leaders for reporters

1. Type of pressure group.

	Relations with reporters	
	Cooper-ative	Antag-onistic
Noneconomic	10	5
Economic	3	7

$N = 25; \chi^2 = 1.930; P = .08; C = .38$

2. Responsibility of
reporters.

	Relations with reporters	
	Cooper-ative	Antag-onistic
Higher	12	4
Lower	3	5

$N = 24; \chi^2 = 1.800; P = .09; C = .37$

3. Helpfulness of
reporters.

	Relations with reporters	
	Cooperative	Antagonistic
Higher	10	2
Lower	5	7

$N = 24; \chi^2 = 2.844; P = .04; C = .46$

4. NGO leaders who are more likely than their colleagues to stress the informational requirements of policy (Factor II) are less likely than their colleagues to perceive antagonism in their relations with reporters $(N = 24; P = .06; r = -.38)$.

5. NGO leaders who are more likely than their colleagues to accept the role expectations of reporters (Factor V) are less likely than their colleagues to perceive antagonism in their relations with them $(N = 24; P = .05; r = -.41)$.

6. NGO leaders who are more likely than their colleagues to stress the informational requirements of the public (Factor VI) are less likely than their colleagues to perceive antagonism in their relations with them $(N = 24; P = .05; r = -.46)$.

VII. Patterns of Perceived Antagonism (Chapter 10)

A. Comparisons
1. Perceived antagonism
among reporters for

	Cooperative	Antagonistic
Policy officers	15	23
NGO leaders	19	6

$N = 63; \chi^2 = 6.695; P = .01; C = .44$

2. Perceived antagonism
among reporters for

	Cooperative	Antagonistic
Policy officers	15	23
Information officers	23	14

$N = 75; \chi^2 = 3.006; P = .10; C = .28$

3. Perceived antagonism
among NGO leaders for

	Cooperative	Antagonistic
Information officers	24	1
Reporters	15	9

$N = 49; \chi^2 = 6.523; P = .02; C = .48$

4. Perceived antagonism
among NGO leaders for

	Cooperative	Antagonistic
Information officers	24	1
Policy officers	19	7

$N = 51; \chi^2 = 3.479; P = .10; C = .36$

5. Perceived antagonism
among information
officers for

	Cooperative	Antagonistic
Reporters	20	18
NGO leaders	26	6

$N = 70; \chi^2 = 5.108; P = .05; C = .37$

6. Perceived antagonism
among policy officers for

	Cooperative	Antagonistic
Information officers	29	7
Reporters	9	26

$N = 71; \chi^2 = 19.308; P = .001; C = .65$

7. Perceived antagonism
among policy officers for

	Cooperative	Antagonism
Reporters	9	26
NGO leaders	20	13

$N = 68; \chi^2 = 7.088; P = .01; C = .43$

8. Perceived antagonism
for information officers
among

	Cooper- ative	Antag- onistic
Reporters	13	24
NGO leaders	24	1

$N = 62; \chi^2 = 20.508; P = .001; C = .70$

9. Perceived antagonism
for policy officers among

	Cooper- ative	Antag- onistic
Reporters	8	30
NGO leaders	19	7

$N = 64; \chi^2 = 15.064; P = .001; C = .62$

10. Perceived antagonism
for reporters among

	Cooper- ative	Antag- onistic
Information officers	25	13
Policy officers	13	23

$N = 74; \chi^2 = 5.384; P = .05; C = .37$

B. Intercorrelations

1. None among information officers.

2. Among policy officers.
   a. Perceived antagonism for information officers is associated with perceived antagonism for reporters ($N = 36$; $P = .05$; $r = .42$).
   b. Perceived antagonism for reporters is related to perceived antagonism for NGO leaders ($N = 32$; $P = .05$; $r = .38$).

3. Among reporters.
   a. Perceived antagonism for information officers is correlated with perceived antagonism for policy officers ($N = 34$; $P = .05$; $r = .54$).

b. Perceived antagonism for information officers is associated with perceived antagonism for NGO leaders ($N = 31; P = .05; r = .42$).

4. Among NGO leaders.

a. Perceived antagonism for information officers is related to perceived antagonism for policy officers ($N = 23; P = .05; r = .49$).

b. Perceived antagonism for information officers is associated with perceived antagonism for reporters ($N = 22; P = .05; r = .46$).

c. Perceived antagonism for policy officers is correlated with perceived antagonism for reporters ($N = 22; P = .05; r = .48$).

Index

361